Upholstery

A Manual of Techniques

Hugh O'Neill

The Crowood Press

First published in 1999 by
The Crowood Press Ltd
Ramsbury, Marlborough
Wiltshire SN8 2HR

British Library Cataloguing-in-Publication Data
A catalogue reference for this book is available from the British Library

ISBN 1 86126 140 3

Line illustrations by David Fisher.

All photographs by the author.

Typefaces used: text, New Baskerville; headings, Optima Bold.

Typeset and designed by
D & N Publishing
Membury Business Park, Lambourn Woodlands
Hungerford, Berkshire.

Printed and bound by Leo Paper Products, China.

Contents

Preface

As a writer, I have always written about my professional work as well as my hobbies and interests (most writers also have a 'real job'!). To date, there have been four books and over 800 articles on a wide range of topics, with some translated into other languages. It started with an article on installing a septic tank drainage system for our first home, which was soon followed by a series on building a racing dinghy, and then scores on the quarry plant and practices that I was then working with.

Other things started at that same time – including an interest in chairs! In fact, since attending auctions to furnish that starter cottage I have had something of a fixation with chairs. Would you believe they came before a table, wardrobe or chest of drawers! Many of the pieces, bought at those early auctions over forty years ago, needed some restoration. And, as my new wife said at the time 'restoration covers a multitude of sins'.

Later, first as a hobby interest, I started making my own furniture, and in time this too became part of the 'day job'. This book marks another major transition in my life.

Although years ago I built and raced wooden sailing dinghies, the focus of my craft interest has for some fifteen years been woodturning. Like most turners I spent most of my time making bowls and decorative items. Eventually craft fairs built sales volumes which eventually well exceeded the writing income. I began to look forward to early 'retirement' so that I could become a writing woodturner. However, sustaining a family forced a more realistic outlook, and I remained a semi-pro

bowl turner. Bowl turning has its limits and the challenge of turning spindles and building them into furniture items eventually took over.

From the beginning my furniture making has reflected that early chair fixation. Some chairs such as Windsors and Glastonburys are 100 per cent wood – seats and all. But as a chair maker you are very soon into the need for upholstery skills. Fortunately, a local school ran an evening class. In the first year of the class I had covered eight drop-in pads for two sets of dining chairs; a high-back easy chair; made and covered a pair of Prie chairs; and rebuilt and totally reupholstered a chaise and a Knowle settee. My wife commandeered all of these items (bar the chaise) for our home.

I found upholstery a fascinating craft form in its own right. At the same time as this interest grew, but quite coincidentally, furniture making and restoration totally displaced bowl turning. One of the greatest satisfactions that I found in upholstery (and restoration) was the aspect of problem solving. Each piece is different and presents a new challenge; and most are deviations from any text book. You have to work out how to do them for yourself – there are no Haynes or maker's manuals.

Crowood, who have published my three wood-turning books, knowing of this change of focus, suggested that I wrote a book about upholstery. So here it is!

There are others to thank for the book's appearance. First is my wife Eve. Had she not wanted those early pieces I might never have been encouraged to push ahead. But it does not end there.

When I moved my workshop from the Home Counties into the rural Marches a number of people expressed an interest in upholstery classes, so I started running an evening class as a part of the Local Education programme. Later, I also opened my own studio and now hold afternoon, evening and occasional weekend sessions there. These have become very popular.

Through these, it became obvious that many people share my interest in chairs. In the country, people do not just throw things away – particularly old and much loved chairs. They keep them – hoping that 'one day ... '. So, many people have old bits of furniture in barns and attics, and once they know there is a class available they are banging on the door. Although they may first attend a course in order to recover a particular piece, many soon become hooked. Even before the first chair is finished they are off around the auctions to buy the next project or two. Most also look for different types of piece so that they can develop a range of different basic skills. Several have identified the satisfaction of problem solving, and one present student will, I am sure, end up as a self-employed upholsterer.

Recognizing their increasing depth of involvement I try to develop in the participants an interest in basic, but universal techniques rather than just how to deal with the requirements of the particular type of chair that they start with. This has led to the development of a series of models and teaching aids for use in the class. Some of these aids have also been used to produce some of the illustrations for this book. I also decided that the book would be more authentic if most of the photo illustrations were of students' (and tutor) work in progress taken during the classes, rather than studio set-up 'perfect' examples. I also persuaded Crowood that although colour photos look pretty, many aspects of upholstery are better illustrated with line drawings.

Any reader should be able to do as well as the work that can be seen in the illustrations, and most, with a little practice, should soon be able to do better.

So I would like to thank my students for their support and for permission to use pictures of their work. Above all, thanks to them for the enormous satisfaction that their many achievements have given me. And finally I would like to say 'Welcome to a fascinating activity'.

Introduction

Upholstery must be amongst the more widely practised crafts in the country. In both urban and rural areas you will find a number of professional practitioners advertising their trade in the local papers. In schools and colleges across the land there are evening classes with anything up to a couple of dozen students of both sexes meeting one evening a week to learn the basic skills. In many homes you will find at least one stool or chair that somebody has had a go at recovering; sometimes the job is a mess, often it is acceptable, occasionally it is superb – always it is much cherished. It is usually shown off with a proud: 'I did that!' Certainly in the area in which I now live there are twenty or thirty DIY upholsterers to every woodturner.

Basically, upholstery is not difficult. There are a number of skills to it, but they are mostly easy to acquire. There are then many 'wrinkles' that make life easier, but once you have been shown these, you are away. Yes, there are some higher-end problems on more complex pieces, but with the basic skills under your belt, you will soon be able to work your own way through most of the pieces that you come across.

Wherever you start, whether it be books, classes or apprenticeships; you eventually have to work some things out for yourself, because not every type of chair or every problem can be found in the project-based upholstery books that are available.

The purpose of this book is to take you through the basics and to introduce you to some of the wrinkles. There is, however, no real substitute for going to a class and seeing several different types of piece being worked on. For some that is not always possible; hopefully, therefore, this book will enable you to make a start on your own.

It is interesting how often adult students coming to a class once a week bring the piece that they are working on and get on quite well. Yet between classes they do not touch it. Yes, we do all lead busy lives, and sometimes there just isn't a spare moment. Occasionally on this 'toe-in-the-water' once a week programme some students even appear to have forgotten what the tutor has helped them with through the previous week. But on some occasions there is a real, but self-imposed block. Because a piece of professionally finished upholstery looks so skilful, the student thinks 'I will never be able to do that (unless 'teacher' is holding my hand)' so they wait for the support of class night. This is a pity – you really can do it if you do but try; so this book is intended to allow you no excuses!

One thing is certain, there is nothing like 'giving it a go' - and then backing it up with plenty of practice.

There are, fortunately, many students who 'get bitten by the bug' as the saying goes. They are shown something at a class, and the following week show up with the piece completed. One student on a one night a week, three-term course started as a complete beginner. By the end of the year, despite holding down a full time day job, he had finished four drop-in seat pads for some antique dining chairs, covered two Victorian balloon back chairs, resprung and covered a wing arm chair and a chaise longue. A professional might have done a more perfect job, but the student's work was definitely acceptable and graced his home.

Before you start to read the book itself, it is worthwhile looking carefully at its structure. It is a manual rather that a 'start at the beginning and read through to the end' type of book.

First, it is assumed that your interest in the skills of upholstery is because you actually want to do some. You have a piece of furniture that has been loved to death and is now sagging so badly that you just cannot live with it any longer. Or you have seen a battered old piece in a junk shop and you can see its potential. Many want to reupholster a classic piece for their own use because the quality of so much new furniture is so appalling (and the price unjustifiably high). Again, you may have a student offspring who needs furniture for the bedsit. Or perhaps you just want an interesting new activity to while away the winter evenings. For whatever reason, you are going to tackle your first piece (or two) and you now need to know how to go about it. This book is primarily aimed at you. It is also, of course, designed to provide a set of permanent notes should you decide to go to a local evening class.

The book has been structured in a particular way. Many books on upholstery are project-based. In these, each chapter takes a particular piece of furniture and then works through the process of recovering it from beginning to end as a project. By choosing the projects included, the authors manage to cover most of the basics.

There are two difficulties with this approach. First, only the problems associated with specific pieces of furniture are covered. But worse, project-based texts prompt some readers/students to look for a book that has a piece of furniture that is exactly the same as the one they wish to work on. It stops them conceptualizing and they get locked into a 'maker's manual' mindset. With this, they need precise, illustrated instructions on how to tackle each

step on a model exactly the same as theirs. It could be that if they have four different items to redo, they have to have four books! This is not necessary – the skills are transferable from one piece to the next, and an introduction to basic skills and the idea of problem solving should be all that is needed. Later, perhaps, they may think about a book on advanced techniques.

You will occasionally come up against a problem of a specialist nature – but you will rarely see these in a project-based text. To deal with everything – such as some of the fancy decorative patterns of chair caning – would require several volumes. For these, you will need to go to books on specialist techniques (and they are not always easy to find), or seek professional advice – maybe even beyond the skills of the local evening class teacher. Or, and this is the best route, starting with a good grounding in all the basics and an understanding of why things are done in a particular way, you then develop the ability to be able to work out for yourself how to tackle the more complex pieces.

So here, we will focus upon basic skills and techniques – such as 'Springing' – in all its common patterns; or 'Making Corners' – whatever the material or stage of the work. There are then notes on how these techniques apply or may have to be modified to suit different pieces of furniture.

After a general introduction to upholstery, we take a look at the finding and preparation of chair carcasses. There are then notes on tackling the most frequently needed aspects of frame restoration.

From here, the book moves into an examination of the basic forms of upholstery – rushing, caning, simple stuffed pads, built-up forms, and then spring-based structures.

In each of these sections we take the process as far as the need for a final covering. There is then a section on choosing, measuring, cutting and fixing the covering fabrics.

We then need to consider some of the variations on basic patterns so we look at buttoning, loose cushions and some of the problems presented by specific types of piece. In the appendix, there are also some summaries of the steps involved in completing the upholstery of various typical chairs to show how the basics link together in sequence.

Finally, there are chapters which are in essence recaps; they also serve as quick reference sources. In the earlier process sections, some skills have been taken for granted. For instance, you are advised to draw together the folds on a corner using slip stitches. Most readers will know what this phrase means – but not all, so there is a chapter on knots and stitches for those readers who are non-sewing, non-angling landlubbers. There is also a listing of tools and a breakdown of the materials used.

So although you may be undertaking one type of project – say re-covering a drop-in pad – you will find most of the core information in one chapter, but you will also need to refer to others such as the chapter on covering. If it is your first piece and you have not built up a tool kit or ever done any sewing, you might have to dip further into other chapters on points of detail.

However, whatever your starting level, you should find, somewhere in the book, all the information that you will need to enable you to tackle a number of different levels of upholstery projects. But please take heed of the comments made in the chapter on carcasses and do not try to run before you can walk. Don't start with a wing arm chair or multiple curve nursing chair, but with something simple such as a stool, or some drop-in pads for dining chairs.

To round off the book in Appendix II there are further reading references and a list of some of my favourite sources of supply. It is not a comprehensive list of all suppliers and by asking around, searching the Yellow Pages for your own area and keeping your eyes open, you will soon be able to build up your own list of favourites. A few months ago when looking for carcasses in antique shops (not an ideal source) in a village near Bournemouth I was advised of a wonderful local upholstery supplies shop. Here the stocks were amongst the best I have ever found – yet he did not advertise anywhere. In Middlesex I used an antiques/junk shop which also sold all the basics at prices only a little above wholesale. So it really does pay to look and ask.

However good your area or your searching, do not expect to find everything locally. I have a nearby sawmill that supplies kiln-dried beech for carcass repairs. I also found a supply of excellent mahogany boards at a local undertakers. Everything else we use in the studio has to be obtained by mail order or on the occasional visit to London.

One area of upholstery has been excluded from this book, and one only touched on briefly. The exclusion is loose covers. Although the upholsterer does need to be able to sew and to use a sewing machine, and may be able to make a reasonable cover, loose covers are not usually made by an upholsterer and have therefore not been included.

The area which is only referred to briefly are those forms of upholstery that have been developed for modern industrial production – hence rubberized webbing, pre-formed spring frames, cut foam blocks and similar are given scant mention. Our focus is very clearly upon what is known as 'traditional methods' and this means using traditional materials (in their original and their contemporary form).

In fact many upholsterers will not even consider the refurbishment of some modern pieces. Many are designed so that they can be covered once only and the construction of some is such that they are best scrapped after a year or two's wear. They are made of matchboard, chipboard and scrap wood; held together with staples; and are

A student's first piece. Stuffed back pad and sprung seat. A braid trim is yet to be fitted.

(Below) *Cattection! Slip-over covers for every day use in a house with three cats.*

stuffed with foam which was often (until recently) highly flammable. Worst of all, in some cases the frames are built up around the upholstery and you have to start by taking the carcass apart – and most were not designed to that end.

It has to be emphasized that not all modern pieces are bad! The construction of a Parker Knoll wing chair is a joy to behold. Often the timber used is of even better quality than was used by the great furniture-making masters of the past. They are solid and 'properly' jointed. Although designed to be upholstered using contemporary methods, many can still be adapted to use traditional materials.

Of one thing I am sure: using traditional materials and basic skills, and applying a little logic and intelligence, you will be able to tackle most pieces that you wish to, whether ancient or modern.

11

Do you wonder that someone started upholstery classes? A nicely shaped but modern wing chair that will be sprung and covered using traditional approaches.

— 1 —

Historical Perspective

'Using traditional methods and materials' does not mean going to the local farmer and cadging an armful of straw! You may come across some pieces that actually are stuffed with straw, or even mildewed hay, but while a number of traditional methods are practised in a manner largely unchanged since they were first introduced, materials have been developed which enable us to cope better with supply problems, convenience, fire and health hazards, storage issues and many day-to-day matters.

So, in faithfully restoring an antique we use appropriate, but not necessarily original materials. Let's put this into a broad context by taking an historical overview – well, part history and part supposition! There are few records that tell us that a certain form of seating was introduced at a particular time or in a specific place. Occasionally, there are early drawings that show a certain piece in use, but, of course, very few of the original pieces have survived the rigours of use, damp and draughty housing, woodworm, fire and so on. In fact, the Great Fire of London caused a major clearout of furniture and triggered the introduction of a huge range of new designs and new materials.

At one time we probably all sat on the ground or upon a handy rock or branch. None was really satisfactory. The ground was damp, and rocks were cold and immovable. Rocks could be made a little more comfortable by throwing an animal skin over them – but they remained immobile.

Tree trunks and blocks of wood probably came next. These could be moved and were 'warmer' to sit on. By using bits of wood lashed together the seats became even more portable than solid blocks of wood. Benches, simple board tables and wooden platform beds followed. But then have you ever tried sleeping on a wooden platform?

Hay wasn't bad – except that it irritated the 'cave-proud' who constantly had to sweep together the bits. So the hay or straw was stuffed into skins and bags to keep the bits together, and the mattress and seat pad were born.

In Mediaeval houses chairs were still not common. Information from the late sixteenth century indicates that a typical dining hall was still largely furnished with benches. The master of the house would often have had a wooden throne-like chair with arms; important guests were provided with stools; while the rest sat on simple benches or forms. In the wealthier houses, and for more important guests, the joynt stools would have had a cushion.

The heavier person would 'bottom out' through the straw palliasses – something softer was obviously needed. You could either have enormously thick stuffed mattresses, or provide a supporting framework that was not simply a solid board. The first springing arrangements were stretched skins or a less 'expensive' lattice of thongs of leather or lengths of 'rope'.

Most chairs were, however, still of solid board or plank construction. By the beginning of the sixteenth century there were also chairs where all legs, arms, rails and the back were of turned elements and only the seat platforms were a wooden board. It was still some time before upholstery became an integral part of the chair.

By now the board seats of chairs in wealthier homes were also sometimes replaced by stretched leather – this came to its zenith in Cromwellian times. At some earlier date, some bright spark had also thought about making ropes out of the rushes that grew in the nearby marsh, and this was certainly cheaper than leather. We do not know when woven rush seating first appeared in England, but the practice was known in Denmark early in the Viking times. It could well, of course, have been started much earlier by Nile-side dwellers in the Egypt of the Pharaohs. Settles and benches were, however, too long to rush, so they were still plain board, but they could be made much more comfortable with loose seat pads – again originally probably hay stuffed.

At some stage and somewhere, somebody probably got tired of picking the cushions up off the floor and decided to fix them permanently to the frame. So stuffed-over upholstery was born! Eventually, there were a few covered chairs, and some existing fabric-covered chairs have been dated at about 1600.

By the middle of the seventeenth century lounging furniture had begun to appear and there are armchairs that can be dated to this period.

The problem with grass and straw as a stuffing was that it quickly became compressed, squashed flat, and the straw started to break up into chaff. Something better was needed. Feathers and animal hair were seen to be much more resilient.

Horse hair was found to be a wonderful material. It was springy and long-lasting and was widely available. So the padding was built up, probably with some straw to give bulk, but then a thick layer of horse hair was incorporated to provide shape and comfort.

What was good to sit on was also nice to lie on, and mattresses were also feather or hair-filled. Back in Tudor times wealthy travellers carried their own mattresses (and bedding) with them – huge bags of feathers were considered to be an essential part of their baggage.

Unfortunately, no form of upholstery is everlasting and even the best-constructed pieces required periodic re-covering. In time, the frames got so holed and splintered that they became useless and were thrown away – very very few early examples still exist. Probably the best are some 600 to 700-year-old rope-sprung beds and a few solid or rope-sprung chairs.

Hessian sacking and then webbing took over from rope and thong. It first appeared as a base for the over-stuffing, and then much later as supports for the coil springs that had by then been developed.

Over the same period, there had been huge developments in society. No longer was there only the furnished castle or hall with everyone else living in 'packing case' furnished hovels. There were by now wealthy merchant and farming classes who could afford to have furniture made for them. It would, however, be a long time before much of the furniture was made by craftsmen cabinet makers; instead, it was usually part of the ongoing output from the estate or village carpenter's workshop – even the local wagon maker would have a go. The so-called 'Inferior' chaise longues that still abound from early Victorian times are a more recent example of this practice. They required only the most basic of woodworking skills and were probably made and upholstered by the village 'chippy'.

With the eighteenth century advent of steel springs, widespread use was made of jute webbing to support sprung frames, and the whole was topped with layers of hair and wadding under patterned fabrics. Very quickly this method of upholstery became a worldwide standard, and was used on furniture of a wide range of qualities.

Coil spring and hair stuffing has remained as a basic technique until recent times. Post-World War II, more modern industrial approaches were developed and

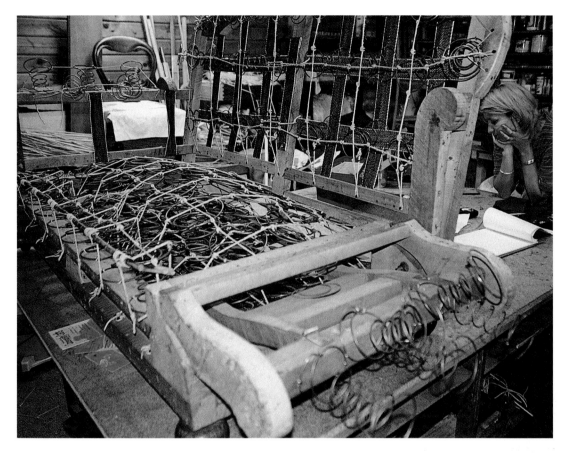

Not to be recommended. This student contemplates the work in progress on her first piece – a fully sprung drop-arm Chesterfield.

long tension springs and rubberized webbing have now replaced coil springs on factory-made furniture. For all this, springs and stuffing remain today not only as 'traditional materials' but as those used by most craftsmen furniture makers.

Of course, other developments were continuing in other countries. In the Far East – and it is uncertain whether it was India or China – use was being made of cane, and particularly rattan. Rattan is a jungle creeper which can grow to lengths of 400 to 500ft (120 to 150m). It was woven into cane and 'wicker' furniture; but it was also sliced so that thin strands of the inner

bark could be used to weave into the seat and back panels of cane-bottomed furniture. This appeared in some quantity in England in the early seventeenth century as London recovered from the Great Fire. It too has remained in its original form since that time.

Of course, there have been developments as well as modifications forced upon us by issues of supply and demand. There are now far fewer horses per head of population than there ever used to be, and so horse hair is not readily available. Some imported hog's-hair is now used. Vegetable hairs (based upon coconut fibres) have been developed and are now widely used. More sophisticated cotton waddings have taken over from rags and cotton waste.

Then, of course, the 'plastic age' hit us – first in the form of rubber and then plastic foams. Today, with pre-shaped blocks it is easy to achieve any desired shape, however complex. All you need now is the very crudest of wood frame and then go to the catalogues of the upholstery suppliers for shaped blocks that will give you a perfect carcass. Square corners and sharp edges cause no problems and because of their precise shape and the predictable sizes of a factory-cut block, covers can be machine sewn to shape rather than be built up panel by panel on the chair frame.

There are many who do not like the perfect shapes and clearly synthetic appearance of the mass-produced items, however; and the cause of the traditionalists was given a huge boost with the introduction of the stringent safety and fire regulations. Some plastic foams have been found to be particularly hazardous. Now fire-resistant stuffings (and foams) are available, and any piece of furniture finished for selling has to use FR-rated materials.

APPROACHES TO RESTORATION

There have been developments in other branches of this main line journey through the history of upholstery. Let's go back to rush seating. Rush is good, lasts reasonably well, but is not the easiest of materials to work. There have therefore been various alternatives. The problem is that rush work requires that the upholsterer has to twist his or her own 'rope' while weaving the seat. This means frequently laying in another rush, and twisting this onto the strand. So you have to keep a twist on the cord while threading and weaving it. Sea

grass is used as an alternative and this can be obtained in pre-twisted lengths or ropes. It is more durable and is not so inclined to dry out, but when compared with true rushing it does look synthetic. Of course, this form of seating has not escaped plasticization. Plastic ropes can be obtained which explore the full colour range available in synthetics.

So today, when you are restoring an old piece of furniture or upholstering a new or reproduction frame, the choice of approaches is wide open. Some Scandinavian designers have gone back to rope, sometimes simply strung, sometimes woven; and this provides not only springing, but finishing material as well. Others use moulded plastic or even shaped stainless steel seats.

Preformed mesh spring units may be found in both antique and relatively modern pieces.

You might at auction be tempted to buy an old rope-sprung bed frame. Ideally (and to the purist), it should be restored with hemp rope to the pattern it was designed for; but there is nothing except time and expense to stop you webbing the frame and using coil springs.

And it works the other way round. Many modern chairs and stools, particularly some nursing chairs, have a pre-formed, built-up mesh-topped spring unit held in place with crude steel brackets. It is a norm amongst upholsterers that you do not reuse old springs. There are still suppliers who will build up one-off spring units for you to your own specification, or you may even be brave enough to really test your engineering skills and build up your own. However, the wooden frames of most chairs will usually accept webbing and traditional coil springing. Yes, of course, you could get a block of foam and cut this into the required shape – but if you really are interested in upholstery then such an approach will not satisfy you. Indeed, if that is all you want to do then you neither need this book, nor an evening class!

BASIC PRINCIPLES

Whatever style or system of upholstery you now opt for, there are some basic principles to take into account. Chairs are intended to support the body's weight with a level of comfort appropriate to the intended use. The longer you are to sit in a chair the softer it needs to be. Hence kitchen chairs which are intended to be sat on for brief periods can be relatively hard (and should probably be washable!). Today, this may mean only a piece of ply, a thin layer of foam, and a utilitarian plastic or leather cloth cover.

Bedroom chairs do not get much use (other than as overnight clothes rails – extending to a week or two for the male child!). They could therefore be firm. But of course many ladies use them to sit at a dressing table and so it is normal practice to make them softer and more appealing. This usually means sprung seats. Nursing chairs need to be very soft and comfortable for those long midnight hours of suckling. This definitely requires deep springs.

It depends upon your dining habits as to what your ideal dining chair is. If you regularly hold dinner parties or long family meals where sitting at table and discussing the ways of the world is the norm, then sprung seats rather than stuffed over-pads are to be preferred. The tops of such seats should also be fairly flat – domed pads become very uncomfortable after a while.

In general, hard/raised front edges are not good, as their pressure under thigh muscles can limit circulation. However, downwards sloping front edges are not good either as these give a mound centre effect. There is now pressure on the lower bones of the pelvis and this can trigger pins and needles. If you do get pins and needles after a prolonged sitting at the dining table, then there is probably something wrong with the chair's design, and particularly with the profile and nature of the upholstery.

Although the ideal top profile is flat, you need to have a little more give in the centre than at the edges. This allows the seat to mould around the buttocks, which in turn increases the contact area, spreads the load more evenly, and ensures that there are no pressure points. For this reason, the walls of stuffed over-seats are built up to be firmer than the centre area.

This is also the reason why the stuffing is fixed over springs or stretched webbing strips, and why only the cheapest low-quality chairs have ply boards. If you ever find an antique chair with a board under the stuffing (and it is not uncommon), then you know that some bodger or cowboy upholsterer has got at it.

BASIC COSTS

Maybe this is the time to introduce another thought – that of cost. Many people are surprised when they get a quote from a professional upholsterer. The cost will often be many times what the owner paid for the second-hand chair. Indeed the cost for properly done reupholstering can be a significant percentage higher than would be the cost of buying a new factory-made chair from a high street furniture store.

In fact, you should not be surprised. Once you take on an upholstery project of your own, you will begin to understand. By shopping around you can often halve the cost of materials from one supplier to the next; but even when you do find a keenly priced supplier, the total cost will still make you gulp! A London upholsterer recently quoted £1,500 for a three-seater settee, and a Parker Knoll dealer says 'two-thirds of the original cost of the chair'.

Six stuffed-on-springing dining chairs will take thirty-six springs, and about 15lb (6.8kg) of hair – animal or vegetable. You might get Filair – black-coated coir fibre – for £2.90 per pound (one supplier's 1999 price). It can be over £4! An average drop-in pad will require about 1 to 1½lb of hair. You have to add the webbing, cord, tacks, cotton wadding, lintels, bottom cloth, hessian and calico; so you are now up to £10 plus per chair. We still have not bought the covering fabric and depending upon pattern and matching you could be in for a total of 3 metres at anything between £10 and £30 a metre according to taste. If you had to pay the overheads for your own workshop and to pay yourself an average wage (currently standing, according to government statistics, at £300 plus per week), then redoing your chairs is unlikely to come cheap. A wing armchair using mid-priced covering fabric could easily cost you £120 to reupholster yourself. Even a professional upholsterer buying all the materials in bulk will still be paying considerably more than half that sum. Add to this overheads and mark-up and you can begin to see why reupholstery costs money. Yes, you can do it more cheaply – you can get a bit of foam down at the market and simply tack a bit of curtain material over it at a fraction of the price of a satisfying, long-lasting, 'proper job'!

The choice is yours, but on my courses, and in this book, we are only concerned with doing a proper job at as reasonable a cost as we can achieve.

There is no monetary value that you can put upon the satisfaction of doing the job properly – of finding out what the original approach would have been and getting back as close as possible to that. Not necessarily back to the original materials, but to the modern replacements or equivalents, and to the age-old traditional upholstery techniques and skills.

— 2 —

A Fine Brown Frame
Carcasses and Where to Find Them

The first piece that you upholster may well be some much-loved utilitarian piece that has simply become worn out. It may be a stool or a bedroom chair. Flushed with your success on the simple piece you may decide to redo the drop-in pads for the dining chairs. After this you should look for an armless chair with a sprung seat. Then, and only then, should you think about that old armchair.

Not everybody does it this way – more's the pity! New students often arrive at an evening class with some quite complex nursing chair that they were lucky enough to pick up at auction. One, for her first piece ever, brought an appallingly badly made modern wing armchair. What followed was ten weeks of mind-stretching and off-the-cuff problem solving! It was like jumping in at the deep end of the baths before you have even learnt to doggy paddle. So if the treasured piece is complex, find a couple of things to cut your teeth on first. Let's think about obtaining carcasses: what to look for, and where to find them.

AT THE AUCTION

Auctions are not very good places for the beginner to find quality pieces. Yes, super pieces can be found there; but if they are of quality and have an antique cachet, you will be competing with dealers. It will cost you to win! At the end of the day you will

Back from auction – a trailer load of frames for restoration and recaning. The price was £18 – the cost two weeks' work (before caning could start).

have a piece of value, but only when your upholstery has reached professional standards and you are buying all your materials wholesale. Start by looking for something a bit more middle-of-the-road.

Auctions, however, are very good for everyday carcasses. Often for just a pound or two you can get a single, relatively modern dining or bedroom chair which will be ideal for practising traditional approaches. Recently, a well-made modern style wing armchair cost me £1, and a trailer-load of Victorian kitchen chairs for caning cost just £18 (although admittedly several of these are still under treatment in the woodworming ward).

Some upholsterers have become very adept at buying at auctions. They have been at it for years, and now really know the ropes.

First, it is essential that you view in advance. This gives you time to look right round and to examine likely pieces in detail. Some amateur potential bidders think that they should not show real interest in a piece because this will let other people know they are interested, which will push the price up. A few even think that they should not draw attention to the little gem that they have spotted because it may have escaped the notice of potential rivals. Forget it!

At any auction today there will be a score or two of professional dealers. According to the level the auction is pitched at, and the type of publicity it is given, that score may treble and it will include not only the local traders with modest budgets but also the wealthier dealers who are buying for the London and other fancy-priced export markets.

If there is *any* piece worth buying, these dealers will know about it – and they will have examined it in the minutest detail. They will know its value, and will have spotted all the defects that only a trained eye would see. They will know where they are going to sell it, and at prices you would not even dream of paying.

As a one-off buyer you do have one advantage, however, the dealers have to make a profit – so if you do succeed in buying a piece its retail value will probably be higher than the price you paid.

It is widely known in the trade that many pieces bought in auction get sold or exchanged within hours of the hammer falling, and that some change hands as many as ten or a dozen times before they are even seen by their final owner. You may be at the umpteenth auction that the chair has been through.

It is not only chairs that can be found at auctions. Old Ottoman chests respond well to simple stuffing and fabric covering.

CHOOSING A CARCASS

Obviously a sound, robust frame will make life a lot easier for you when you come to reupholster it. So, before you buy, test that the joints are tight, and particularly that the back does not move in relation to the seat. Legs should certainly be vertical and firm. Arms are better if tight but slackness here is the easiest defect to put right.

Avoid carcasses with a lot of woodworm. Heavy infestation almost certainly means that some of the spigots and dowels of the joints will need major surgery. This really is not worth bothering with, so such pieces are best left to the professional furniture restorer.

Almost anything is repairable, even broken legs, provided that you have the time and skills, tools and equipment. Note that very few furniture problems are simply a matter of 'applying a little glue'! For example, if the joints have become unstuck the only real answer is to dismantle the piece – this may mean steam injection or some other treatment to break apart any remaining sound joints, then cleaning out all traces of the old glue. You can then re-glue, reassemble and clamp up. This probably also means that there is a need for a set of large sash cramps to hold the frame square while the glue sets. Are you geared up for this?

So look hard at any piece you are interested in. Make absolutely sure that it is worth buying and that it does not require repairs that are beyond your capability. Remember that it will cost you not only the auction price, but also the cost of all of the tools and materials you will require and possibly an extra 20 hours of work.

Unfortunately, the fact that the piece needs recovering will not bring the price of a quality item down at auctions. On the contrary, dealers often know that a properly reupholstered antique will more than repay the work done on it. Indeed, in some instances the fact that the upholstery is falling away, or that the carcass has been stripped, can put the price up. That way, you can see the frame and you know the quality of what you are buying.

BIDDING

Stay around a while at the auction viewing. See how much other interest your chosen lot is attracting, and by whom. You will soon learn to spot the dealers, and quickly build up an idea of what they will go for and what sort of prices they will pay. You will see them openly take out their note books and jot down the lot number and their maximum bid price.

Now set your own price. From here on, you must be hard and not go above that price. Even though the piece may be knocked down to the next bid after you have dropped out, you will never know how much further your rival(s) might have gone had you continued. Bid up to your limit but no more. Your limit should reflect your real interest and should have been carefully set. If you really want the piece you will have set a higher limit, and that limit should win other than in exceptional circumstances. If you lose at that level then it is just as well – let someone else waste their money! Often I have some interest in a piece, but nothing particular, so some of my limits are 'flyers'. I don't mind if I lose, but if I win under such circumstances I know that I have got a really good deal. Naturally, I lose many more flyers than I win on; but then sometimes I am surprisingly lucky. When I am, it is not because I spotted something that others had missed – it is just that nobody else happened to want it. Unfortunately, you are then left with that niggling doubt – 'I wonder why nobody else wanted it?'.

It is not recommended that you position yourself where you can see those who are bidding against you. If you eyeball a bidder

This beech chair was bought for £24. One arm was loose and the finish was poor. It has been repaired, sanded, stained and button polished. (the working trolley will be referred to later.) The stool is a repaired job but is now part of the workshop furniture.

it can become a gladiatorial contest, and if you then win, you will find you have lost – your shirt! Also eyeballing a professional is dangerous for another reason. They can read the signs – they can see that you are twitchy or nervous as you near your limit – they *know* when *you* will stop.

Don't start the bidding, and don't get excited when the auctioneer started with a 'Who will bid me £50?' and has not been able to get a bid right down to a fiver. If he still cannot even get a pound, then don't worry. You have probably missed something that others have spotted. You can always go and have another look at the piece after the auction and then go to the auctioneer and make an offer. On the other hand, if he had asked £50 to start, that may be what he intends to try to get – and sometimes will. Dealers and bargain hunters wait until it has got down to the fiver in case they are lucky – but they never are! And do not be fooled by the price estimates that you see on some auction lists. These are often set well below what the piece eventually sells for – it could be the auctioneers' ploy to attract potential bidders to the sale!

You have to learn when to come in. Some auctioneers want to keep the pace going and as soon as bidding lags they drop the hammer. Ideally, and to play safe, wait until there are only two bidders left in the contest and the pace has just started to slow. You will become the 'new bidder' and you will probably have to make three or four more bids before you convince those who were bidding that their cause is lost. Make sure that the auctioneer sees your first bid – it is useful if you have earlier made some flyer bids on items because he will then know that you are a potential buyer and will be watching you. If not, and he does not appear to be looking your way, make your first bid bold. After that he will watch and you can be much less obvious.

So what might you expect to pay? At 1998 prices a mixed lot of three or four kitchen and bedroom chairs, two of which might be workable, can go at some regular 'household and antique furniture' sales for a couple of pounds. Two or three matching period dining chairs may fetch £10 to £20. As soon as you get to four matching chairs prices start to climb. Four modern dining chairs with drop-in pads might go for £20, but if they are relatively plain Edwardians you are unlikely to get them for under £50 and according to character and age you can soon add a nought to that. Sets of six really nice walnut or rosewood chairs with a carver may run to over £1,000, and for a really special antique set expect telephone bidders to far outstrip the local dealers. I saw a set of six plus two carvers recently fetch £7,200. The area in which the auction is located can do anything from halving all of these figures to doubling them. You just have to research your own auctions, and

avoid all those that are given national advertising, or are promoted as 'antiques and collectors' events.

Sometimes you can get a modern, semi-reproduction wing armchair for £25, but for a relatively nice period piece even in poor condition you would be lucky to see any change out of £250. Any wing, tub or library chair of antique quality but requiring reupholstery is likely to go for over £400 at a furniture and antiques sale. Knowle settees – lovely to do – range from £250 to £750 (unless special), whereas Chesterfields – quite difficult to tackle, particularly if buttoned – will be much lower.

OTHER SOURCES

Unless you are after a character piece you will often do better by watching the adverts in local papers. Around us (the Marches) there are regular offers of wing armchairs of Parker Knoll quality (well made and nice when recovered) at £25 to £40. Occasionally, you will find nice period items but often the price asked for middle-range antiques in the local paper is higher than you would see at the right auction. Some people have grossly inflated ideas of the value of any piece that could even vaguely be classified as 'antique'.

The customer adverts on the supermarket noticeboards are also a useful source, and occasionally a large second-hand furniture store can turn up trumps. But remember that most of the goods there will have been purchased at auctions and that the price has already been doubled (at least!). Be prepared once again set your own price and bargain – hard!

There are times when you might place your own ads. Try both the local papers and the free advertising papers such as *Loot* or *Bargain Pages*. Quite often, people have items that they simply want to get rid of. You can be their golden opportunity – and they yours!

You can, of course, buy carcasses that have been specially made for upholsterers, and the catalogues of many upholstery suppliers will carry a range. Most are made in beech but they are very expensive and are often not particularly well made. Some even use short life, modern factory jointing techniques (staples and so on). A ready-made dining carver could be £200–300; and a quite poor Victorian balloon back nursing chair over £200.

Throughout this book, stress will be laid upon the quality of construction. Of course, once covered you do not see the woodwork, so does it really matter? The answer is: it all depends. 'Country Chip' or 'Inferior'* furniture from the past has lasted fifty to one hundred years already – it will certainly last a few years more, and once recovered it will look very nice. However, it will never be worth much and you will be very disappointed when your lovingly restored chaise fails to make £80 at auction; but if you are doing it for yourself, does that matter? Unless you really know what you are doing, buying furniture for reupholstering and then trying to sell it on is a non-starter. You are better rewarded by selling your services as an upholsterer.

What must be avoided at all costs is modern factory-made furniture that is designed for one-owner use and to last two to five years at best. The wood is of the lowest grade white wood and is left rough sawn. Often all joints are butts and are held with white glue and staples. Because they were designed to be foam-upholstered they do not have the necessary strutting to provide anchors for the various layers of stuffing and covering. The exposed legs will be held on with screws (which often pull out) and the legs may even be made of 'wood effect' plastic.

Actually, if you are considering 'country chip', then why not make the carcass yourself? You really could do better than some of the stuff that is on the market and there are many 'how to' books with good, easy

A Prie Dieu chair. The construction of the frame is extremely simple and is well within the capability of a handyman.

designs. If you hanker after a Knowle settee for instance, it is both easier and cheaper to make your own frame than it is to find an old one for recovering.

* *'Inferior' is a widely used term applied to chaise longues made by the local carpenter. Woods are stained to look like mahogany and carving is often crude.*

— 3 —

The Full Monty
Stripping Off

So you have dragged it out of the loft; been given it by a parent; or fallen in love with it and paid money for it at an auction, and now it is sitting in front of you.

The cover is worn through, the stuffing is oozing out of the arms, and broken lengths of webbing are hanging down underneath. Probably a leg is loose. So where do you start?

Sorry, whatever the apparent condition of the stuffing, there is only one answer – take it *outside*, either into the open air, or a workshop or shed. You just have to strip the chair down – remove everything, and start again with new materials. Old stuffing has compressed down, is dirty and is probably infested with cat fleas. Some of the springs, although they may look all right, will have lost their tension. Hessians will have dried and denatured. Ultimately, you have to throw *everything* away. In actually stripping it you will create mess and a lot of dust. This is not a job for the kitchen table, at least not at this stage.

There are three exceptions to the 'bin everything' rule. Keep one example of each of the sizes of spring that there were. You may need these as patterns when finding replacements. Unless it is a very simple design of chair, you might also find it useful to remove the top cover carefully and even if it is damaged, keep this as a guide pattern for cutting the new covering fabric. The third exception is different. If the chair is stuffed with genuine horse hair this is worth keeping for later use.

Proper hair is wonderful to work with, but it is both very difficult to obtain and expensive. If you find a supply of new hair, it will probably be an imported mix of hog and cow's tail. This is good, but nowhere near as nice as horse hair. So hang on to any hair you find. Some of my students have a deal with the local tip – any old horse hair mattresses are put on one side for them.

The hair is removed (once you have the chair outside), and is put into old pillow cases which are then sewn up. These are taken to the local launderette and put into the industrial clothing machine. Do not risk your own domestic washer. The cleaning process kills off any vermin and bugs; removes the accumulated dust of ages; and restores the wonderful springiness of proper hair. However, do not expect to restuff the same chair with the hair you have removed unless you can supplement it with hair from another source. Keep the reclaimed hair in store until you have enough to tackle another chair.

Unfortunately, nothing else from the original can be restored. Occasionally, you find good quality down and feather stuffing that is contained in a dust-proof fabric case and this may be reused. Everything else is thrown away, including the old tacks.

STRIPPING DOWN

Let's look at the actual methodology of stripping down. First, get a notebook and pencil, and possibly even a camera.

In the early days of your involvement with upholstery you should study how each piece was done. Don't just rip everything off, but try to reverse the order of the original covering process. You will find that it was built up in layers, so remove the materials layer by layer. Make a sketch of how the corners were formed. Note particularly to what each layer was nailed. Identify the precise sequences of laying the webbing, springs, hessian, hair, hessian, cotton wadding and calicoes. Note where and how the springs were fixed and laced. As you progressively strip your piece down, note particularly where the layers from one part – say the wings – were nailed over the finishing fabric from another part – possibly the seat or back facing.

You will find this information absolutely invaluable when you start to rebuild. You will also discover that there are few standard routines and sequences, but that each carcass is different; and there will be specific variations in each piece. Each will require its own modified treatment.

You may want to press on, but the need to take time in stripping cannot be overemphasized. A beginner stripping a fully sprung, Edwardian drop-arm settee may take 10 to 12 hours to reduce to a bare carcass. Yes, it can be done in an hour, but you will learn nothing!

The first thing to remove is the bottoming cloth (if any). This will be held in place with a row of upholstery tacks. A ripping chisel and a mallet (NB *not* a hammer!) are used to remove all tacks. A proper ripping chisel is unique to upholstery. It has a chisel end, a bit like a single bevel wood chisel, but the shank is cranked. This enables you to drive the edge under the head of the tack and then to lever it out. *Always* drive the edge of the ripper in from the side by pointing it along the grain of the wood. This helps to push the tack out. If you rip across the grain, the tack will cause the wood to split and you can easily break long splinters out of the frame. If the chair has been reupholstered many times and the tacks have been ripped out across the grain, the frame members can be so broken that retacking is not really possible.

It is worth noting that you can make a spare straight-bladed ripping chisel by grinding the end of an old screwdriver to a sharper chisel edge.

The stripping set.
From left to right – a tack claw; round-nosed pincers; a good claw hammer; a plastic-headed mallet; a homemade ripping chisel (ground screwdriver) and a proper cranked ripping chisel.

A cranked ripping chisel being driven under the head of an old tack.

Once the tack has started to lift you can get under the head with a tack claw and lever the old tack right away. Many standard DIY hammers have a nail claw on one end of the head. These tend to be a little too large for the smaller upholstery tacks, so a separate tack claw tool should be a part of your basic kit.

There are times when the heads break off old, rusted tacks. You may be lucky in that there is a sufficient nub standing proud that you can grip with a pair of round nose pincers. Gripping tight, the pincers are rolled on the nose and the tack may draw out. The few that will not come away should be driven right in with a hammer and nail punch.

The next piece to be removed is the back panel. This will usually have been tacked under the frame and sewn in down the sides. The stitches should be cut away with a Stanley knife. There may then be a tacking strip under a fold at the top of the panel.

Proceed on to remove all the top covering fabric. Again, you may find several panels have been sewn in, particularly the outside faces of the arm covers. The seat and the facing of the back will be wrapped around lower layers and will probably have been drawn around or under the frame to be tacked down. You may have to pull away braiding to reveal the tacks, and there may be piping or flanged cord along some edge joints.

Carefully undo the corners, and make a sketch noting how the material was cut and folded. Again, the seams or pleats on the corner may have been tack-stitched together.

There will probably be a calico layer under the top fabric, although there may be an interleaf of skin wadding.

You will now be down to the stuffing. There will be a covering of hessian over old hair or brown coconut fibre. In older chairs, there will be a layer of blue/black cotton or wool waste; this will be tied to perished hessian. In some very old chairs you might find a stuffing of straw or rotted hay. Under these will be another layer of hessian.

Unfortunately, most of these layers will have been broken up and it may be difficult

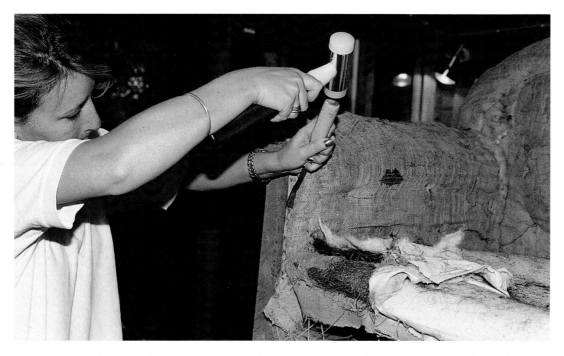

Milly strips the hessian off her old Chesterfield. Note the chisel is driven along the grain so that the wood does not split.

to establish how they were originally sequenced. Just pull them away and bin them for burning.

If the seat was sprung, you will now have reached the top of the springs. These may still be tied together with runs of lacing cord. Again note, sketch or photograph the position of the springs and the system of lacing. The springs are supported on webbing, some strands of which may be broken and hang loose. The springs should have been sewn down to the webbing – again note how.

Now, another important point to note. If the chair was sprung with coil springs the webbing to support these will have been nailed to the underside of the frame. If there were no springs, the platform of webbing will have been fixed to the top of the frame and the stuffing then fixed over this. This latter is a form of upholstery which is called 'stuffed over'. Springs are always

underslung – stuffing on hessian is always fixed on top of the frame.

You may, in removing the hair layer, find that there were rolls of hair wrapped in a 'tube' of hessian – these are known as dug rolls, and this is a device for building up a raised, firm edge to the seating pad. Note particularly how these rolls were made and fixed.

Do not be surprised at two things. First, cowboy upholsterers have been around a long time. Also, some of the country carpenter/furniture makers had only scant knowledge of proper upholstery techniques. You will often find that both groups have skimped on the webbing and that there are only two runs in each direction where you would prefer the strength of three. On larger sprung seats you would choose to use six, where they have used only four or five. On some really big pieces that I want to last, I put double runs of webbing. Rely on *your* judgment. Although much stress has been laid upon noting what you find when stripping down, you will learn to use this as a guide and not necessarily a strict pattern to follow.

The second thing you find could be an appalling cowboy trick. An original length of webbing has perished, but instead of removing it, a botched repair has been done and a new piece of webbing has merely been tacked over the broken bits. No attempt has been made to retie the bottoms of the springs. Just say a prayer for the repose of the souls of those who did it – they should now be languishing in perpetual torment!

One other thing to note in the stripping-down process is that when dealing with more complex pieces such as wing armchairs, particular attention should be paid to how the fabrics were fixed on the arms and wings. On modern Parker Knoll wings you may find that the wing was covered separately and then screwed in place. On older chairs the seat and back were covered right to finished fabric and the insides of the arms were then covered and the fabrics were nailed on top of the seat materials. Again on older chairs, seams may not have been nailed down as they were laid, because the materials for another part of the chair had to be drawn through the gap before nailing down would close it.

If you had not noted this, and in re-covering the chair you are following a normal upholstery sequence of getting every part

An Inferior chaise in the process of being re-covered. The webbing is the older brown jute. It is very strong but does stretch and sag. Here it had been applied as a double lattice – there are four strands under each spring.

A daybed webbed with modern 'old English black and white jute webbing'.

covered in calico before any covering fabric is fixed, you may suddenly find that you cannot run the fabric properly and you have to devise some quite bad bodge to get round the problem.

After you have done a few chairs you will find that you will have developed your own sequences and problem-solving skills. Notes are not now as important, and eventually they may become totally redundant.

So now you are down to a nude carcass – I hope that it is a pretty sight, but I doubt it!

It may look even more tired than it did when covered with tatty fabrics. I can almost guarantee one thing, that unless you paid a lot of money for a piece by a known maker, you will probably be appalled at the quality of timber and construction. In fact, it is at this stage that you begin to think that you were robbed at the auction. You weren't! What you now see is the norm. Be positive; it *will* look wonderful again when you have finished it. But before that time we may have to do something to the frame.

Sanatogen Or Surgery
Carcass Restoration

By the time a chair needs reupholstering it will probably need some repairing as well.

At best it may only require cleaning and repolishing; often, unfortunately, some of the joints will have gone and there is movement in the frame. The first to come apart are usually the joints between the seat and the top of the front legs. More of a problem is that the dowels or tenons inside some of the joints will have disintegrated. At worst, a frame member will have broken, and the nastiest of all is that a rear leg has split through or the main frame of the back rest will be in pieces.

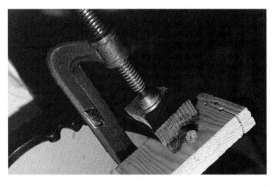

Repairs to a Victorian balloon back chair.

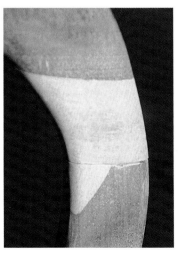

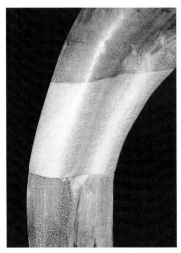

(Top left) *In the original botch repair the broken bits had been stuck together and a long pine dowel fitted.*
(Above) *The rails were tapered off and new pieces of mahogany were scarfed on (around a temporary dowel).*
(Far left) *A complete new piece on the top rail and a new lower corner below as seen from the back.*
(Left) *The front face is carved to profile and then sanded smooth.*

THE CHALLENGES AHEAD

Before you start to reupholster the seat, the frame has to be repaired and refinished. Let's now work through the various problem scenarios in increasing order of severity.

AVOIDING THE FULL STRIP

Most pieces of furniture for reupholstering arrive bruised and scratched. It is often the case that the finish – polish or varnish – has dulled, been chipped or marked. Often it has partly worn away and now looks not just 'aged', but tatty, unloved and unsightly.

Occasionally, the condition is such that there is no alternative to stripping the piece right down and completely refinishing; but do not be too anxious to go down this route. There are a couple of things against it.

First, the appearance of new or completely stripped wood is stark, bland and characterless. It looks even worse if placed next to a piece with normal wear and coloration. Secondly, the moment that you apply abrasives – even the finest grade of sandpaper – you can loose the crispness of square edges and carved decoration.

An antique, or in fact any piece of used furniture, will have a wide range of colours. Areas subject to wear, such as the front edge of the seat frame, are usually lighter in colour. The ends of spindles are darker. Deep corners and hollows often have very dark areas of built-up polish (and grime), euphemistically known as 'patina'. It is these colour variations that give the piece character.

So an action as drastic as completely stripping the piece is better avoided if possible. Totally removing the old finish also means that you will have to restain completely before repolishing and this can also lead to problems.

Using Furniture Cleaner
If a full strip can be avoided, our first possibility is to use a furniture cleaner,

The furniture stripping and cleaning set. Left to right: Two wood-handled scrapers. A tungsten carbide stripper for window frames. Two steel cabinet scrapers. Tin of Nitromors that will remove anything. Tin of furniture cleaner which does not attack the old varnish. Wire wool grade 0000. Sandpaper and wet or dry grade 180 to 400 grit.

but first there may be a little damage to repair.

The lightest damage may well include bruising and chipping. Here any jagged or splintered areas will need to be smoothed. Start with a medium grade of sandpaper – say 240 grit, and rub along the grain. With the splintering rubbed away remove the abrasive scratch marks with 400 grit paper, and smooth the whole area. The damaged area should then be burnished by rubbing it with a block of hardwood. An oak 'rubber' and a little pressure are ideal.

Next, touch up the area with a little wood stain of the appropriate colour. For this, a spirit-based stain is useful. Although spirit stains can fade in strong sunlight, they do not lift the grain in the same way as do water-based stains or dyes, which can be a plus at this stage of the process.

Scratches and small bruises are best treated with wax filler sticks. Rub the stick in the mark until a layer of wax is deposited, then burnish with a rag. Again, filler sticks are available in colours to match most woods.

Finally, the frame is cleaned down using a proprietary furniture cleaner and restorer. These are non-aggressive liquids which are rubbed on with 0000 grade wire wool. Some of the more aggressive have a base of Methyl Chloride (as used in brush cleaners). They will remove all the old wax and grime but not the stain; nor do they lighten (too much) the darkened corners. Once dry, wipe the surface clean with a dry cloth. It is now ready for re-polishing.

STRIPPING DOWN

Let's now notch one point higher up the problem scale. If the old finish was so bad that it had to be completely removed, this now becomes our first task. Whatever you do, avoid having the chair stripped in a caustic soda bath as this really does attack the glue joints. You can consider the use of brushed-on caustic soda, although even this is something of a specialist job and there are proprietary products that are both safer and easier to use. They do, however, involve a little more hand work and take time. Nitromors and a set of scrapers will totally remove most finishes, and recently Ronseal have brought out a pair of products that are extremely useful. One appears to be at least as aggressive as Nitromors, and will strip anything, including polyurethane; the other is a much gentler product designed for use on shellac varnishes and polishes. This latter is more appropriate for French-polished period pieces as it is less likely to etch into the underlying colour.

If you are planning to completely refinish and restain your piece it is important that you start with a clean carcass. All traces of the old shellac or varnish must be removed, as must all signs of glue that may have spilled out from the joints and repairs. Old glue and varnish remnants impede the absorption of dyes and stains and leave light coloured patches.

Often when you strip a piece you will get a surprise. Much of the furniture we work on when reupholstering starts out as 'mahogany'. Sometimes it is genuine, but more often it reverts to being beech on stripping. A great deal of Victorian furniture, even the quality reproduction work, is made of stained beech. Sometimes the stain was applied directly into the wood, but at other times it was incorporated into the varnish or shellac. In the latter case, all surface colour will completely disappear with the stripping; in the case of some dyes, traces will remain after using a mild stripper, but the piece will now be much lighter and will require recolouring.

STRUCTURAL REPAIRS

You will not always be so lucky that all that is required is a simple stripping job; in any case your developing interest in upholstery will soon lead you to being more adventurous in your purchase of carcasses. It will not be long before you decide that the time has come to accept the risk and you acquire a chair needing more fundamental refurbishment.

You are now faced with structural repairs. We will again look at this in terms of a range of different problems and consider the implications of each, again dealing with them in increasing order of complexity.

DISASSEMBLING THE CARCASS

First, many repairs will require either partial or total disassembly of the carcass. Occasionally, you will have a nice simple problem where just one of the members has come away and you can access the joint for regluing. Here, the joints are cleaned out, reglued and cramped together. More of this process in a moment.

More likely, however, is that some of the joints will have gone while others have held, and the free ones cannot be simply pulled apart and cleaned out. You are faced with doing some dismantling.

If the chair is modern, or has been repaired using modern synthetic glues, you have a problem. These are particularly difficult to 'unglue'. Some joints made with modern adhesives are stronger than the woods that they are bonding, and there are no solvents that will unbond the glues. This is the point when we make make a strong plea for restoring period furniture using the original animal glues.

Older pieces created using traditional methods and 'proper' animal glues are much easier to deal with. At one time old joints were steamed – often injecting steam into holes drilled into the joint. Some people try soaking in water – this really does not work and can result in refitting problems. All that is needed to separate most animal glue joints is to pour a little methylated

spirits into the joint. This will soften the glue. Two or three applications may be required, but usually the joints can be pulled apart after soaking for a few minutes. The process is so easy that if there are a number of loose joints, it is often easier to dismantle the whole (or most) of the chair. This greatly facilitates later joint cleaning and rebuilding.

If modern glues have already been used, the only answer to loose joints may be to try to introduce more glue into the recalcitrant joint. Veritas have produced a suitable product. It is a gap-filling glue which comes in a squeezy bottle and is supplied with three 'hypodermic' needles of different diameters. Glue is injected into the joint, if necessary through a small drilled hole. Alternatively, thin grade superglue can often be persuaded into the joint.

Not infrequently when a carcass is dismantled you will find some parts are broken – often one or more of the dowels or tenons are broken inside the joint.

Types of Joints
Basically, there are three types of joint used in chair construction. The first is where the end of one element, usually a stretcher or style, is rounded in section and has slightly tapered ends which are simply pushed in and glued into a round hole in the main frame member. The seat frame members of rush chairs are jointed in this manner, as are the stiles – the cross rails under the seat – on many Victorian balloon back and caned chairs and similar.

The second and third types of joint are where two adjacent members abut – often at right angles – and some form of key is used to strengthen the glued joint. There are two types of key. One is a dowel – a separate round peg which fits snugly (and is glued) into holes in the two adjoining members. Usually there are two or three side-by-side dowels to each joint. The third type is a mortise and tenon joint where the

To break open an old glue joint, simply pour in a little meths, wait a few moments and then pull the joint apart. Two or three meths applications may be needed. This method will not work with modern synthetic glues, however.

end of one member has a squared or rectangular tongue cut on the end and the other member has a matching squared mortise cut into it. Again they are cut to a snug fit and the joint is bonded with glue.

A variation of the mortise and tenon joint is often found on early oak and elm furniture where a hole is drilled through the side of the mortise member and into the tenon. A locking peg or dowel is then pushed through the two. Sometimes the hole in the mortise and the one in the tenon are ever so slightly offset so that the effect of driving in the dowel is to draw the two sides of the joint tightly together.

Broken Dowels

Broken dowels are frequently encountered, particularly where there has been some woodworm. Here, both ends have to be drilled out, the holes cleaned and new dowels inserted. Today, ready-shaped beech dowels can be purchased, but these will be in metric sizes so that old imperial holes will have to be drilled out. You will most frequently need 8 and 10mm dowels. The advantage of using commercial dowels is that they are made to be a tight fit, are already ribbed down their length to hold glue, and, being beech, they are tough, strong and long lasting. One other advantage of this approach is that drilling out to the marginally larger metric equivalent will clean up an old or damaged hole.

On older pieces of furniture you will find that the dowels were often hand hewn and are fitted into holes where the drill size seems 'variable'. Certainly the socket can be of larger diameter than that of a commercial dowel. The best answer now is not to try to replicate the hewn dowel but to drill out the socket to a clean diameter, to turn a plug to fit, glue this in place and then drill it out to the size of a standard dowel.

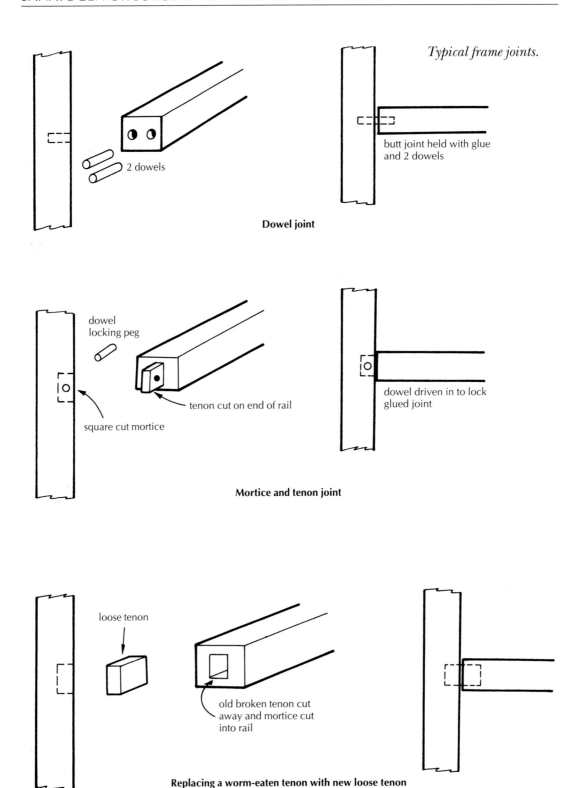

Typical frame joints.

2 dowels

butt joint held with glue
and 2 dowels

Dowel joint

dowel
locking peg

tenon cut on end of rail

square cut mortice

dowel driven in to lock
glued joint

Mortice and tenon joint

loose tenon

old broken tenon cut
away and mortice cut
into rail

Replacing a worm-eaten tenon with new loose tenon

WORST-CASE SCENARIOS

Now to some of the worst-case scenarios. A frame element may be broken. Possibly it is the spigot end; maybe a stile or seat frame member; or, worst of all, a leg is sheared through.

If it is a stile joint rather than a main frame joint that has broken, then this is not so difficult to deal with. Stiles are not fully load-bearing.

Sockets and Spigots

A broken end to a round socket fit has to be replaced with a new piece. The old end must be drilled out (or meths-removed) from the socket; the remaining part of the original stretcher is then cut to a long taper or 'scarfered'. A new end section is cut and shaped and is then also tapered off so that a splice or 'scarfed' joint can be made. You will then either have to turn or hand carve the make-up piece. Of course, there are times when it is easier to turn a complete new stretcher. This is especially the case where the stretcher is in easily replaceable wood such as oak or beech and where the frame can be sufficiently dismantled or sprung to make the fitting of a new length feasible.

To fit a new end, a whole new piece, or even to reglue an original member in place you must first clean out the old socket, removing any bits of broken wood and *all* traces of the original glue. Again, if the old spigot hole has broken edges it needs to be drilled out and plugged and redrilled.

The spigot end of the new piece is pushed into the hole and then the tapered end of this and the original stile are glued and bound.

Replacing the end of a broken stile with a new section.

Mortise and Tenon Repairs

Clearly if a tenon is broken (or is badly worm-eaten), the old bits have to be removed from the mortise and any remaining pieces cut from the rail end. The mortise is cleaned and a new mortise of exactly the same size is now cut into the end of the rail where the tenon used to be. A rectangular

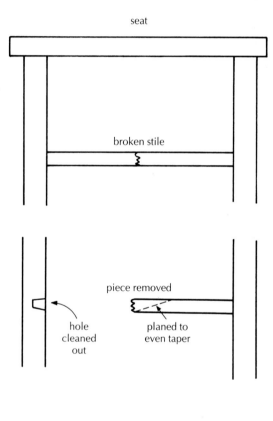

seat

broken stile

hole cleaned out

piece removed

planed to even taper

new piece tapered to make scarf joint

end shaved to fit hole

glued in and joint glued; bound with twine while glue sets

A common problem. Woodworm has got into the tenon on the side rail and it has snapped. The mortise has to be cleaned out, a new mortise cut into the side rail and a floating tenon made to fit.

key (or double-ended tenon piece) is now cut to sit into the two mortises.

The essence of all these repairs must be to ensure that a tight wood-to-wood fit is achieved between dowel hole and dowel or tenon and mortise. The purpose of glue is to bond the wood faces together, not to infill huge gaps. Almost any glue used as a gap filler will shrink on drying and will eventually split within the joint. Before long, the joint will be as bad as ever.

Joining Other Breaks

Most other frame repairs are based upon one or other of these joint repairing methods.

A clean break in a non-load-bearing member where there are no missing splinters can be glued together, but even here a simple butt joint will not have the necessary strength. It will probably need the additional support of glued-in dowels.

Metal brackets or wooden corner blocks can be used to provide additional support to a repaired joint, but it must be remembered that they are additional supports, not substitutes. You should not rely upon brackets without first regluing the joint. On their own, brackets do not provide sufficient rigidity or strength. One old design of wing chair was built using six internal metal plates or brackets to strengthen the carcass at particularly heavily stressed junctions, but the joints underneath were still properly dowelled. When restoring an old 'inferior' frame it is a good idea to add a few corner blocks even if the frame is not in need of repair.

GLUING THE JOINT

When it comes to the question of which glues to use, there are a number of considerations. First, if you are undertaking a period restoration, or you think the piece might require redoing at some time in the future, then you really should use Pearl or animal glue. This is purchased in pellet form and has to be melted slowly in a water-bath glue pot. Put the pellets into the inner pot the night before you wish to use the glue and cover them with cold water. The pellets will swell as they take up the water, so do not fill the pot to the brim. The following day, put the pot on a low heat half an hour before you wish to start work. Neither the glue in the inner pot, nor the water in the jacket, should be allowed to boil.

When you are going to make the joint, first heat the timber to be joined. You may use an oven but a hot-air gun (the so-called electric paint stripper) is fine. Quickly spread on a layer of glue and bring the joints together before the glue can cool. You may even have the paint stripper mounted so that it plays hot air onto the joint as you are reassembling it. Clamp up the joint with G or sash cramps and leave overnight.

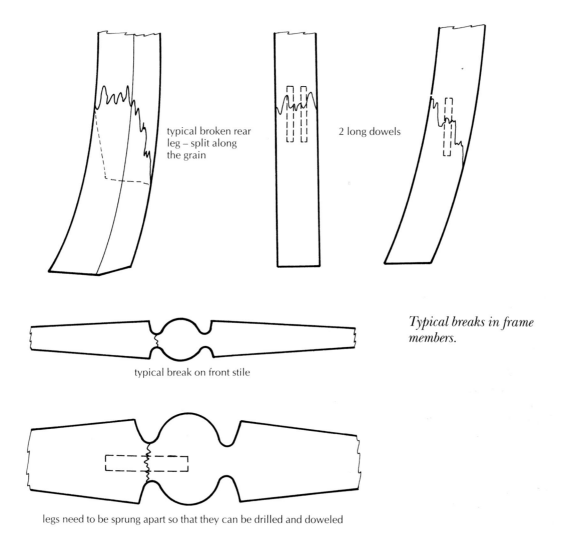

typical broken rear leg – split along the grain

2 long dowels

Typical breaks in frame members.

typical break on front stile

legs need to be sprung apart so that they can be drilled and doweled

For most work we tend not to be quite so fussy; but I still like to use a good glue. When boat building and for the strongest permanent joint my preference was Aerolite 604. (Aerolite *not* Araldite!) It was originally developed during the war for the building of the wooden-framed Mosquito fighter-bomber. This is a two-part urea formaldehyde-based glue. The powder is mixed with a measured quantity of water, and this syrup is spread over one side of the joint. The catalyst which hardens the glue is an acid and this is brushed onto the other side of the joint. Setting time is about half an hour. The beauty of this glue is that the thin liquid nature of the acid allows it to soak into the wood and a very strong bond is formed. Unfortunately, Aerolite has not been easy to find for some time.

Next on my list of preferences is Cascamite, a casein glue where the glue powder also contains the catalyst. Carefully measured quantities are mixed with water and the glue is used immediately. It takes a little longer to set but gives a very good bond (but again *not* for gap filling).

When sticking two large areas together, as in two boards face to face, then the PVA wood adhesives are very good. Personally, however, I do not find them totally satisfactory when making furniture joints and if laminating a load-bearing curved piece my preference would always be to use Cascamite.

There are, however, two problems with all the modern synthetic glues and adhesives. First, as already mentioned, they can not be easily opened if you are trying to strip a carcass. The other problem is that they dry white and will not stain. Hence if the joint is not absolutely tight they often create a white line. With the semi-transparency and brown colour of animal glues the mend is much less obvious.

There is one other gluing practice which can be useful, although I am not yet sure of its longevity. Woodturners make a lot of use of superglues to seal hair cracks in timber blanks. These glues can be introduced and will move by capillary action along very fine splits and into cracked joints. A hairline fracture can be glued, cramped together and will set in only a few minutes.

With all glues it is important that you wipe away the surplus with a damp cloth before it has a chance to set.

Frequent re-covering has badly pierced and splintered the chair frame. Liberal quantities of wood hardener were poured into the ragged timber and allowed to dry. Heavy duty resin-based wood filler was then pushed into all holes and splits. The chair is now good for another 100 years.

TREATING THE OVERTACKED FRAME

Some of the pieces of furniture that you work on will have been re-covered many times during their life. This will mean that on a number of occasions old tacks have been pulled out and new ones driven in. Over a number of 'redoings' this will have caused the tops of some frame members to become very holed, often split and splintered, and occasionally almost broken up. Certainly it is questionable whether you could get yet another set of reasonable-sized tacks to hold. We have been experimenting in the workshop with a solution to this problem and it seems to be effective.

First, the ragged area is given two or three very liberal coats of Ronseal wood hardener. This is a highly penetrating acetone based liquid resin which is designed to harden up rotten wood – 'rotten' being wet or dry rot. As the solvent evaporates, it fills the pores with the resin and this can make rotten wood hard enough to hold a screw.

Once the tack-ragged areas have been liberally treated with hardener – and a large tin may do only two or three small chairs – the holes are filled with a fibreglass resin-based wood filler. This is mixed to a soft consistency and is pushed right into the holes with a flexible applicator. Only small quantities of filler should be mixed to allow for the time involved in pushing it into every hole. When hard, it is sanded smooth. While this process does involve both time and effort, it does appear to add a new lease of life to a valuable frame.

USING DYES AND STAINS

As was suggested earlier in this chapter, for touching up a small damaged surface area spirit dyes can be quite useful, but I prefer water-based wood dyes for the restaining of a whole carcass for a variety of reasons. A drawback is that water dyes do tend to lift the grain slightly and have to be sanded down before polishing, but against this they penetrate well into new wood; seem to be more light-fast; and do not then lift off with either varnish or spirit-based polishes (such as Button or French polish). They are also easier to mix or overlay to subtle shades. Spirit stains are quick and easy to use, dry very fast, and do not raise the grain – but they do lift off when varnishing, and I have yet to find a range that is totally light-fast. With water stains, by using your own mixes and multiple coats laid on with a sponge applicator, you can reproduce darkened corners and lighter coloured 'worn' zones.

One thing you will quickly discover is that you should not restrict yourself to using only a dye or stain which is labelled as the wood you are trying to recreate. Some of the darker oak stains do not always give the depth required and a splash of a black colour such as ebony may be needed. Certainly the yellowish green of walnut stain can be effectively introduced into medium oak. In most cases several applications of a colour are used to achieve the required depth. Overall, in the workshop we have found that the Liberon wood dyes offer the widest range of colours and are the most intensive of the wood dyes.

CONTEMPORARY COLOURS

In a book based upon traditional techniques of upholstery, I am not sure that the following should be mentioned at all! You are, of course, not necessarily stuck with trying to recreate a natural wood look. Today, many people are using spectrum colours to change the appearance of furniture. There are regular programmes on television where pieces of furniture are given a contemporary 'makeover'. A lot of use is made of acrylic paints, scumble glazes and so on. And why not? Some pieces of furniture look so much better in bright colours. And, let's face it, most antique pine furniture was made to be painted. Stripping them to bare wood and exposing all the carpenters' short cuts was not what the makers intended! Unfortunately many of these television programmes also promote restoration and upholstery techniques that are very questionable. Not only are they positively offensive to the traditionalists but they are often structurally dubious, ergonomically disastrous, and many will only last a few weeks in normal use!

READY-MADE DYES

This book is not the place to go into the finer points of furniture staining and certainly not into painting. Some professional furniture makers still make up their own colorants using various chemicals, natural stains and agents. There are excellent texts available should you wish to pursue these subjects further. In the last few years, however, there have been such developments in the ranges of ready-made products that most people's total needs can now be met off the shelf.

For instance, in restoring a beech-based 'mahogany' chair you will find that amongst the wood dyes of the Liberon range are two which meet most needs. These are the Georgian Mahogany and the Victorian Mahogany (and you can add home-made blends of the two). My tins and bottles of Vandyke Brown powder, bichromate of potash, oxalic acid, ammonia, tannic acid, and quicklime have not now been touched for some years.

Whatever stain or dye you are intending to use you should first try it on a scrap of wood. It is important to ensure that the wood is the same as that of the piece you wish to stain. Different grades of mahogany can respond very differently to the same stain. Make several colour 'swatches' with various blends and dilutions. Let them dry and then give them a coat of varnish (even if you intend to shellac polish the finished piece).

FINISHING

A completely stripped and restained piece now needs finishing. There are basically three choices. Some people are quite happy with varnish and for hard-wearing utilitarian surfaces it has to be admitted that satin finish polyurethane is workmanlike and effective. Three or four coats will be required, with a flatting down using very fine grit wet or dry paper and water between each. Finally comes a wax polish.

The second is to use something like a beeswax-based polish and apply several coats and a lot of elbow grease. This is probably the route you will take if you have not stripped the piece but have used a proprietary cleaner.

The traditional way of refinishing a piece of furniture is to use a Button, French or other shellac-based polish. Shellac comes from Sri Lanka. It is a residue extruded by the Lac bug (*Laccifer lacca*). It is commercially available in a number of grades. The finest, which is almost colourless, is made into what is called (and is bought as) French polish. This produces a beautiful golden sheen on whatever wood or stain it is applied to. It feeds the wood and brings out the natural grain and colour beautifully.

French polish is most widely used on quality furniture, but the slightly browner Button polish is the one usually chosen for chairs. Button and French polishes are very similar. They are made and applied in the same way, but the shellac in Button polish is slightly lower in quality and gives a deeper, brownish coloration when applied. There are two other grades normally available. Pale, which is a superfine French, and black. The Black polish is a relatively recent introduction from Liberon. It is still a shellac-based polish but has the addition of carbon black. It is applied in exactly the same way as the rest of the family, but produces a beautiful ebony finish. In fact, a crude, whitewood, caned country chair can be turned into a superb salon piece by first staining it with ebony dye and then 'French polishing' it using the Black polish. The technique of applying all the shellac polishes is not difficult to master and many students now regularly do their own French polishing.

Before Black polish appeared on the market we used to make our own by dissolving old shellac 78rpm gramophone records in a jar of meths.

The fact that at least some of these polishes can be obtained in any DIY store is some indication of the ease with which they can be used. The mystique of French polishing has now totally vanished; but there are excellent books and videos on the subject for those who need convincing. Let's now give it a try.

FRENCH POLISHING

Start with some of your upholstery waste. A ball of cotton wadding about the size of a hen's egg makes an ideal core for a 'rubber'. Place this in the centre of a 10in (25cm) square of strong calico. The corners are drawn together and twisted to make a little bag. Actually I use two squares. The inner is a heavy grade and the outer much finer.

A pair of white wood kitchen chairs. They have both been stained with ebony wood dye. The one on the left has then been polished with black French polish and is now ready for re-caning.

To use the rubber, open the twisted neck of the calico, and pour a little of the polish into the centre of the wadding. Close the neck and twist it. This will cause some of the polish to ooze out through the face of the rubber.

Rub the polish onto the surface of the wood using long strokes along the length of the grain. Try to squeeze enough polish through to ensure that the surface of the area being polished is evenly wetted.

Continue the long strokes for a moment or two, then start making small circular

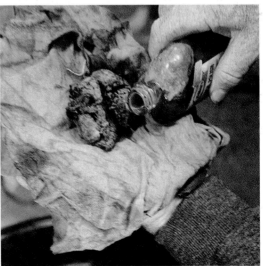

The rubber for French polishing is made from a ball of cotton felt in a twist of calico. The polish and a little meths is poured into the centre.

43

French polishing – the rubber traces paths along the grain and then moves in tiny circles.

strokes working across the whole area. Repeat the movements of long and then circular strokes, squeezing the rubber every so often to apply a little more polish. If the surface of the rubber becomes dry, you can dip it very lightly into a saucer of meths.

After a few moments, recharge the rubber with polish and continue the process of long and circular rubbing. You are aiming to build up a layer of polish that completely fills the grain and forms a definite film. Eventually, you will produce a shiny, absolutely 'grainless' surface.

By applying a little pressure, you will see a glass-like polished effect beginning to materialize. At this stage, you may find that there is some stickiness between rubber and polish, so dip the rubber very lightly into linseed oil to lubricate the polishing action.

Continue to build up the film of polish until you are satisfied that it is even across the whole of the area. You will soon get the hang of it, though a little experimentation may be necessary before you get a good overall sheen.

When the outer calico wears through it is replaced so that the core can be repeat-edly reused. When you have finished your polishing session the rubber sprinkled with a few drops of methylated spirits and put it into a sealed jar. A small snap-catch Kilner jar is ideal. This keeps the cloth moist and ready for instant reuse.

A few tips. Do not overdip in the meths during the polishing process – although the meths helps the polish to spread, too much will soften the film and allow it to rub off; so it really is the tiniest of dips. While too much polish is difficult to buff up, you do need to build a definite film; most beginners do not apply enough polish. The moment you take a linseed oil dip you get a beautiful shine and it looks as though you have finished. Sorry, but a little more rubbing will dry out the oil and you will see that you still have areas requiring more polish. Also beware of using too much oil – this will produce an oil film which will remain tacky for days. Shellac polishing is easiest on large flat surfaces – a table top is an absolute doddle. It is more difficult on fiddly items such as chair legs; you really have to be patient and use pinched corners of the rubber to get into the coves and corners of beads.

And, really, that is all the upholsterer needs to know about French polishing. It is not difficult, although it does require a little practice (don't do that treasured antique first!). There is, however, one further point about ebonizing. Natural ebony wood when polished has a sheen, but not quite a gleam. This is due to its particular grain characteristics. Black polish produces a real gleam – as do all the shellac polishes when properly applied. You can reduce this to a sheen if, after polishing, you stroke along the grain with 0000 steel wool dipped in a little beeswax polish. This produces minute scratches which simulate the wood grain of true ebony quite closely.

So you have a carcass that is now sound and gleaming; let's now – at last – get down to covering it.

— 5 —

An Express Job
Rush Seating

Unfortunately rush, reed and straw do not last forever – even houses thatched with best Norfolk reed have to be redone every sixty or seventy years. There are therefore no existing examples of early rush work on furniture, and the origins of this form of 'upholstery' are unknown.

Archaeological finds have shown that rushing was certainly practised in Viking times, although its origins probably date back even further. It is also merely speculation that links its origins with the colder, wetter marshlands of northern Europe. It seems unlikely that the Egyptians, who in the times of the Pharaohs were already weaving rush baskets, did not also use the Nile reeds for some form of seating. Certainly, they used rushes to make mats, and we also know that reeds were used to make fish traps.

Rush seating can look very nice in spite of its limited lifespan; it is undeniably comfortable. In fact, it probably lasts longer than most upholstery fabrics. It is not difficult to do, but today sources of suitable materials are not always easy to find. For this reason many of the 'Country Chip' chairs that were originally rushed are now seated in other materials. At best, they are seated with ready spun Sea Grass 'rope'; at worst, they have a ply board nailed across the top.

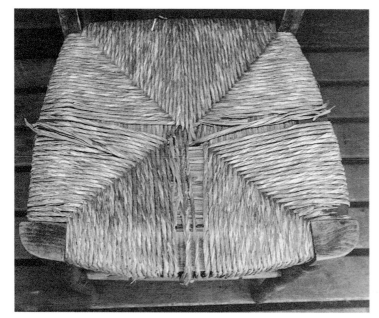

A rush seat for redoing. The photo above shows how rushes are joined on the underside.

Rushes are still grown and harvested in the UK – there are sources in the Fens, the Somerset Levels, parts of the Thames and a few other local areas. One of the problems is that cutting the rushes requires a particular skill and many hours of wading through mud and water. One of my main sources of supply, although based in Somerset, now actually imports most of its rush from Holland.

THE BULRUSH

The traditional material is the common bulrush. It is harvested when it is about 5–6ft (1.50–1.80m) tall and is bundled into 'boults'. A boult is normally about 5.6lb (2.5kg) in weight and at 1998 prices costs about £20. Plus, of course, a heavy postage and packing charge.

There are three grades normally available. It is 'chair seating rush' that most interests us here, but there is also the softer and more expensive 'salt rush' (all of which is imported). The third grade is a thicker rush that is used in basket and hat weaving.

When used for seating, two or three rushes are twisted or 'spun' together to provide the required thickness. Further strands are then knotted on as weaving proceeds, to form a continuous length. To make the rush pliant and easier to spin it is kept damp. The skill in rushing is not so much the weaving itself, but in squeezing the air out of the rush and in spinning the strands between finger and thumb as they are laid on the frame.

It is easy to identify a frame that was made for rushing. The rails are usually rounded on the leading and trailing edge but are flattened on the top and bottom. They are narrower in section than the frame members used in any other form of seating.

The ends of each frame rail are tapered down to a round spigot which is push fitted into a round hole in the legs and back. The seat rails are still glued into the main frame, although the rush rope will almost bind the seat frame together.

Unfortunately, the smaller cross-section of the seat frame members does often mean that the front rail will have broken – often close to a spigot end. Restoration usually therefore starts with carving and fitting a new front seat member.

Using a piece of beech of suitable thickness, draw on the profile. Cut it out on a bandsaw and then shape the rail and the two spigot ends with a spokeshave or even a whittling knife. An exact shape is not important as the rail will be totally hidden once the rushing is laid. Finish off by sanding, particularly taking any sharp corners off the outer edges. It is certainly much easier (and makes a stronger job) to make a new rail than to try to graft on a replacement spigot end.

SOAKING THE RUSHES

Rush has to be made pliable before it can be used. Step one means soaking it, a handful at a time, in hot water. It should be immersed for about half an hour, then taken out of the water and wrapped in a damp towel. A small garden hand sprayer is also useful for keeping the working weave damp, particularly on hot, dry days.

The initial soaking may present a problem. If you are only doing one or two chairs, you may find that using the bath is the best solution as you can then immerse the whole length of the strands without needing to bend them.

For more regular work, consider making a soaking trough. Three 6ft (1.82m) lengths of boards are used. Suitable sizes are 9in (23cm) wide for the base and 6in (15cm) wide for the two side walls. Timber of about 1in (2.5cm) thickness is ideal. You will also need two end caps. The whole is

if so, you can skip to step 2 and most of 3 in the following sequence. (Soaking the rush is step 0!)

SQUARING THE FRAME

Most rushing jobs involve chairs of a standard form where the front rail is longer than the back and the two side rails are somewhere between. Hence a front rail of 16in (40cm) and a back of 12in (30cm), is likely to have side rails of 14in (36.5cm) in length. If, as in the occasional case, the side members are longer than the front, then it is known as a 'deep seated' chair.

First, step one, is to find and mark (a light pencil line) the centres of the front and the back rails.

Step two (not needed on square seats) is to measure up and mark off the seat to establish the central true square. The process is known as 'squaring the weave'.

To do this, measure the exact length of the back rail that forms the open hole in the seat – that between the inside faces of the two side rail abutments. Now, using the centre mark on the front rail and working out from it, mark off on the front rail the exact length of the back rail. These are your 'squaring marks' and you now have the central square defined. The two side triangles outside the square are known as 'gussets'. The next step is to lay rushes to infill these triangles – hence 'squaring the weave'.

A soaking trough. This is made of creosote-treated larch and has a simple lining made from damp-proof membrane. Rush should be given a 15-minute soaking in warm water prior to use. They are then kept wrapped in a damp towel.

screwed together. My trough was then creosoted for added protection.

It is made waterproof by lining it with a layer of thick damp-course membrane – a tough polythene that is available at most builders' suppliers. This is folded into the trough and brought up over the top of the sides and end caps where it is tacked in place with large-headed galvanized felting nails.

Occasionally, you will find yourself lucky enough to be working on a square frame –

TWISTING AND WEAVING

So in step three we actually start the rushing. As was mentioned earlier, the 'rope' is made by spinning two (or three) rushes together. Take the first pair of rushes from the towel and place them side by side in a head-to-toe pair.

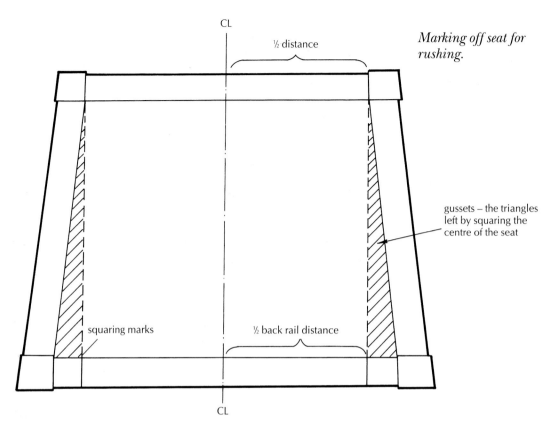

Marking off seat for rushing.

CL

½ distance

gussets – the triangles left by squaring the centre of the seat

squaring marks

½ back rail distance

CL

Until the 'square' has been achieved the weave is built up with short lengths of rush. These are tied off to the inside of the frame using fishing line. The rushes to the left have been well pulled up, those to the right are too loose.

In rushing, as later in caning, always work in a set sequence. The standard practice for both right- and left-handed people is to start work on the left side of the seat as it is facing you. All subsequent notes are based upon this principle. In rushing, you start with the front left corner.

Today, the standard practice is that the gussets are infilled with multiple shorter lengths of rush. Each end of each length is tied off to the frame using a fine twine. Monofilament nylon fishing line is widely used but I prefer the cheapest available woven fisherman's 'reel backing line, as it is more pliant and easier to knot. Backing line is available at any angling shop – it is very fine but has considerable strength (25lb (11kg) breaking strain). The tied-off ends eventually disappear under the subsequent weave of rushing.

Tie the end of the rope onto the inside of the left side rail a couple of inches back from the corner with the main length of the rope hanging over the top of the front rail.

Draw the finger and thumb along the working length of rush, pinching the rush to flatten it and to squeeze out the trapped air. If, like mine, your fingers are on the aged and arthritic side, use the thumb and the back of a knife handle. This is the 'stroking' process.

Now pull the rush rope to apply a little tension and start to 'spin' the strands. This means twisting them between finger and thumb. Always twist by rotating away from the nearest corner of the frame. Your rope is coming from the side rail over the front rail towards you. It is lying immediately to the right of the front left corner of the frame. You are therefore twisting with a clockwise motion as in driving in a screw with a screwdriver.

Maintaining the tension and twist, lay the rope on the top of the frame and then

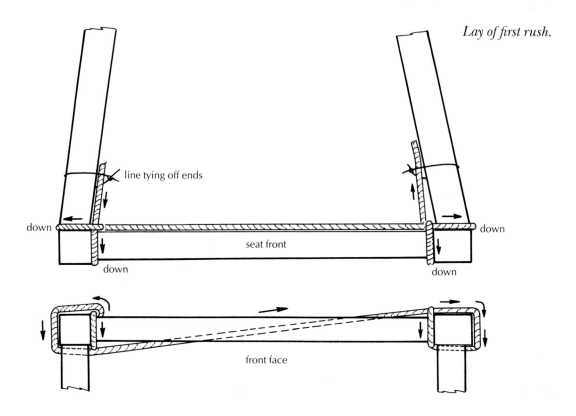

Lay of first rush.

line tying off ends

down

seat front

down

down

down

down

front face

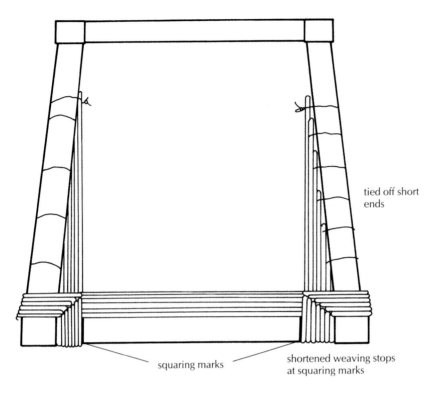

Squaring the weave.

tied off short
ends

squaring marks

shortened weaving stops
at squaring marks

pull it down over the front face. Feed it under the rail beside the front leg. Now bring the rope back up through the frame up the inside of the left side rail and tight against the front leg. At the top of the side rail, still maintaining the spin, lay it over the top of the tied-off starting end and then over the top of the side rail, bend it down over the outside face and take it back under the side rail (against the back of the leg). From here, the rope is taken across the seat, coming up through the centre hole, and heading for the right front corner. The free end will now be lying against the inside of the front rail. As the rope crosses to the next corner maintain a little tension, but you do not need to twist it. This section of rope will eventually be sandwiched inside the seat. Take the rope over the right side rail tight into the corner.

Now rotate the chair through 90 degrees in a clockwise direction. What was your right front corner has now become your working left corner and the rope is already lying across the top of the rail at the new left-hand front end. It is time to restart spinning, while taking the rope down the front face, under the rail, back up through the hole, crossing over the laid rope and the now left rail, on down the face, under the rail (pressing against the leg) and back along the inside of the present left rail. Tie the rope to the frame 2in (5cm) along with a little fishing line. Cut off the waste.

Keep the waste end. It may be long enough to make another gusset infill line. Alternatively, you can use it for stuffing at a later stage.

Now rotate the chair 90 degrees anti-clockwise and the true left (starting) corner will be back to the left. Lay your next (and subsequent) infill rushes in exactly the same way. With each strand, you will be getting further away from the corners, and

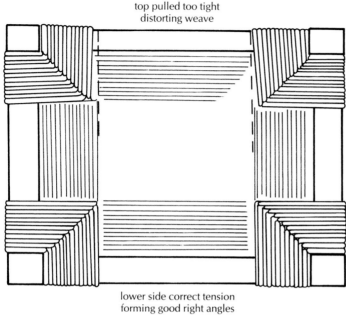

top pulled too tight
distorting weave

Squaring the weave.

lower side correct tension
forming good right angles

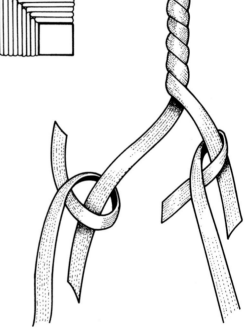

Tying on new lengths of rush.

you will be tying off further along the inside of the side rails. Keep the strands close together and always twist that part of rope that will be seen on the top of the weave. As you come up through the hole and make the right-angled turn to go to the side rail, you must put on just enough tension to keep the weave tight, but not so much that you distort the corner. The right angle must be a true right angle. If it becomes distorted, there is no way of correcting it later.

There are three aims involved in twisting or spinning. One is to get the rushes to an even and regular diameter, and this achieves our second aim of creating a neat appearance. The third aim is to provide added strength and wear resistance to those surfaces which are subject to wear – hence the top of the seat, and, particularly, the front edge. As none of these 'aims' matters underneath, we do not spin those lengths which are overlain, hidden under the seat, or not subject to wear. What this means in practice is that the strands near the corners

are only spun for a short distance – an inch or so. The spun length then increases as you get towards the centre of the seat.

Continue to lay short lengths until you reach your squaring marks on the front rail. You should now have a true square remaining in the centre.

FILLING IN THE CENTRE

Step four involves infilling the square. Again, so as to establish the habit, start at the left front corner. This again means that the starting end of the rope has to be tied off on the inside of the left rail – just behind the last of the short strands.

From here, the rope is continuous. This means two things. First, that as you get to the end of a twisted pair of rushes you need to knot in another pair. Second, every rotation of the chair is now made clockwise so that you continually bring the corner you are working on round to be your front left corner. You are still spinning the rope with a clockwise twist.

Let's make a small diversion. Rushing (and caning) can be back-breaking, and certainly can give you neck spasm. Your working position is ergonomically very important. Obviously by standing the chair on a work bench you bring the seat up to an ideal working height – your hands are at chest level, your shoulders can be relaxed, and there is no tilt or tension on the neck. The only problem then is hours of standing.

Some sit. The chair is now on the floor and you have to lean over; back curved, shoulders hunched and neck bent. Many hours of this and long-term spine trouble can result. The answer is two-fold. First, have a stool or, preferably, an old typing chair, where the height of the seat can be adjusted according to the task that you are working on. The second is to make a work platform that brings the seat up to a proper working height. Ideally, when seated, this will bring the weaving area to about elbow height so that the forearms are parallel with the floor. By mounting the platform on castors it means that the continual rotation of the chair is greatly facilitated.

Actually, the platform can be designed to accommodate chairs of different footprints and it can be used so that you can sit for many regular upholstery tasks. Taking the time now to make one will make the rest of your working life so much easier.

You are now starting to fill in the square. Tie off the end to the inside of the left rail. Weave the left corner, rotate 90 degrees and weave what started as the right front corner. Rotate 90 degrees. You are now working on the original rear right corner but it is now in the left corner position. The process is the same – over the top spinning the rope and keeping the rope tight against the inside side of the chair back, down the outside face, under the back rail, up through the hole, over the side rail, down its outside face and under. Holding the rope against the inside of the back rail, rotate another 90 degrees. Weave what will be the last corner of the first circuit. Rotate 90 degrees and the chair is now back in its starting position. Continue on round in exactly the same way.

It will not be long before you reach the end of the first pair of rushes. Take another pair (head to toe) and tie them on to the end of the first rope. Make sure that the knot is in an underneath section that will be sandwiched and therefore covered by

Chair trestle. The platform slots into the top of a piano trolley, and can therefore be removed. The wood rail is reset to whatever size chair is being worked on. It is held in place by two nails. This trolley brings the chair to an ideal working height, and is simply turned as each corner is completed.

top and bottom layers. When the chair is finished, you should see no knots from the top and only two or three underneath if the chair is up-ended.

The knot used is a simple half hitch (*see* Chapter 14). You will need two hands to knot in a new length. This means releasing the tension that you have been maintaining as you laid the rushes. It is advisable to use a large spring clip to hold the rushes pinched to the rails.

As the weave develops, keep a vigilant eye on the right-angled corners, as mentioned earlier. You will soon find that you can maintain the right balance between tension on the rope and the angle of the corner.

STUFFING THE SEAT

When about half of the seat has been woven, clip down or tie off the working end of the rope. You now have to stuff or pad out the seat area that you have already woven. The space between the upper and lower layer of rush is known as 'pockets'.

If you are working on a chair that you had to strip down you may have been surprised to find a stuffing of other material between the top and bottom layers of rush. In a properly rushed chair, it may have been off-cut ends of rush, but commonly clean straw will have been used. In some really old pieces you could find hay – often mildewed. Occasionally you may find other things! Crumpled newspaper is not unknown, cotton wadding is another, and once even a small dead mouse!

Today, some upholsterers use layers of corrugated cardboard, which have been cut into triangles to fit tightly into the corners. Certainly it gives a good shape, but may well eventually compress and lose its shape. Hence I prefer rush ends or clean straw, but make sure that whatever you use, it is dry. There should be enough stuffing to lift the centre of the weave slightly above the top of the rails.

From here on, the pockets are packed regularly – probably every 1½in (3.8cm), a process that gets much more difficult as you approach the centre.

TAKING A BREAK

Somewhere about now, it is advisable to leave the job for a while. Assuming that you have been working continuously and completed two-thirds to three-quarters of the seat, the rushes will still be damp – even those laid whilst squaring the frame. As they dry, they will shrink and tighten up. Tightening is no problem, but it could mean that adjacent rows are now no longer close enough to each other. A rest of 24 hours will allow them to dry out so that you can push the strands together before the final runs are laid.

A useful DIY 'pushing up' tool is a piece of hardwood about 6 to 8in (15–20cm) long by ¾in (1.9cm) wide. This is wedge-shaped, and starts at about ½in (1.27cm) thick and tapering down to nothing.

So, after a break, it is back to the weaving – push up the ropes, and unclip the working end and continue to lay this.

Although we talk about 'squaring up the seat', most chairs have a centre rectangle rather than a true equilateral square. This means that you will eventually reach a stage where the side strands (those running from side to side) are complete to form two full triangles, but there is still a gap of an inch or so running through the middle of the seat between the points of the two triangles where you can still see unwoven front-to-back strands. It is again time to complete some other task to allow the rushes to dry, before taking the next step of 'bridging the gap'.

BRIDGING THE GAP

The final ropes of rush are taken front to back only, and they are laid in a figure of eight. Starting from the front, the rush will go on top of the seat towards the middle of the chair; it will cross the middle cross run of rush and then be pushed through. From here, it will continue under the seat to the back rail where it will wrap round from underneath to emerge on top. It is now brought back to the middle where it again crosses the middle cross run before being threaded down through the seat. It has thus made a figure of eight across the seat.

As these runs are laid, you will of course continue twisting the rushes for those areas that are on top of the seat, and laying the rush flat as it passes underneath.

Eventually the rush line you are working with will reach the centre marks that you drew on the front and back rail. From here on, you will need to twist the rushes in the opposite direction as it moves towards meeting the lays coming from the other side.

As the gap reduces in size it becomes increasingly difficult to poke the rush through and a rush or upholsterer's needle is very useful. In fact, many rushers make their own bodkins from a small piece of metal strip with a rounded point at one end and a large rush hole at the other. Once the gap is fully bridged the rush ends are tied round a laid line and the ends tucked into the underside.

The last task is to go over the underside of the seat, trimming off any loose ends and tucking knots into the pockets.

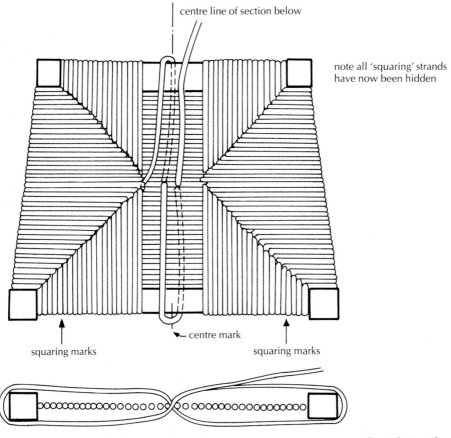

centre line of section below

note all 'squaring' strands have now been hidden

squaring marks

centre mark

squaring marks

figure of eight weave of verticals across centre

Completing the middle gap.

Six Of The Best
Caning

The source of the first two chairs that my wife and I caned is lost in the dim and distant past. I remember that they were started as a means of relaxation from working life.

Our handiwork was acceptable as seen from the top – the chairs were not beaded or fully pegged but they were serviceable. One, after a period as a nursing chair, was later painted white and is still in service in the bathroom; the other did not last long as the frame was not too robust and the appearance very poor. The children soon exploited its weakness! If you chose to turn either of them over you could see a very amateurish finish – many large, ugly knots and twisted loops.

The point of the story is this. We found all of the materials in a handicraft shop opposite the back door of Foyles bookshop off Tottenham Court Road, London. All we had for guidance was an illustrated article from a woodworking magazine – I still have the article in my files. There were no classes or workshops, and the amount of information in that article was only about half of what you will find in this chapter. So – give it a go!

THE HISTORY OF CANING

The idea of using cane as a furniture-making material came to England at about the turn of the seventeenth century. We are not completely sure of the origin, but it is widely held that caning came from China where it had been practised for centuries.

Certainly, the process arrived in Europe as a part of the trade boom with the Far East. Very quickly, furniture makers in Portugal, Spain and France became skilled in the use of cane, and the development took two paths. One was to weave round cane to make the whole carcass of the piece – what is often known today as rattan, wickerwork, or basket weave furniture. The second path is the one that interests us here. Instead of using the whole cane, thin strips of the outer skin of the rattan vine are used to form a resilient woven pad to the seats and backs of wooden carcass frames. The introduction of furniture of this nature came at a time when many English householders were seeking an alternative to the heavy, solid wooden furniture that was then the norm.

After the Great Fire of London in 1666, and those in other cities during that century, there was a huge demand for new furniture. This, coupled with the wish for lighter and more delicate furnishings, turned the market for this new approach into a boom.

Since that time, the fortunes of cane have waxed and waned many times. One thing is certain: the making of caned furniture was not confined to a few specialist furniture makers, nor its use to the houses of the rich. Many of the more able village craftsmen who made chairs as a part of their regular output also found cane easy to use.

Today at local auctions you frequently find frames that require recaning and these are usually at very affordable prices.

You will often come across sets of chairs that now have perforated, slightly dished, ply seats nailed onto frames that were originally caned. They look so much nicer if properly recaned!

The cane material used today still comes from the Far East. It is sliced into long lengths from the surface – the inner bark – of rattan creepers. The vines themselves can reach lengths of up to 500ft (150m), but the ribbons that we use are usually between 10 and 20ft (3–6m) in length. They consist of the hard shiny bark on one face backed by some long, softer pith fibres. The thickness is usually about 1/16in (1.58mm) and the width runs from about 1/16in (1.58mm) to 3/16in (4.75mm). The material is classified into a number of standard sizes, and an appropriate grade should be chosen for each specific job.

THE BASIC TECHNIQUE OF CANING

We are going to deal with basic caning as applied to the most common type of kitchen, dining or bedroom chairs. This will normally mean a seat pad of four straight or slightly curved frame members with the front rail somewhat longer than the back. Occasionally, we may also find a caned back pad which is usually rectangular in shape. Some caned kitchen chairs have circular seat pads. All of these use the middle range of cane sizes.

As with most upholstery, once you have gained an understanding of the basic techniques you can usually work out how to tackle the more complex jobs. It has to be said, however, that there are some chairs, screens and table tops that are not only caned to oval and more complex shapes, but in which the cane is woven into elaborate sunburst and other distinctive patterns. These require a very fine grade of cane and

specialist caning skills, and are certainly not for the beginner.

The size of cane required for a chair is determined according to the number, diameter and spacing of the holes. However, and this is an important point to note, many of the frames that you will come across are 'Country Chip' – that is, made by a local village carpenter. The hole drilling can be very irregular! In the workshop we have just had one nice chair which had a different number of holes on each side.

The simplest means of assessing the cane required is to measure off a distance of 6in (15cm) from the centre of a hole on one of the frame members, and then to count the number of holes along the row in that 6in length. There could be anything between ten and sixteen. The greater the number of holes, the finer the grade of cane used.

The table opposite shows English caners' sizes worked out on this basis. It also cross-refers to American caners' named sizes. In the States, caners work on a hole diameter/spacing measurement basis.

THE SIX STEP PROCESS

The basic caning pattern produces a series of small squares, each of which is constructed of six strands. The weaving of this pattern is often known as the Six Step Process. Although caning is a weaving process, the first three strands (two from front to back and one from side to side) are not woven. They are simply laid one on top of the other. The fourth strand (the second side-to-side strand) is the first that is actually woven (over and under the earlier strands). The fifth and sixth strands are the two diagonals, and both are fully woven. It is these two that are the most complex. They are woven into all of the four earlier strands, are difficult to align, call for some strength of thumb and forefinger, and require care to get them correct.

Cane Size Table

Number of Holes In 6in (15.2mm)	Hole Diameter Inch	mm	Hole Spacing Inch	mm	Cane Width Inch	mm	English 'size'	American 'size'
10	$5/16$	8.0	$7/8$	22.0	$5/32$	3.7	6	Common
10	$1/4$	6.5	$3/4$	19.0	$1/8$	3.0	5	Medium
11	$1/4$	6.5	$3/4$	19.0	$5/32$	3.7	4	Narrow Medium
12	$7/32$	5.5	$5/8$	16.0	$7/64$	2.5	3	Fine
13	$3/16$	4.75	$9/16$	14.0	$7/64$	2.5	2 and 3	Fine
14	$3/16$	4.75	$1/2$	12.0	$3/32$	2.1	2	Fine Fine
15	$1/8$	3.0	$3/8$	9.5	$5/64$	1.75	1 and 2	Super Fine
16	$1/8$	3.0	$3/8$	9.5	$1/16$	1.3	1	Carriage
Finishing Cane								
Beading 10–12	$5/16$	8.0	–		$3/16$	6.0	Beading 6	Binding 6mm
Beading 12–14	$1/4$	6.35	–		$13/64$	5.0	Beading 5	Binding 5mm
Beading 14–16	$3/16$	4.75	–		$11/64$	4.0	Beading 3	Binding 4mm
Pegging 10–12	$1/4$–$5/16$	8.0			$13/64$	5.0	Pegging 5mm	Pegging 5mm
Pegging 12–14	$3/16$–$1/4$	6.35			$11/64$	4.0	Pegging 4mm	Pegging 4mm
Pegging 16	$1/8$	3.0			$3/32$	2.0	Matchsticks	

CHECKING THE FRAME

Of course, the first task is to check the frame, complete any necessary repairs, and restore the finish. At this time ensure that the caning holes are clear by pushing a fine nail punch through each. I have made a simple set of tools for this. They consist of a 4in (10cm) and a 6in (15cm) nail driven into turned handles. The heads of the nails are then sawn off with a hacksaw and the ends cleaned and faced on a grind wheel. Sometimes in a chair that has been fitted with a ply seat, the old cane will have been cut off without the holes being cleaned, leaving behind tight-pegged holes. The force required to knock the old material out with a punch and mallet is likely to be too close to the structural danger limit of the chair and the old rattan will have to be drilled out.

PREPARING THE CANE

The cane itself needs a little preparation, which involves two tasks. One is to make the cane pliable, and the other is to find the threading end.

The cane needs to be made pliable by soaking it in water. Opinions differ on precisely what this means. Some caners give each length 15 minutes in a hot water bath, while others give a quick soak and then wrap the cane in a damp cloth until required for use.

To find the threading end of the cane, you will need to study the surface texture. Most weaving cane has a series of little blimps or knots where a leaf was attached. If you examine the nub carefully you will find that on one side there is a smooth slope, whereas the other makes a little step. The steps will catch as the cane is drawn through so it is woven with the slopes leading and the steps following. To find the threading end run your thumbnail along the bark (the shiny) side of the strand. In one direction it will catch on the bumps; in the other it will pass along easily. If you weave with the steps leading they will not only catch on the laid strands, but they can actually cause the earlier strands to break.

Certainly cane that is left in water for a long period will blacken. If it is too wet it will lose its shiny skin on weaving – on the other hand, if it is too dry it can kink and split.

THE CANING PROCESS

Start the caning session by loosely coiling some lengths of cane into separate skeins and around each put a loose rubber band that just holds the coils together. The threading end is laid to the top of the coil. A plastic bucket of hot water is then drawn from the tap. The first three coils are dropped into this and these are left for 15 minutes.

As the first (and later each subsequent) skein is taken out of the bucket, another dry coil is dropped in to replace it. Should there then be a delay in the weaving process for any reason, take the skeins out of the water and wrap them in a damp towel.

The original three coils, being simply laid, are disposed of fairly quickly. Once

weaving is imminent – second side to side and the diagonals – the process becomes slower and some coils may get a useful, slightly longer soaking.

The advantage of using cane freshly drawn from the bucket is that once each coil is woven into place drying starts, and they contract. This tensions up the weave quite nicely – in fact, it ends up drum tight.

If there is a break in the process, such as for lunch, all skeins should be taken out of the bucket and wrapped in a towel. When work restarts (or after any real delay), give the underside of the strands already laid a light spray with a small garden mist sprayer.

A word about the working environment. You can cane anywhere – even in the kitchen or in front of the television! Sitting out in the garden in the sun is fine, but you will need to use the spray a little more often to keep the weave from getting too dry too soon. There is absolutely no need for you to stand provided you do not create a situation where you continually have to bend over. The frame and working position that was recommended in the chapter on rushing is ideal, and if you skipped that bit because you are not interested in rush seating, it is worthwhile going back to have a look (see page 52). The rushing trolley illustrated in Chapter 5 is also ideal for caning.

One of the problems of caning is that few seats are perfectly square, resulting in different numbers of holes on the various frame members. The back will have the fewest, and there will be a number more along the front rail. There will be the same number on each of the two sides, but this will usually be halfway between the numbers on the front and back rails. A typical small chair will have twenty-four on the front, eighteen on the back, and twenty-one along the sides. Consequently some of the front to back strands out towards the two front corners will be short and will terminate somewhere down the side rails.

SEQUENCE OF BUILD-UP OF CANING

Step 1

The first run (Step 1 in the Six Step Process) is laid front to back. It is always started in the centre of the seat back rail, so find the centre holes on the front and back rail. Mark these off by inserting a peg in each.

You cannot have too many pegs for caning. I regard two dozen as being a working minimum. Mine were made by turning them from 8mm dowel, but if you go to any of the golf sales that are presently plaguing most cities, they will sell you a 'handful' of trees for about £2 (go with somebody who has a big hand!).

Check again which is the threading end and then feed the tail end of the first strand down through the centre hole in the back rail until about 3in (7.6cm) hang below the rail. Hold it in place with a peg. The shiny side should be uppermost when the strand is laid across the seat.

Run the strand through your finger and thumb to ensure there are no twists, and push the threading end down through the centre hole on the front rail. Pull it tight (tension it) and fix it in place with a peg. If

plucked, it should 'ring' (about soprano middle B for the musical).

Again ensuring that there are no twists, push the threading end up through the hole immediately to the right of the centre hole on the front rail. It should emerge with the shiny side uppermost and facing the front. Draw it up tight and peg it off. The strand is then taken to the hole to the left of the starting peg on the back rail and fed down through the hole. Again tension it and peg in place.

As you move along, you can remove earlier pegs provided you do not withdraw the anchor peg for the start of the strand.

If, as you move to the right, you reach the end of a strand (or have pulled too tight and snapped it!), peg it off leaving a tail below the frame. Starting with the next free hole on the opposite frame member, peg the tail end of a new strand and continue weaving.

As you get towards the right side you will reach the stage where you have filled all the holes on the back rail *with the exception of the corner one*, but there are still one or two empty ones along the front. (The corner holes are usually left free until you weave in the diagonals.)

The caning sequence:

(1) The centres are found and the first lay is from centre back to centre front and then out towards the right. Always work with the front of the chair facing you. Text instructions are for your right, left, chairfront and back.

If your last complete front to back run finished on the back rail, peg it off and cut it to leave a tail below the frame. Take a new short length to continue from the next vacant hole on the front rail. If, on the other hand, you were fortunate enough to finish on the front rail, continue to the next hole to the right. Come up through the hole, peg the cane in and lay the strand so that it is absolutely parallel to the strand to its left. It will end up at a hole somewhere about halfway or two-thirds along the right side rail. Push it through and peg it off.

If there is another free hole on the front rail (except the corner hole), lace this to the side rail – this will probably be to a hole about one-third along the rail. Ensure that the strand is parallel to the rest of those already woven.

Now starting on the front rail immediately to the left of the first (centre) front to back strand work out to the left, mirroring exactly what you did when working right from the centre. Take particular care when filling in the triangles that you go to matching holes along the side rail.

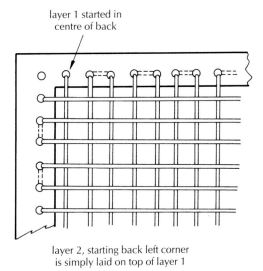

layer 1 started in centre of back

layer 2, starting back left corner is simply laid on top of layer 1

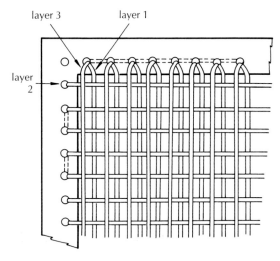

layer 3   layer 1

layer 2

layer 3 is started in the back left corner; it must lie to the left of strand 1, and it simply sits on top strands of layer 2

Layers 2 and 3 of standard seat caning pattern.

Step 2

The next layer is a very simple job as you will be working across the seat from side rail to side rail, and both of these will have the same number of holes (provided the original frame maker was sober!).

This time, start at the back left corner (still leaving the actual corner hole free). Do not interweave the cane with the first layer – merely lie it on top.

Step 3

The third layer is another front to back run and it matches the first layer. With the first layer, however, you started at the centre in order to ensure that the outer triangles were even. The third layer starts from the left side. Start by filling in the left triangle with short lengths until you get to the first working hole on the left-hand end of the back rail. From here, continue across the seat, finally filling in the right triangle.

Again, this third layer is not woven, but it is important to ensure that the strands

(2) Lay 2 is from side to side. It may be started from the middle of the side rail but more usually from the back left corner.

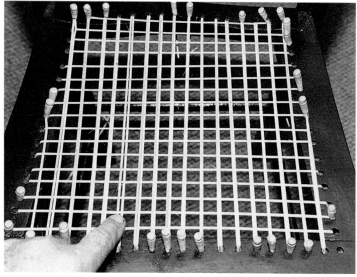

(3) Lay 3 is from back to front and starts at top left corner. The strands are simply laid on top of layer 2 and are placed to the left of the strands of layer 1.

always lie beside and to the same side of the first layer. Most caners work with strand three to the left of strand one. Although the strands are not woven you will now begin to see a weave pattern emerging due to the successive layering of front to back, side to side, and front to back strands.

At this stage, some caners tie off the tail ends that have been produced so far, while others who are working more quickly complete all layers before tying off. If you do plan to take a break, you should tie off while there is residual dampness in the cane. We will be examining the methods of tying off after completing layer six.

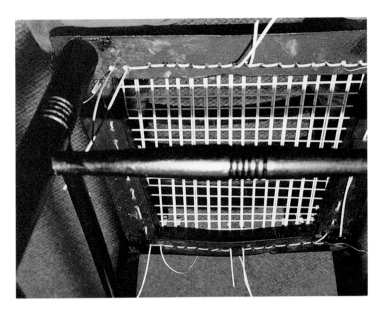

(4) The ends of strands laid so far are tied off.

(5) A simple half hitch knot is all that is needed.

As with all the work so far – and from here on in – keep a good even tension, ensure that there are no twists and that the shiny, coloured side of the cane is always uppermost. So far, this will not have been difficult. It is in the next three layers that maintaining the 'no twists' rule becomes a little more tricky.

Step 4
Layer four is the first woven layer and consequently requires more care. It is the second side to side run, and it weaves over and under each of the strands of layers 1 and 3. It again starts at the back left corner and it is placed so that it parallels run 2, but is to the far side of it – that is, it lies closer to the back rail. Now the importance of finding the threading end becomes apparent.

If you have worked exactly as described so far, the strand will start by crossing over the first vertical strand (layer three, the left one of each vertical pair) and then pass under the right-hand one of the pair (layer one). It will always be over–under, over–under; and every strand in this layer will be the same. Constantly look back over your

work and see that you have not deviated. If you have made a mistake, go back and unpick it – that will teach you!

By using a short length of the leading end of the strand you can weave about twelve over and under loops and can then pull the strand through until it is tight. You

(6) Layer 4 is the first truly woven strand. It runs side to side and is placed so that it is closer to the back than the line of layer 2. It weaves over the strands of layer 3 and under those of layer 1. Unusually this corner has started front left not rear.

(Below) *Layer 4 in place.*

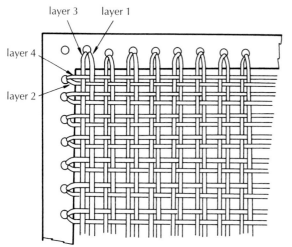

layer 4 is first truly woven layer; woven over layer 3 and under layer 1; this effectively also weaves in layer 2

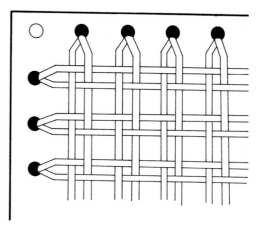

layer 4 completed; the strands now have to be pushed together into tight squares

will find that by working through a number of strands before drawing up, it is easier to keep the strand flat with the shiny side up. Drawing up after each strand or loop both wastes time and is more likely to lead to kinks. Four or so sets of about twelve will get you to the other side. It is particularly important to ensure that there are no twists before you start each set of twelve. When you are pulling through, control the diminishing loop with the free hand – this loop can be very prone to rolling over and creating a twist. So put a finger or a length of dowel in the loop and keep it square on to the pull. If it does twist, you will need to draw it back and untwist without kinking it or straining the lie of the fibres. If you greatly exceed the twelve you may find, particularly in later layers, that the tension required is too much and the strand will break. If it does snap, you must unpick back to a hole and peg off the end.

It is at this stage that the garden sprayer really comes into its own – it helps to keep both weaving and already laid strands pliable. Sometimes also drawing the weaving cane across a damp sponge can be helpful.

It goes without saying that at the end of each pass the cane is tensioned and pegged off.

When layer four is completed, your caning will probably look a mess. You will now have woven 'squares' of all sizes and shapes and the pairs of vertical and cross strands

(7) Layer 4 is completed but the weave looks messy with varying spaces.

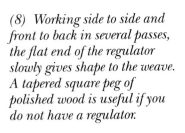

(8) Working side to side and front to back in several passes, the flat end of the regulator slowly gives shape to the weave. A tapered square peg of polished wood is useful if you do not have a regulator.

(9) All the squares are now nicely formed and we are ready to weave the diagonals.

will be well separated. You must now square everything off and give the weave shape. An upholsterer's regulator is ideal but the side of a screwdriver blade may be used. First, push the pairs of the vertical strands as close together as possible. At the same time, ensure that the strands are straight and do not wander from side to side. Do the same with the pairs of cross strands. A much cleaner pattern of even, true squares will

now emerge. You may need to go across the whole surface two or three times before you are satisfied that the squares are as tight as you can get them.

Step 5
The fifth run is tricky. It starts from the back left corner hole. You are therefore normally starting with the hole empty and into it you insert a tying-off length of the

(10) The first diagonal is laid from the back left corner towards the front right. It is moved until the lie of the cane fits neatly across the diagonal row of squares. It usually ends up one or two holes back from the front right corner. It crosses over each pair of verticals and under each pair of horizontals.

65

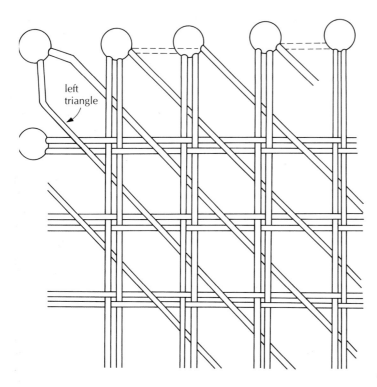

The first diagonal.

layer 5 – the first diagonal – started back left corner, working to right; woven under each pair of verticals and over each pair of horizontals; left triangle starts from same back corner

(11) You will need a bodkin or awl to lift the strands to feed the diagonals close to the frame.

trailing end of a new strand. You now have to establish the line of this run and it is here that you will find out how accurately and evenly the maker of the chair drilled the lacing holes.

With the top left end of the strand anchored in the back left corner hole, lie the strand across the weave aiming for the front right corner. End with the strand across the first or second hole back along the right side rail. Draw the strand tight. Now look back along the length and move the free end until the strand passes neatly over a continuous and straight diagonal row of squares. Ideally, it will lie towards the top right-hand corner of one square and the bottom left corner of the next square along the line of the diagonal. From then on it will alternate – top, bottom, top, bottom, and so on. Move the free end until you achieve the best lie and put a peg into the receiving hole to mark the weaving line. This will mean that the strand will

cross over the middle of a pair of verticals and the middle of a pair of horizontals – or vice versa according to the position of the starting square. On 'Country Chip', with its irregularly spaced holes, the best line may be something of a compromise.

If, however, the holes are well positioned and you are looking at a fairly standard kitchen or dining chair you may reach an ideal position where the back left corner brings you to one or only two holes down the side rail in from the front right corner. On 'deep seats', it could be hole four or five.

What you must avoid is having to bend the line of any diagonals. At worst, if the line is not true, you can cause the edge of the diagonal that you are tensioning to saw through and break one of the earlier lines, resulting in the tedious process of having to replace the broken length.

Now weave from the back corner towards the marker peg. Once you have reached it go down through the hole, tension the strand and peg it down. Bring the threading end up through the next hole back along the right side rail and weave diagonally back across the seat exactly paralleling the first diagonal. You should end up at the first hole in along the back rail from the right rear corner. Continue on, working to the right of the first line, and fill in the right rear triangle.

All the earlier comments about tensioning and avoiding kinks (now quite difficult) still apply, and most important of all is to ensure that the overs and unders are the same across the whole seat. This will normally mean going over each pair of cross strands and under each pair of verticals. Whichever way round you start, the pattern must be maintained (and constantly checked) for the whole of the layer.

There will be times when, due to the shape of the seat or the placement of the holes, the ends of the diagonal strands will have to be kinked in order to get them to a side hole. There comes a point where to avoid excessive kinking the strand is taken either to the same hole that the previous run used, or is positioned to skip a hole. This may also happen as you reach a corner.

Once the upper right triangle has been completed, start again with a second strand also pegged into the back left corner hole. If your first diagonal ended in a hole one back from the right front corner, this new diagonal will parallel it but will end up in the actual front right corner hole – this is ideal. Now continue to fill in the lower left lower front triangle.

If on a final check you find that you have gone off track – and it is very easy to get two unders where the second should have been an over – you really do need to try to rectify this as it can create major difficulties with the next layer. If a small length can be unpicked, fine. If not, cut the offending strand, draw the ends back, peg them off, and weave in a new strand.

Step 6
Layer six is the other diagonal and it is at right angles to the strands of layer 5. It is, in fact, a mirror image of the previous diagonals, skipping holes or doubling up in exactly the same way. It also reverses the under and over pattern of layer 5, in that it may pass under each pair of cross strands and over each pair of verticals.

This time, start at the back right-hand corner and come down to the left-hand rail hole which is the same offset as the first strand of layer 5. In fact, the strand is easier to lay for two reasons. First, the tensioning of the diagonals in layer 5 will have helped to square off the holes. Also you can quickly see where there should be over and unders because they have the previous layer there to mirror.

TYING OFF

So the weaving is complete, and all the loose tails have now to be tied off. Let's look at the method.

Some of the ends may have been exposed for some time and have now dried off. So the first task is to moisten them.

The final weave.

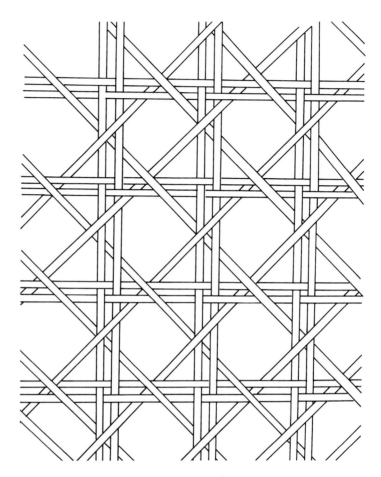

The sixth and final layer has now been laced in but has not yet been pushed tight into the corners. It goes over all vertical pairs, and under all horizontal pairs. It is woven from the back right hole and mirrors layer 5 (missing or doubling on opposite holes).

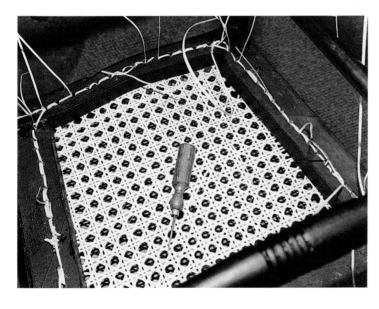

(12) Both diagonals (lays 5 and 6) are completed and the ends are now tied off.

Working under the seat, liberally sponge all ends and leave them for a few moments to soak.

All that is required in tying off is a simple knot. A good caner will do a job that can only be seen on close inspection. The knot is tight and flat and the end cut so that there is a tail of less than ¼in (6mm). To make the knot, the tail is pushed under the nearest adjacent loop (you may need an awl or bodkin to lift the loop slightly). The tail is then drawn through and the end is passed through the loop now formed. The whole is then gently tightened and the knot flattened with the thumb.

Just as a matter of interest, the underside of the chair will probably tell you more about the skills of the caner than will the top. On a well done job there will be very discreet knots, no build-ups of multilayers of loops, and there will be at least one loop between each pair of holes. For the first chair or two you can be forgiven a couple

of gaps or so; the problem often lies in the chair design and the sequence in which you started and ended strands.

The novice, overcautious caner, will usually overdo the knotting, ending up with a bird's nest of multiple loops and ends. A simple single loop is all that is required because under tension these pull up on themselves; furthermore, the final beading and pegging give a firm enough anchor.

TIDYING THE WEAVE

The next task is to tidy up the weave. If you have not already achieved it, the aim is to produce a regular pattern of even squares, so you may need a little further articulation with the regulator or equivalent. Again, push the pairs together and straighten up any wavy lines. In pulling the weaving strands through you will have pulled off a few hairs of cane edge. The way to deal with this is to flash quickly over the chair seat with a gas lighter and singe away the hairs.

We are now into the finishing straight. On your first chair it may have taken you 8 to 10 hours to get this far – with experience and improving skills you should be able to halve this time, particularly if you are working on a number of similar pieces.

PEGGING AND BEADING

If you are restoring an early caned chair you will now need to peg each hole. For this you need pegging cane of an appropriate diameter (according to the maker's drill size). The softer centre of the rattan vine is used for pegging and it is normally available in 4 and 5mm diameters. Cut the cane into short lengths – usually about ¾in (2cm) and push a length into each hole. They should be a tight fit against the strands of cane already passing through, and they are finally driven in with a nail punch until the top is about 1mm below the surface of the top of the hole.

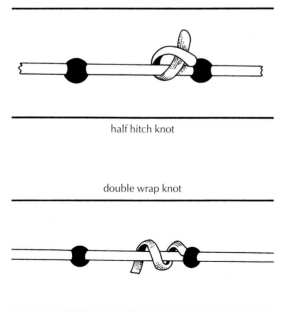

half hitch knot

double wrap knot

Knots to tie off cane tails.

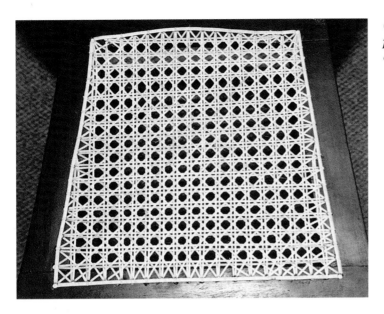

(13) Finally the holes are pegged and a beading cane is couched in around the top.

From the middle of the eighteenth century it became the practice to fit a beading to cover the tops of all the holes. For beading, we use a 5 or 6mm wide, flat beading cane. If you are planning to bead the top, leave alternative holes clear when at the pegging stage. The beading cane is cut into lengths such that there is a piece (with pegging tails) for each of the four frame members. Again, the cane should be dampened with a short dip in hot water.

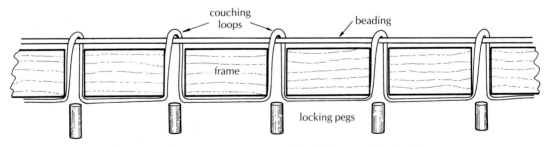

the pegs are driven in against a wooden dolly held on top of the beading; here couching loops use every hole; normally only alternate holes are couched

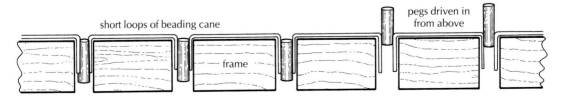

Couching the beading – alternatives.

Fit the beading and temporarily peg it down at each end. Using the non-pegged alternate holes, a strand of soaked 'couching cane' (basically a piece of seating cane) is brought up through the hole, looped over the beading cane, taken back down the hole, tensioned and then taken on to the next free couching hole, and from there along on round the seat.

Although not always done, it is good practice also to peg the couching cane. For this, you will need a slightly smaller diameter pegging cane, and this time the short lengths are pushed up from the underside. You may need to keep pressure on the top of the beading cane to ensure that the pegs do not push up any seating cane.

The description above is the most widely used standard beading practice, but there is a not uncommon alternative method. Here, the couching cane consists of small 'U'-shaped loops, which are pushed down from the top together with a small wedge-shaped peg. You may even find examples where it is the couching cane that has been cut into loops and bridges from hole to hole. Again it is locked in with wedges.

CIRCULAR AND OTHER FRAMES

We have been looking only at square or near rectangular seats. Some bentwood chairs were caned, and here the seat had a circular frame. These are approached in the same way as the 'square' frames, with front to back and side to side strands forming regular squares. Here, Steps 1 to 4 are laid from centre to centre. The diagonals are taken from exactly half way (on the 45-degree angle) between the cross and verticals. In fact, they are very easy to work.

Other patterns of chair have rounded corners or bow front rails – again no problem if woven front to back. Bow backs and saddle seats where the top and bottom rails or the front and back frame members of the seat are not flat are again not difficult

provided you start with the strands that lie along the trough. Layer 2 needs to be only lightly tensioned and has to be laid under layer 1 so that it adopts the curve set by the strands along the trough. There may then need to be slight modification to the weaving in layers 4, 5 and 6. Layer 4 is not hard tensioned as it has to be pulled down to the curve and the diagonals hold it in place. However, if you are planning a project involving radial, sunrise or sunburst patterns, you may need to seek advice or further reference before completing them.

A MODERN APPROACH

Finally, mention must be made of one of the modern approaches to caning, in which instead of holes along each seat member there is a shallow channel. For this method, the cane is bought ready woven just like a roll of cloth. A piece of the required size is cut from the roll, allowing a 1in (2.5cm) margin overlapping the groove all round. The cane is soaked and the ends of all the strands are pushed down into the groove with a wedge-shaped wooden rammer, keeping the seat as taught as possible. When the cane is firmly home the edges are trimmed back to just under the shoulder of the groove using a sharp bevel chisel, taking great care not to damage the wood of the frame. Finally, a long length of pegging cane is forced into the groove to wedge the woven cane in place. Hey presto – No fun at all!

Caning really is fun and is very satisfying, despite the occasional irritation at missing an over or under and having to unpick a row. It is also a very pleasant wet afternoon job that can be done in the warmth of the house. At all stages it is much more delicate than a lot of upholstery work, and, in fact, you see results much more quickly. Why not join my campaign to remove the ply seats and restore the caning on every bastardized chair that we can find?

Fitting prewoven cane:

*(1) A chair with a prewoven
cane seating that has been
cat-attacked.*

*(2) The beading cane has to
be levered out and the old cane
cut away with a narrow chisel.*

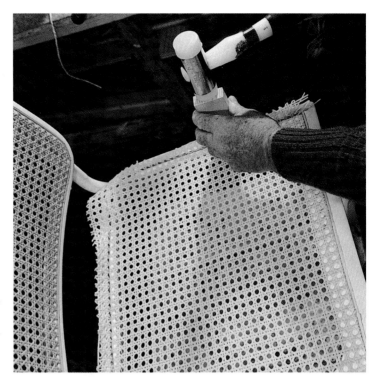

(3) and (4) The woven cane is cut to overlap the groove and is soaked for 15–20 minutes. It is then pushed into the groove using a wooden wedge.

73

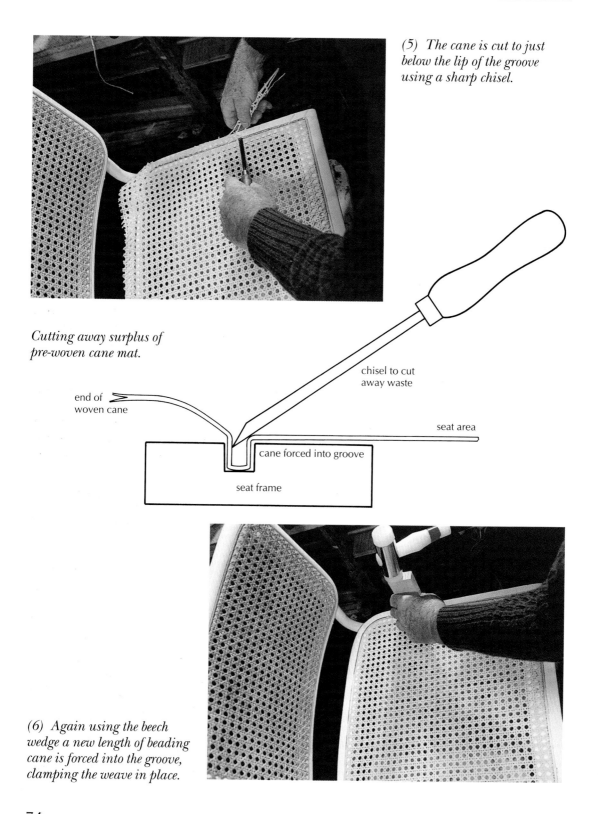

(5) *The cane is cut to just below the lip of the groove using a sharp chisel.*

Cutting away surplus of pre-woven cane mat.

end of woven cane

chisel to cut away waste

seat area

cane forced into groove

seat frame

(6) *Again using the beech wedge a new length of beading cane is forced into the groove, clamping the weave in place.*

7

Under Cover
Basic Stuffed Pads

The simplest of all forms of upholstery, the loose pad, is found in many stools and dining chairs. It is the first of the three forms which between them comprise the basics of most upholstery.

The loose pad provides the ideal item for the beginner to start with. It consists of a stuffed and covered wooden frame which drops into the main seat frame of the chair. The seat is fairly thinly padded – it has a dome top with no special shaping – and being removable from the frame it is easy to reupholster, possibly even as a laptop job. Because the stuffing is applied directly onto the top of the pad's frame, it is known as 'stuffed over'.

The second form of seating is also classified as 'stuffed over', but in this case the stuffing is not applied to the top of a drop-in frame, but is fixed directly to the top of the chair frame itself. Ordinary stuffing materials are still used – usually natural animal or modern vegetable hair, cotton wadding, hessian and webbing – but because the stuffing is often deeper or thicker it has shaped side walls and is therefore a little more complicated.

The third form of seat upholstery uses springing, which is then topped with the same types of materials as are used in the stuffed-over approaches. In its basic form sprung upholstery is quite simple, but on larger pieces with more complex shapes,

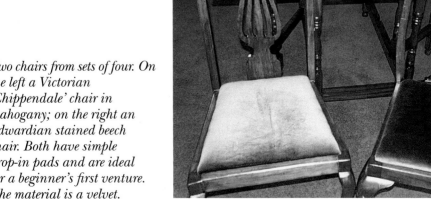

Two chairs from sets of four. On the left a Victorian 'Chippendale' chair in mahogany; on the right an Edwardian stained beech chair. Both have simple drop-in pads and are ideal for a beginner's first venture. The material is a velvet.

such as drop-arm settees, it can become quite 'interesting'.

The springs are always housed within the frame of the chair and are supported from the underside of the seat frame. These chairs are therefore 'undersprung' as distinct from being 'stuffed over'. In fact, other than the springs themselves and the heavy string used to lace them, undersprung chairs use exactly the same materials as the simple seat pad, although a considerably greater quantity of hair and the other materials is required.

THE STUFFED-OVER DROP-IN PAD

In this chapter we are going to deal with the first of these approaches in some detail – the stuffed-over drop-in pad. Although this form of upholstery is simple, it introduces us to many of the basic skills that are required in most of the traditionally upholstered chairs (the *only* exceptions being cane and rush).

The outline steps are:

1. Fixing a lattice of webbing to support all that follows.
2. Tacking a layer of hessian over the top of the webbing. This is known as a platform.
3. Stitching in rows of stuffing loops.
4. Stuffing hair into the loops to cover the top of the whole hessian pad.
5. Covering the hair with a layer of lighter grade hessian or skrim.
6. Applying a layer of cotton felt or cotton wading.
7. Covering the wadding with calico.
8. Putting on a thin layer of skin wadding (optional).
9. Fixing the finishing fabric cover.
10. Covering the underside of the pad with bottoming cloth to hide the webbing.

Sometimes we do not bother with step 10; also when we are aiming for a thin pad and the calico of step 7 has produced a smooth and tight finish, the skin wadding of step 8 can be eliminated.

So, we are starting with a bare frame. It will be a 'square' with the two sides tapering in to a shorter length back member.

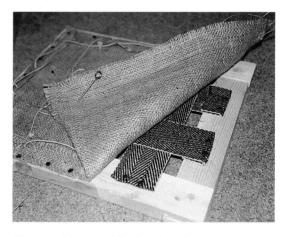

Two teaching models showing the processes in simple stuffed-over drop-in pads.

(Above) *The frame with webbing and hessian in place. The stuffing loops have been sewn in.* (Below) *Hair has been stuffed into the loops. It has been capped with skrim, a layer of cotton felt and then calico.*

First, check how well it fits into the carcass of the chair. If it is one of a set, check each pad and if there is any variation from one to the next, match them into pad/frame pairs and mark them off.

What are you looking for at this stage?

There are several problems you may face. If the pad is a tightish fit in the frame, you may only be able to use a light covering fabric. You will also take only the finishing material down over the side of the frame. All the materials of the earlier layers (even the calico) have to be fixed to the top of the frame and not overlap the edges.

You need a gap of about ¹⁄₁₆in (1.5mm) all round. If it is less, and particularly if you are planning to use a tapestry or other heavy material, you might have to plane down the side of the pad frames. (When making a new set of frames I allow about ¹⁄₁₆in (2mm) all round.)

Assuming a reasonable (normal) fit with about a ¹⁄₂₀–¹⁄₁₀in (1–2mm) gap all round, and if you are planing to use an average weight covering fabric, you can proceed as normal.

WEBBING

First, any seat needs to be 'springy'. On drop-in pads we need a little 'give' to be comfortable for a long dinner or an evening homework stint. Hence a solid wood or ply under layer is not appropriate. The give in stuffed-over seating is achieved by building everything up on top of strands of jute webbing. Only on the very cheapest dining chairs do you find a ply layer.

Today, all quality work is based upon old English black and white jute webbing – or its equivalent. The cheaper, old-style plain brown webbing can be used, but this stretches over time and needs more frequent replacement if the seat is to remain comfortable (not sagging!).

The webbing is fixed to the top of the pad frame and a number of lengths are criss-crossed to produce a lattice. The aim is to have about 3in (7.5cm) between each parallel length front to back and side to side. On an average small dining chair this means three front to back runs and two or

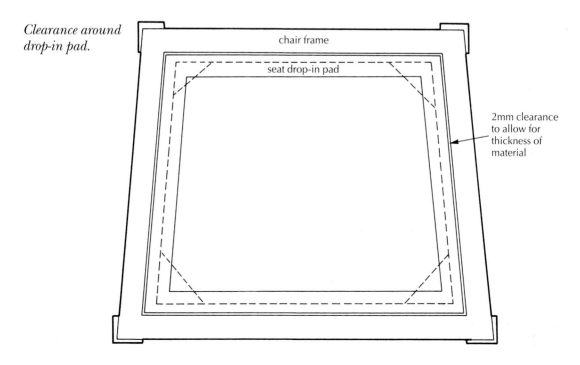

Clearance around drop-in pad.

chair frame

seat drop-in pad

2mm clearance to allow for thickness of material

Three types of webbing. The older brown jute is strong, a little over 2in (5cm) wide, but does stretch in time. The top roll is the best available. It is 100 per cent jute black and white, and is 2in wide. The third is known as 'old English black and white', it is the pattern most widely available today and is a little under 2in wide; it does not stretch but can tear away from the tacks if over-tensioned.

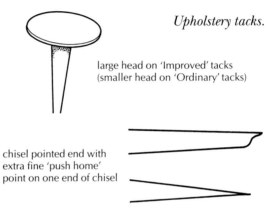

Upholstery tacks.

large head on 'Improved' tacks
(smaller head on 'Ordinary' tacks)

chisel pointed end with
extra fine 'push home'
point on one end of chisel

three side to side. On larger carvers you could have a 4 × 4in (10 × 10cm) lattice.

The webbing is nailed on under tension using 13 I or 13 Imp (Improved) upholstery tacks. These are ½in (13mm) long, and the 'I' or 'Improved' means that they have large heads. They are made of a blued steel and have a very sharp double point, which consists of the larger, slightly chisel-shaped main point, but on the tip is a very fine, pin-like point. This extra sharp element allows you to push in the tack with thumb pressure alone until it holds. It is then driven home with a tack hammer. Once the tack has been hit, the fine point often breaks away, so it is rarely practical to reuse old tacks.

Later on in your upholstering career you may learn to drive the tacks straight into place with a magnetic head hammer, thus avoiding the thumb push. However, it is not easy to place the tacks accurately.

Web first from front to back, starting with the middle strand. Judge the approximate centre of the frame by eye, and do not cut the webbing into lengths, as this is very wasteful. Lay the free end of the webbing across the centre of the back rail with the end corresponding with the inside edge of the frame. The main length of the webbing is now outside the frame. About 1in (25mm) in from the inner edge of the frame knock

in a row of three 13 Imp tacks; this will mean that the row is ½ to 1in (13–25mm) in from the outer edge of the frame. One tack will be in the centre of the jute and the other two near the outside edges of the webbing.

Fold the length of the webbing over the nailed tail and position it so that it crosses the centre of the opposite rail. Now drive in two more tacks to hold the fold in place – space these so that they fall between the first three fixing tacks.

When nailing on webbing (and any subsequent) layers, try to position the tacks so that they are not into a badly holed area – aim for sound wood. Equally, do not go too close to an edge as this is a weak zone.

The next task is to tension the webbing and fix it to the opposite side of the frame. A webbing stretcher is used for tensioning. This is simple and effective, and with some suitable timber and a dowel you can make your own. There are a number of designs

Starting a drop-in pad:

(1) The first web is placed on the centre line. It is tacked with three 13 Imp tacks and then bent over.

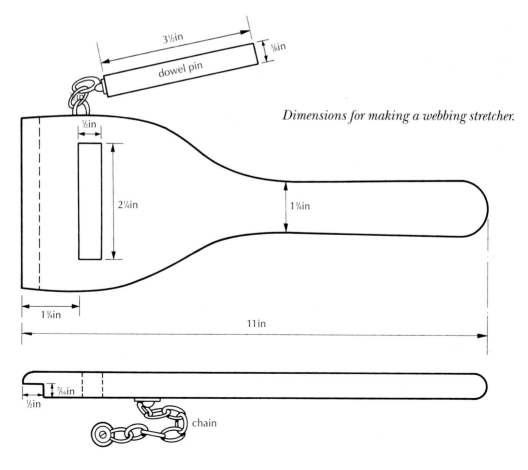

Dimensions for making a webbing stretcher.

3½in

⅝in

dowel pin

½in

2¼in

1¾in

1¾in

11in

⁷⁄₁₆in

½in

chain

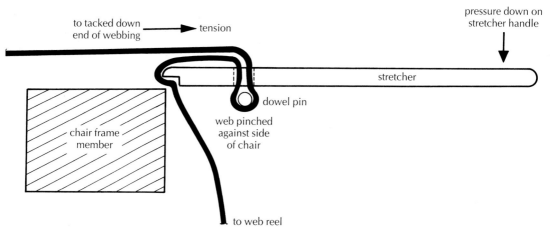

to tacked down end of webbing → tension

pressure down on stretcher handle

stretcher

dowel pin

web pinched against side of chair

chair frame member

to web reel

(2) Path of webbing through the stretcher.

used but a simple slotted spade and dowel pin model is the most effective.

The principle of the stretcher is that it grips, then clamps the web against the side of the frame so that leverage can be applied to tension the webbing.

While gripping the stretcher in one hand (or wedging it against the chest), drive three tacks into the webbing to hold it. These will mirror the position of the first three tacks at the other end of the length of webbing. The stretcher is now removed from the webbing, the end is folded over and two more tacks are driven home. The webbing is now cut from the main length. If you had used separate pre-cut lengths of webbing you would have had to have enough to grip in the stretcher and this would now be trimmed away as waste.

The folds in the tacked ends of the webbing are important. The tension that can be applied with a stretcher is such that the material would tear away from a single row of three tacks. It does not matter that the fold over is seen at present, because it will eventually be covered.

You may question why we take such care to fold under the first end of the webbing while we simply fold over the second end. Good question – put it down simply to tradition.

Having placed the middle web, the two either side of it are now fixed in the same way.

Now turn the pad through 90 degrees and again judge the centre line. Feed the end of the centre web through the three already in place to give an over and under weave. Fix this as before. The two webs either side are now placed using an opposite under and over to the centre piece.

To support the hair (and hold it in place) on the webbing we first cover the top of the frame with a piece of hessian. Cut the hessian about 1in (2.5cm) wider than the frame on all sides. Place it on the frame and turn the edges up so that the hessian comes to about ⅜in (9mm) from the outer edge of the frame. Tack the hessian in place, stretching it as you go. Here, use the shorter 10 Imp tacks.

(3) Two more tacks are driven into the fold and the web is then stretched across the frame. The end of the stretcher butts against the frame and the handle is held under tension hooked on the upholsterer's body.

(4) Three tacks are driven into the stretched end. The end is trimmed and folded and held in place by two more tacks. Here the first side-to-side length is being fitted. It is woven under and over the first lay.

(5) The final web is laid. The different weaves can be seen.

(6) A hessian platform is tacked over the webbing (below).

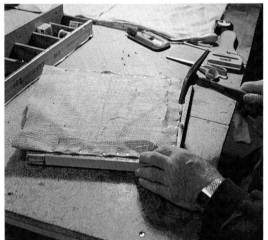

(7) The hessian is in place. The corners are crude and the edge is folded up. This will be completely hidden by the hair layer (above).

(8) A neatly fitted platform hessian on a large dining chair.

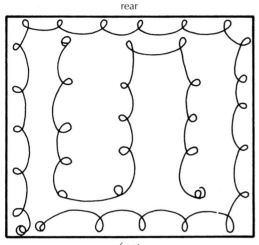

rear

front

pattern for drop-in pad or small stuffed-over seat

STUFFING LOOPS

The hair is held in place by 'stuffing loops' of twine, so these are stitched in next. The string used is no. 4 or no. 6 Barbour twine. In my studio, we use no. 6 twine as the students and I frequently pull no. 4 to breaking point. The twine is sewn on in loops using a 10 or 12 gauge curved spring needle, as mattress needles are too flimsy for this task.

The loops must hold a layer of hair that will compress down to about 1 to 1½in (2.5–3.8cm) thick. Which of these thickness

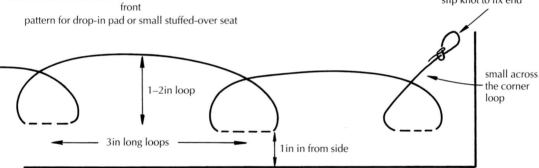

slip knot to fix end

1–2in loop

3in long loops

1in in from side

small across the corner loop

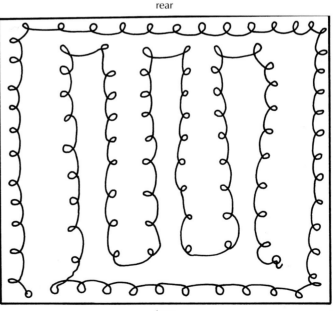

rear

pattern for large seat; multiple front to back lines; loops deeper for thicker pads

Arrangement of stuffing loops.

front

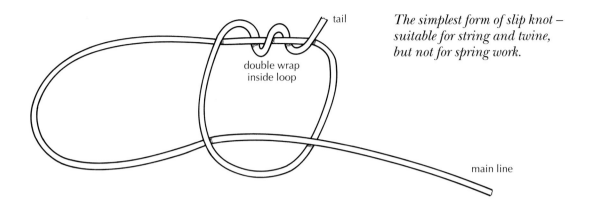

The simplest form of slip knot – suitable for string and twine, but not for spring work.

tail

double wrap inside loop

main line

you veer towards will be very much a matter of choice. Personally, I prefer the extra softness of a 2in (5cm) layer. The hair has to be held in place so that it provides an even layer and does not move when the chair is used – hence the stuffing loops.

To achieve this, run a continuous line of loops right around the top of the frame at a distance of about 1½in (3.8cm) in from the edge. The line is then continued to provide three parallel, evenly spaced lines across the top of the seat from front to back.

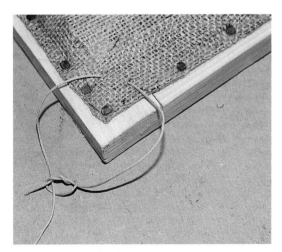

Stuffing the pad:

(1) The stuffing loops are sewn in using twine, starting at a front corner with a slip knot.

To start the loops, knot in the end of the twine at one corner of the frame. A slip knot is ideal. My standard practice follows on from rush seating, in which the starting point is the front left corner. The loops are made using three or four fingers to size them – three for a drop-in pad, four for larger chairs. Having crossed the fingers, the needle is angled back along the line of the thread and re-emerges about a fifth of the way along. This makes each subsequent loop overlap the end of its predecessor.

If you start with lengths of twine that are twice your arm span, you will not be continually joining on new lengths. When the end of the twine is reached, simply tie it off and knot in the next length.

STUFFING THE PIECE

In stuffing most pieces you will use modern vegetable hair. This is a treated, black-coated coconut fibre. It must be fire resistant, and the type I use comes under the trade name Filair. This is moderately resilient and long-lasting. The slightly cheaper untreated brown coconut fibre may be used, but this does tend to squash down and mat.

Occasionally, you may have the luxury of using real animal hair (*see* the reference to saving old materials, page 25). The actual procedure for stuffing with this or with Filair are exactly the same.

(2) Stuffing loops are sewn in using three or four fingers to give width and a clear loop. Note each loop end is oversewn to give an overlap in the stuffing.

(3) Each loop overlaps the next; here there is also a small loop across the corners.

(4) Loops are sewn right around the edge at about 1in (2.5cm) in from the side. The loop thread is continuous. Three rows of stuffing loops are also taken across the pad surface. The rows are always about 3in (7.6cm) apart so a wider seat has more loops.

To stuff, take a pull of hair and tease out any coils or lumps. Fold it over to give a rounded front edge and push this through the first loop, working from the inside of the pad out towards the edge. The rolled edge of the hair is push/pulled until the front corresponds with the outer edge of the seat pad. By pulling on the next twine loop along you now tighten the twine down onto the hair, firmly clamping it in place. Repeat the process with the next handful into the next loop along.

Continue working round the perimeter loops until you get back to the starting point. Only when the outer ring is complete do you start to infill the middle – but still work round from the edge in towards the centre.

(5) The first pull of hair is taken.

(6) It is folded over to give a round front edge.

(7) The rounded edge is pushed through the corner loop from the inside. The loop is pulled down onto the hessian by pulling on the next loop along.

(8) Continue on around the outside and when this is completed work along the inner rows of loops (left).

When all the loops have been stuffed and the twine pulled tight, check to see that you have an evenly dense layer across the whole of the surface. If you come across a hole, stuff it with a little more hair. You will often find that the corners of the frame are peeking through. Tease out the hair on either side, and, if necessary, add a little more. Once you are satisfied that the layer is smooth, go round the edge teasing out the hair to give a slight batter and an even coverage, with none of the hair actually covering the side of the frame members. These must be kept clear.

(9) Feather off the hair around the outside edge and build up corners. In the picture the nearside corner requires more hair.

COVERING WITH SKRIM

Now cover the hair with a layer of skrim – a close weave 7½oz hessian which is closely woven to prevent hair poking through. Applying a little tension, tack this down just inside the top edge of the frame. Skrim is more expensive than plain hessian, and so some upholsterers just use a light to middle-weight hessian instead.

The skrim layer holds the hair in place, but it also shows up any unevenness in the

(10) Tack a piece of skrim to cover the hair. The pad shown has sufficient clearance to allow the skrim to be wrapped around the outside faces. All tacks are only driven half in.

(11) The heel of the hand 'massages' across the surface of the skrim compressing the hair and tensioning the fabric. The wave front of loose skrim can be seen. The adjacent tacks are removed, the skrim pulled down and the tacks driven home.

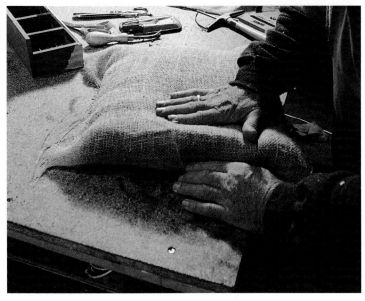

(12) The tensioning process from the other side. This important process, known as 'articulation' is done in each of four directions. It is also used on all layers of fabric (left).

surface. If you do find any bumps or hollows, drag the hair into place using a regulator. This is a long steel 'needle' which has one pointed end and one spade end; it may be anything from 8–12in (20–30cm) long and is about ³⁄₁₆in (5mm) in diameter. A size 8 steel (not aluminium or wood) knitting needle is an alternative.

The point should be inserted through the skrim and angled so that it lies in the hair but near the surface. Position it just behind the bump and then pivot it sideways, dragging the hair with it. The fact that it makes holes in the weave of the hessian does not matter.

An 8in (20cm) and a 12in (30cm) long regulator. These are the upholsterer's best friends.

(Below) The regulator used to even out the hair layer. It is pushed through the skrim and then swept sideways to move bumps of hair.

(Below left) The regulator used to clear out any hair trapped along the edge under the skrim.

(Below) The regulator is very useful for holding down a piece of tensioned material while the first tack is driven in.

Here the spade end of the regulator is used for folding round the corners of materials.

Regulator to the right of a lump.

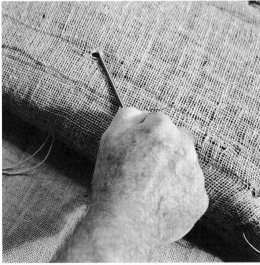

Regulator sweeps left, dragging surplus hair with it.

STUFFING WITH COTTON WADDING

Another layer of stuffing is now applied, but this time it is a cotton wadding. This has several functions. First, it provides another layer of padding; second it smooths out any bumps left after regulating; third, it smooths the surface and rounds out the edges down to the frame; and fourth, it prevents the hair from sticking through the top fabric and irritating the sitter.

Cotton wadding or cotton felt looks like untreated raw cotton 'waste'. In fact, it is treated and is fire resistant. It is available in two weights: 2½oz (70g) and 4oz (113g). The 2½oz is about 1½in (3.8cm) thick and the 4oz is about 2⅜in (6.3cm) thick. The heavier grade is only used on heavy pieces of furniture such as settees and pieces where you are trying to build up a depth of stuffing.

To apply a layer of wadding, the piece is cut with a square edge, but for a drop-in pad to a size of about ½in to 1in (about 1–2.5cm) smaller than the top of the pad. The edge of the wadding is then pulled out or teased to feather it down to the edge of the frame, again taking care to ensure that it does not overlap the edge.

THE CALICO LAYER

The next layer is the calico. For a chair pad a lightweight calico is used (2½ to 4oz (70–113g)). This is cut wide enough to go right over the top, down the sides and be tacked off under the frame from the underside (provided that the fit of the pad to the frame will accommodate this). On drop-in pads, the calico is often the last layer before the covering fabric is applied, so let's assume that this is the case for the moment. It therefore has to provide a perfectly smooth and unmoving platform for the finishing fabric. By careful fitting, tensioning, smoothing and proper corner-making, this can be achieved.

Working on the underside, tack the calico along the front edge of the frame. Use ten 'ordinary' tacks and space them about 2in (5cm) apart at about ½in (1.3cm) in from the edge; but only hammer the tacks

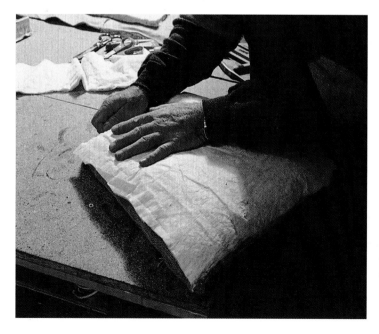

The final layer before the finishing fabric is a tissue-paper-like, fire-retardant, skin wadding. Here the edge is being torn away to feather it down.

In tacking down the covering calico the tacks are only driven in a short distance to allow them to be removed for articulation and tensioning.

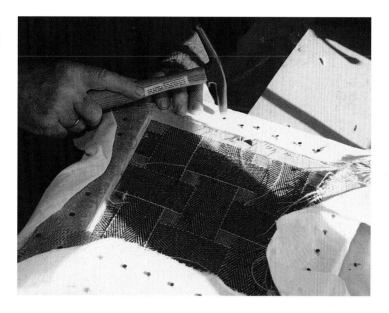

partially in, because you will be removing them in a moment. Leave the last 2–3in (5–7.6cm) of calico by the corners untacked. The calico should not be folded to give an edge seam as the cut edge will soon be covered.

Smooth the calico over the top of the pad and pulling it tight now tack the opposite side down, again from the underside, and again only partially driving in the tacks. After this, tack the two sides. All corners will still be free.

Working on the top of the pad and using the heel of the hand push across the calico from front to back. Despite the tensioning you gave by stretching the calico when first tacking it you will find a 'wave front' of slack build-ups in front of the hand. Upholsterers describe this process as 'stroking' and call it 'articulating'.

As the hand's sweep reaches the edge and pushes over a ridge of slack, withdraw the nearest tack or two, pull the material tight and retack. Articulate the whole of the surface in one direction, pulling down and retacking the material as you go. Then turn the pad round and articulate in the

opposite direction. Having completed this front to back and then back to front pass, rotate the pad through 90 degrees and do side to side articulation in both directions.

This process smooths and tensions the surface. It is continued until you can create no more wrinkles. Often two sets of passes is all that is needed if your earlier work (stuffing and hessian stretching) was reasonable.

Once the pad is really firm the tacks are all driven right home and we can turn our attention to the corners.

Working into a firm, vertical faced, true square corner is the easiest of all upholstery corners.

The process is simplified by first cutting across the corner of the material. To do this, a diagonal cut is made across the corner to cut away the excess material. It is made at a distance out from the seat corner which is the same as the width of the calico which has been tacked along the underside of the frame.

Next, draw a pencil or imaginary line out which bisects the right angle of the frame corner and comes out to the middle of the diagonal across the corner ear that you

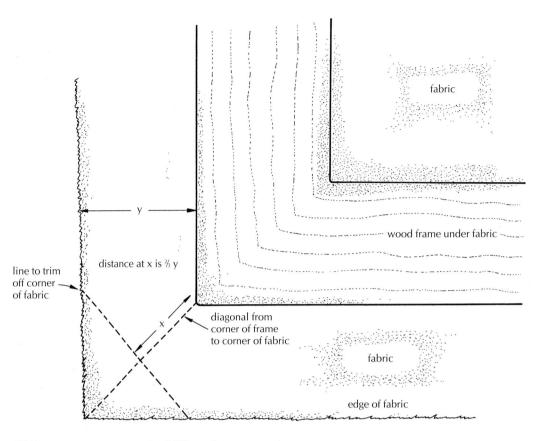

fabric

wood frame under fabric

y

distance at x is ⅔ y

line to trim
off corner
of fabric

x

diagonal from
corner of frame
to corner of fabric

fabric

edge of fabric

Trim away corners to make folding of corners easier.

Examples of making a plain, single vertical seam squared corner.

(1) The covering fabric is first tacked in place along all sides, leaving the corners loose (here shown on a finishing velvet).

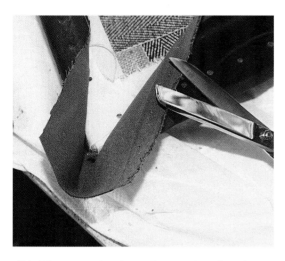

(2) The corner is trimmed away (see drawing opposite).

(3) The wings are pinched together and the fabric is cut down the fold.

have just cut. Cut along this line from the edge of the material until you reach the point at the frame corner.

Fold the cut edge of the material under until the fold lies directly down the corner of the frame. Pull the material under the frame

(4) The first wing is pulled round and tacked down. (This is a teaching model.)

and tack it off. Repeat with the material on the other side of the cut. Complete all the other three corners of the frame. (Note, this method of corner folding is used only on the calico layer and is done so that no tacks have to be driven into the sides of the frame.)

A little earlier in the Chapter I said that we were working on the calico as platform for the finishing fabric. There are, however, some exceptions. If we are using a very fine fabric which might allow even the tiniest imperfections in the under layers to show through, then we may also need to use the tissue-paper-like skin wadding between the calico and the dressing fabric. This should be cut so that the edges coincide with the edges of the seat pad. Two or three dots of adhesive spray may be applied to the calico to hold the wadding in place, although this is not really necessary, then fit the finishing fabric directly over the wadding. We will be looking at the subject of top covers in a later chapter.

In working through a stuffed-over pad we have used a number of basic techniques, and that is why we have dealt with the subject in some detail. In all styles of

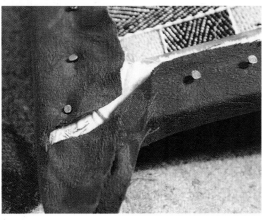

(5) The second corner is folded round using the regulator to square the corner.

(6) The seam may be slip-stitched to a tight closure (on another model).

(7) An alternative method of cutting a simple corner, the upper ear is folded down over the second side (left).

traditional upholstery we use webbing, and this is stretched as it is fitted. Whatever the application, whether stuffed over or under-slung, the webbing is tacked down in the same way. We also always use hessian as a platform layer, and stuffing loops are employed in both over stuffed and sprung forms of upholstery. So although we have been looking at a simple stuffed-over, drop-in seat pad, we have been considering a number of the most fundamental of all basic upholstery techniques.

In the next chapter we will be developing these further as we consider stuffed-over upholstery as it is applied directly to

the chair frame. Here, we will detail two additional techniques. One of these is the use of through stitches to shape and square up the sides of deeper seats.

In the later chapter on fitting the finishing fabrics (Chapter 11) we will also examine a number of different ways of making corners. When fixing the hessian layers, corners do not matter much – provided they are firm and hold together, their appearance is not particularly important. However, we do need to take a little more care with the calico layer because a badly made corner with a bulky fold will certainly show through a delicate covering fabric.

8

Overeating?
Deep Stuffed-over Chairs

Because of the purpose for which they are intended – fundamentally day-to-day eating – stuffed over drop-in pads are relatively thin. Most chairs where the upholstery is applied directly to the frame, however, are intended to be more comfortable: they are for use in the bedroom; as salon chairs for visitors; as library or study chairs for use at desks; or for the dinner party where sitting at table may extend over a period of hours.

It is both a matter of tradition and practical ergonomic/comfort considerations that the platform (seating area) of these deeply padded seats is reasonably flat and that the edges or side walls of the seat are built up to the full depth of the pad. There is, in fact, no clear line in terms of the overall appearance between some stuffed-over chairs and those that have springs incorporated into the platform.

Examination of the underside, however, soon highlights one key difference. Stuffed over is built up with the webbing on the top of the frame, whereas springs sit on webbing that is fixed under the frame.

BUILDING UP STUFFING

The process of building up a deep-stuffed seat starts by webbing the frame exactly as we did for drop-in pads (*see* page 77).

The actual sequence followed in building up the stuffed layers will depend upon the structure of the frame. There are important notes in Chapter 10 on frame variations that should be read before covering anything

more complex than a simple seat and back dining chair.

Most basic deep-stuffed chairs are wider and a fraction deeper from front to back than the normal drop-in pad seat. Hence there could be four front to back runs of webbing, and according to the design of the seat platform there may be both space and need for four side to side webs. As already emphasized, the webbing is always fixed to the top of the frame whatever the arrangement for the subsequent layers of materials.

FIXING THE HESSIAN PLATFORM

Step two, as with drop-in pads, is to fix a platform of hessian over the webbing. A medium grade is used and 10oz is ideal until you move up to big armchairs and settees. The hessian platform is nailed over the webbing and is fixed on the top of the frame. However, for the moment let's take a step forward in the sequence.

There are two major type variations in how the finishing fabric is fixed on stuffed-over chairs. In one, the calico and the finishing fabric are carried down right over the sides of the frame members and are secured to the underside of the frame. In the second form, the materials terminate in a straight line somewhere down the face of the side members. Sometimes there is a step or beading in the exposed wood of the chair's frame, and the materials are brought to the

seat area

frame

fabric (and) calico
wrapped round frame
and tacked under frame

seat area

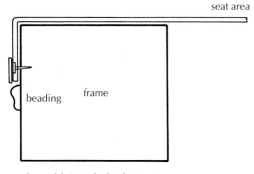

beading   frame

frame fabric tacked to butt onto
beading; tack heads covered
with glued-on braiding

seat area

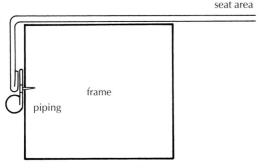

frame

piping

flanged piping cord tacked
to frame and folded edge of
covering fabric stitched to
cord with slip stitches

Various methods of fixing fabric on seat frames.

top of this. On others, there is no beading but simply the edge of the material. In both beaded and non-beaded forms there is usually a line of braiding (or even a tasselled fringe) over the edge of the material. The braid, of course, hides the tacks along the edge of the material. The exposed wood below the line of material is always stained and polished.

Whatever the arrangement for fixing the finishing fabric, the platform hessian is always fixed to the top of the frame. Bring the hessian to about ¼in (6mm) from the edge of the frame, fold it over (up or down) to give edge strength, and tack down with 10 Imps (the bigger head gives a better grip in the open weave of hessian).

APPLYING STUFFING LOOPS

Stuffing loops are applied to the top of the hessian as on the drop-in pads. They are, however, made looser, to a width of four fingers rather than three, with the outer circuit about 1in (2.5cm) in from the frame edge. The extra size of these loops allows us to get a deeper filling of hair and particularly to build up a good outer ring, which is essential if we are to achieve nice vertical walls to the seat pad.

VARIATIONS

At this stage, we are faced with some possible variations. It all depends upon the thickness of the pad that we wish to build.

A square-edged seat pad of about 3in (7.6cm) thickness may be built with a single layer of hair. If we wish to go deeper we may put the first 3in layer on, cap this with another layer of hessian, then sew in another set of stuffing loops to take a second layer of hair. Alternatively, the extra depth may be achieved by incorporating

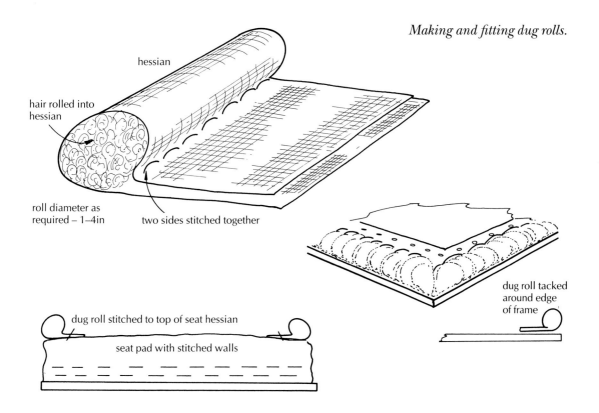

Making and fitting dug rolls.

hessian

hair rolled into hessian

roll diameter as required – 1–4in

two sides stitched together

dug roll tacked around edge of frame

dug roll stitched to top of seat hessian

seat pad with stitched walls

an 'edge' or 'dug' roll. This can appear with two variations.

In one, the roll is made by building up a tube of hessian around a hair core. It is made rather like a flanged piping cord. The roll is then tacked to the frame immediately above the platform hessian. The stuffing loops and hair are then placed to fill in the well inside the roll.

In the alternative, the first stuffing is completed in the normal way and is covered with skrim, then shaped. Next an edge roll is made and sewn on top of the skrim. In this case, while the roll is usually hair filled, it could also be filled with waste cotton wadding.

The making of a roll is rather like the hand-rolling of a cigarette. Cut a long strip of hessian, the length of which will depend upon how long a roll you need. The width of the strip is typically about 9in (23cm).

Handfuls of hair are placed along the centre of the strip and are hand-rolled into a loose sausage; try to get the thickness of hair fairly even down the length. Fold the two edges of the strip of hessian together and with a spring needle and length of twine tack stitch them together, sewing close to the hair sausage. The roll should not normally be tight stuffed as you will usually wish to shape it to the wall of the seat pad. Should you need a long roll to go right around the top of a big seat, bear in mind that it is sometimes better to make two or three sections and join them together.

For the moment, we will continue the description of building up the seat on the basis of a single deep layer of hair. The actual sequence and procedure is similar to that used for the drop-in pad, except that we use larger handfuls of hair and ensure a very generous stuffing around the

99

edges. This usually means that the hair substantially overhangs the outer edge of the frame. We also level off the top and make sure that there is plenty of hair in both of the front corners.

With the hair in place, pat it and feel over the top. Look for any lumpy masses and hollows. Add hair to fill out all holes, and tease out the hair to remove lumps. The top should be smooth and flat and the pad thickness even. Do not worry that the outside edges overhang and are not yet square, but do ensure that the overhang is even all round. Build up any hollows and tease out to make the edge even and continuous.

A cover of hessian is now fixed over the hair. Here a lightweight hessian or proper skrim is used – 7½oz (210g) is a typical weight. The covering hessian may be fixed to the very edge of the top of the frame, but it can be taken down and tacked somewhere down the side of the frame. It may also be taken to the lower edge and wrapped under. If the fabric is to end at a step, the hessian/skrim should end about 1in (2.5cm) above the fabric edge line. Fold the edge of the hessian in or out to give a double thickness to the edge and again use 10 Imp tacks.

With all patterns of chair, whether step edge or wrap under, you will now encounter a new set of problems. These concern the front and rear corners where there are now legs to contend with. Although the hessian will be hidden from view by later layers, the corners do need to be fairly neat as they form an important part of the shaping of the seat pad.

CORNERING

Whether the finishing fabric ends at a beading or wraps under the main part of the frame, it will always terminate in a straight edge across the open face of the upper part of the front legs. On the back of the seat there will also be the two side members of

the back of the chair rising above the pad. Obviously all material layers have to be worked round these legs.

Start by fixing the hessian along the four sides of the frame but leave free the last 2–3in (5–7.5cm) either side of all four corners. There is an ideal level of tension for the hessian. There should be no slack, but equally it should not be pulled so tight that it compresses the hair, and particularly it should not round off the edges. It should just pull back some of the overhang and firm it up, but not completely remove it. To assist in getting the tension right it is a good idea to tack it loosely in place the first time round, then to go round again, remove a few tacks, shape the edge of the pad and tack the material home. If in the hessian placement process you see areas that are clearly not adequately stuffed, feed in a little more hair to bring them to the required shape.

Now we need to look at the actual corners. Start with the front pair. Here we do wish to pull back most of the overhang and to get as close as possible to the required final shape. Some chairs do have rounded front corners, but the upright chairs that we are presently looking at tend to have squared corners and vertical edges all around the seating pad.

The easiest way of making front corners in hessian is to square off the two walls either side of the corner and to pinch the corner of the hessian so that it sticks out in an ear. Cut the fold of the ear right up to the apex of the corner. Fold one side of the ear around the corner and tack it down. Next fold the other ear round the other corner and tack this down – to get the shape and the right angle of the corner the hessian can be bent around the flat end of the regulator needle.

An alternative corner is also made easier if you fold the uncut hessian around the regulator needle which is held precisely where the finished corner will lie. The hessian is

Making corner around rear leg.

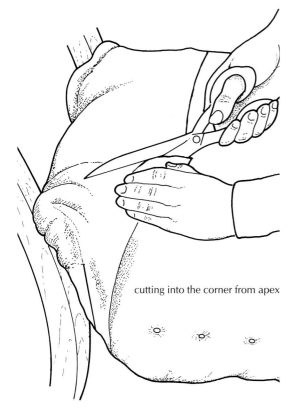

cutting into the corner from apex

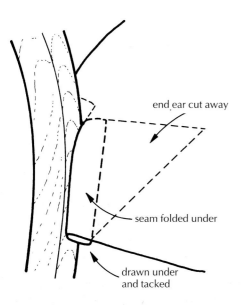

end ear cut away

seam folded under

drawn under
and tacked

now pulled gently down to form two ears either side of the corner. Tack the hessian down to the frame either side of the corner but tacking inside the fold. Use just one tack on each side and place them about 1in (2.5cm) back from the corner. Remove the regulator.

You will now have two ears of hessian sticking out from either side of the corner. Cut a V-shaped notch into the hessian behind the two holding tacks, tuck these notches in and fold the two ears in until the folded edges meet in a vertical line on the corner itself. Tack these down to the frame. If you wish you can sew the two folds together to give an even crisper corner – four or five slip or tacking stitches is all that is required.

The rear corners are much easier. Pull the corner of the hessian back from the frame member such that it lies across the seat. Assuming you started with a 'square' of hessian, cut in diagonally from the corner of the material until the cut reaches the inside corner of the frame member.

Cut away the two ears, fold the edges in to lie neatly down the side of the leg and pulling down the hessian on both sides of the frame member, force the hessian down into the corner. If it will not go right down and ends with a small ruck, you have not made the diagonal cut long enough (beginners often make this mistake), so go back and cut deeper. Once it is firmly down tack it off. Do not worry if the hessian frays a little where the diagonal cut ends.

ROUNDED CORNERS

As noted above, many upright chairs have square front corners, although this is not always the case and Victorian balloon back and similar chairs often have rounded front edges to the seats. Here you cannot achieve a single vertical seam up the front corners, so there will be at least two seams.

To make a rounded corner, the point of the front corner of the hessian is pulled

Making corners around the frame of the back-rest.

(Note on the teaching models – scraps of striped material are used to show how directions change. This material would be unsuitable for a simple corner.)

(1) As seen from above (the chair top), the material is folded over and pulled back from the corner. Here it has been marked on the underside to show cutting lines (above).

(2) The first cut is made deep into the corner (usually going ½in (1.3cm) further than you think necessary).

(3) The corners are cut away leaving two fold-under wings.

(4) The wings are folded in.

(5) The folded fabric is finally tacked down (left).

vertically down the corner of the leg. It is then wrapped round the leg and a single tack is driven in either side of the corner and about ½in (1.2cm) back from the apex. Again, you will have two ears, one either side of the corner. These are drawn together until they meet at the bottom exactly on the corner but the two folds rise in an outward, even V-shape. The regulator is used to get an even lie.

On a small radius corner it may be possible just to get the two inclined folds to meet at the lower edge. On larger radii there is likely to be a small gap. What is important is to manipulate the material and the folds until the two are equally spaced either side of the apex of the corner, and that both lie back at the same angle of slope. Again, the spade end of the regulator is very useful to shape and position the folds.

You may think that taking this much care with the corners on the hessian layer is over-icing the cake. In fact – yes, but there are two justifications for this level of perfectionism. First, the better you make the corners, even at the hessian stage, the better will be the finished shape of the chair. Second, you will find minor variations between every chair you work on, and by spending a few extra minutes achieving the best corners for the piece in hand while you are still at the hessian layer, you can make mistakes and modifications without ruining any of the finishing fabric. When you do come to apply the top layer, you should know exactly how to approach each corner.

STITCHING TECHNIQUES

With the hessian under appropriate 'tension' and tacked down all the way round, we can now start to square up the platform. Here we call into play a series of stitching techniques.

Stitching lines for wall forming on built up seat pad.

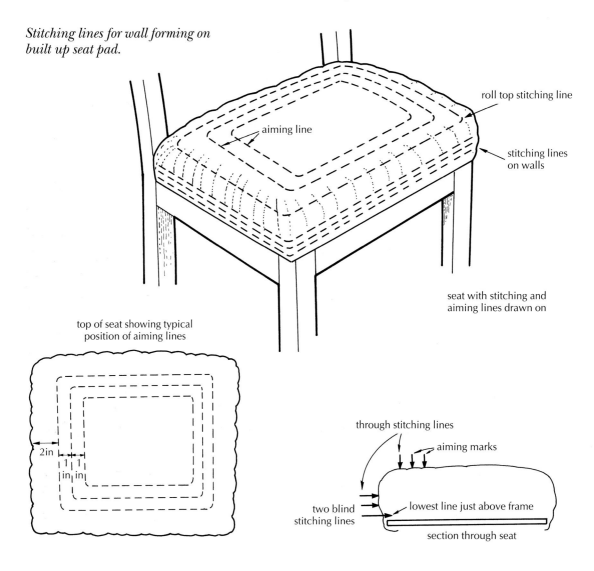

aiming line

roll top stitching line

stitching lines on walls

seat with stitching and aiming lines drawn on

top of seat showing typical position of aiming lines

2in

1 in 1 in

through stitching lines

aiming marks

two blind stitching lines

lowest line just above frame

section through seat

First, using the regulator, level off the hair across the top of the platform, and particularly draw as much of the hair as possible out to the edges all the way around the top of the seat. Make sure you get a good filling into the two front corners. Check the edges under your hand and test that they are even all round. Also check that the top of the pad is smooth and level.

We use three or four rows of stitching to shape the walls. The lower rows are 'blind' – they do not go right through. The purpose of these is to draw hair towards the side and to pull back the hessian so that it rises vertically from the frame. The hair pinched by the stitches makes the side walls stiff and gives them extra rigidity and resilience.

This, in turn, gives greater resistance to crushing and deformation.

The top row of stitching is 'through'; here, the loops enter near the top of the side wall and emerge a short distance in across the top of the seat. Their purpose is to form a crisp roll along the edge. By adjusting the depth of the stitch, you can end up with a near right-angle corner.

Stitching to shape seat pad. Deep over-stuffed back pads are similar.

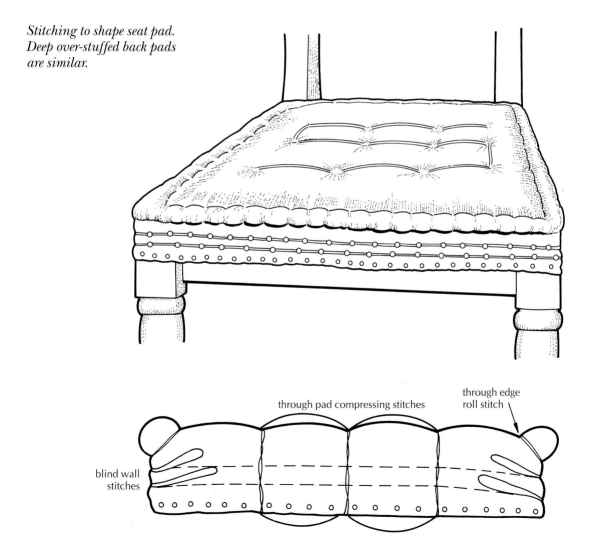

blind wall stitches

through pad compressing stitches

through edge roll stitch

It is a good idea to draw on the hessian the position of each line of stitching using tailor's chalk. You also mark the aiming line on the top of the pad for each row, particularly for the blind stitches.

The lowest line runs right round the front and the side of the seat pad. It is traced about ½in (1.2cm) above the top edge of the wood of the frame. The top aiming line for this row is traced on the top of the seat and may well be 4–6in (10–15cm) in from the edge of the pad. The deeper the side walls, the further in this aiming line.

On some chairs, particularly with a deep seat pad, the design is such that the back of the pad also requires a vertical wall. In this case the blind and through stitching rows should be continued around the back of the pad.

The next row – also blind – is traced halfway up the side wall; it may be 1in (2.5cm) above the first row. If the distance exceeds an inch it may be better to think of

(Above) A seat pad is marked off for stitching. The inner square is the 'aiming line' for a row of blind stitches. The outer square will be the top line of the rolled edge stitches.

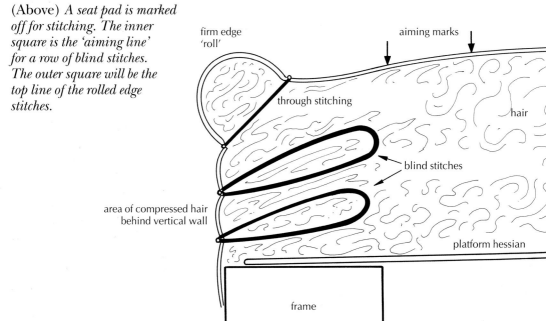

Section through stitched wall of seat pad.

adding an extra row. Again, it may be taken round the back according to the seat pad shape required. The aiming line for this row will be an inch closer to the edge of the seat. A third blind row will then be drawn on deep pads.

The final, through line of stitching is traced on the top and the sides of the pad and is usually between 1in and 1½in (2.5–3.8cm) in from the edge.

To form a crisp corner along the edge you can make this through row smaller. However, you get a better finish by making the roll to the dimensions already given and then pinching the apex of the roll with a smaller row of through stitches.

The dimensions given above are an average 'basis to work on'. As you gain in experience you will find that you vary these according to the particular chair that you are working on. Some require more rows of quite close stitching, while others will need only a few, widely spaced stitches to give you the necessary shape and firmness that you require.

A long (10–12in) (25–30cm) double-ended straight needle is used for the stitching processes – these have an eye at one end but both ends have points. The end with the eye is referred to as the short point, the other the long point. The needle is threaded with a double arm's length of twine. Many upholsterers use No. 4 Barbour twine for this task, but again I prefer to stick with No. 6 as this allows me to pull harder without snapping the string.

Starting at a corner (usually a back corner), the long point is pushed into the hessian on the tailor's chalk line just above the frame. The point is angled to the aiming line on top of the pad which is furthest in from the edge. The needle is driven in until the long point emerges on the aiming line, and is then pulled from the top until the bottom point carrying the thread vanishes into the hessian to a depth of about 2–3in (5–7.6cm) (halfway between the side wall and pad top).

At this stage the needle is angled so that when it is pushed back down, the point and thread emerge about 1in (2.5cm) further along the stitching line from the entry point. The needle is drawn right out and the free end of the twine is knotted to the sewing line with a slip knot. The thread is pulled up tight.

The long point is now moved 1in further along the sewing line and is pushed in until the thread is again halfway through the pad. The needle is angled back towards the end of the previous stitch. As the threaded point emerges, the running line is wrapped round the needle with a couple of turns. When the needle is now pulled right out these turns form a knot on the running line.

As the twine is tensioned the knot pulls up tight. This will cause the hessian to pull back – it also packs hair in behind the wall of the hessian. Draw the twine until the wall is vertical with the seat frame, and make the next stitch – again 1in further along.

This process is continued right around. When the twine runs out, knot it off and start with another length.

Subsequent blind rows are stitched in exactly the same way. With every stitch, and with each row, the wall will strengthen and the vertical face will progress.

The final through row starts in the same way. Here, however, the needle is pushed right through and is drawn out on the top of the seat pad. The threaded point is then moved 1in along the sewing line and is pushed back in. As it re-emerges on the side wall make double wrap knots as before.

The needle is drawn right out, re-enters 1in along the stitching line and emerges 1in along the aiming line. Again, it is drawn right through the top of the seat. Now it backtracks to the end of the previous stitch and it passes through the pad alongside the previous track.

The aim of this final row of stitching is to complete the forming of the vertical wall right up to the top edge. It will also, however,

Forming the knot on shaping stitches. The line is wrapped round the needle in three turns.

The knot is pulled tight and the vertical face begins to form.

top views

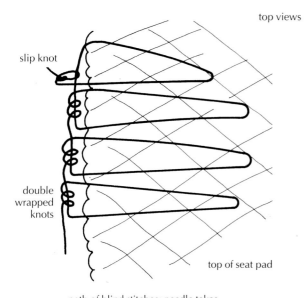

slip knot

double
wrapped
knots

top of seat pad

path of blind stitches; needle takes
thread in to half depth then angles back

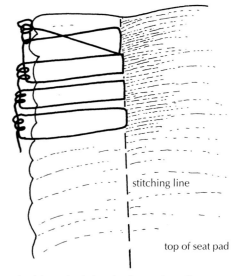

stitching line

top of seat pad

path of through stitches that form edge roll

Paths of blind and through stitches used to form side walls.

create a slight hollow on the top of the seat pad – more of this in a moment.

If you have got the stitching right, you will find that you have also produced nice sharp vertical corners at the front. Any residual slackness in the hessian should have been pulled up. But it does not always work, and you may need to make any necessary final shaping by sewing through stitches inside the corner using one or two vertical rows.

There will be times when you are stripping down a piece of furniture that you will come across a little trick that has been used to deal with the problem of shaping front corners. A semicircle of cardboard has been cut, folded and tacked over the corner. While this does give a very crisp shape, it also leads to problems: the card needs to be strong enough to hold the shape, and it should never rise more than half the height of the corner. If the card is too deep, someone sitting on the corner of the chair could crush the card and you then have a permanently misshapen corner. It is better to avoid the use of card if you can – the secret is in getting the shaping stitching right.

A cardboard reinforced corner revealed when stripping down an old chair.

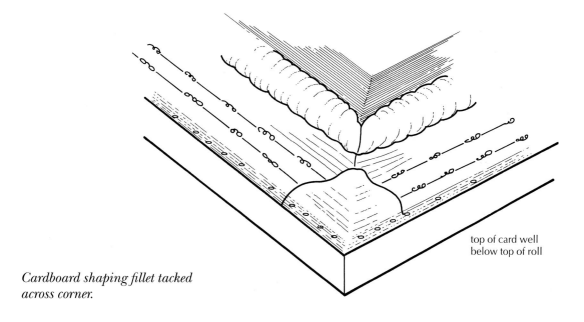

top of card well
below top of roll

Cardboard shaping fillet tacked across corner.

USING THE REGULATOR

Now is the time for some serious regulating! Particular attention should be paid to the roll edge. It is unlikely that you will now be able to move any hair in the vertical walls but the top edge and the top platform need to be worked to give crispness and smoothness.

For an average stuffed-over seat you may now have fixed all the hair that you need. The slight top hollow will be filled with cotton felt.

Let's however, consider where you will require a very deep pad – for instance where the seat has to be buttoned. It is at this stage that you might consider using a dug roll. This is stitched onto the top of the pad so that the roll goes right round the top edge.

At this stage it is usual on very deep seats also to stitch through the hessian and hair, working through the seat pad from top to underside. Three or so rows of wide loops (6in (15cm) each) are taken through and these are drawn very tight to pull the centre hair down. It is this step that finally smooths out any tendency towards a central dome.

You will in your previous through stitch have effectively produced a roll edge – it was this that produced the centre hollow mentioned. The through stitching may have emphasized this well.

Inside the hollow (or dug roll edging) lay down another set of stuffing loops and build up another layer of hair. If you do have a second hair layer, you can stitch on a hessian cover to hold it in place, but this is not usually necessary as the form of the pad is now well established. This does, however, presuppose that you can get an even layer of hair without having to rely on a regulator to smooth out your work.

Through stitching to shape pad top.

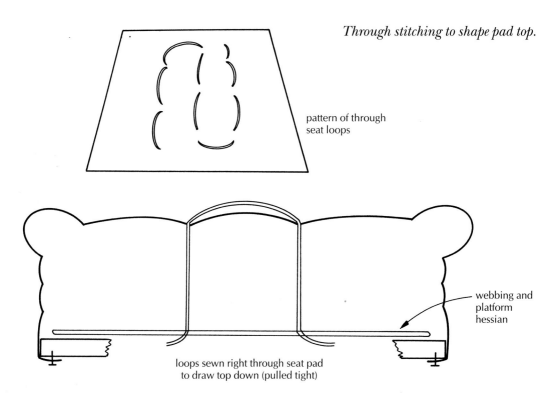

pattern of through
seat loops

webbing and
platform
hessian

loops sewn right through seat pad
to draw top down (pulled tight)

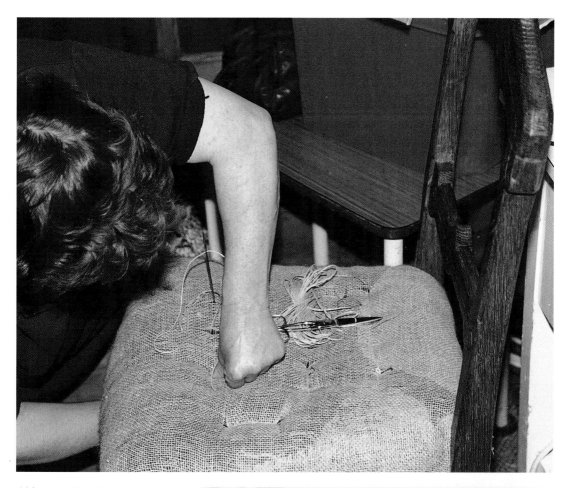

(Above) *Stitching right through the seat pad to flatten the centre dome.*

A stitched pad with one blind row, a roll edge and centre stitching. This piece is quite rough but it will be covered with a second layer of hair. The student will do a better job on that – or else!

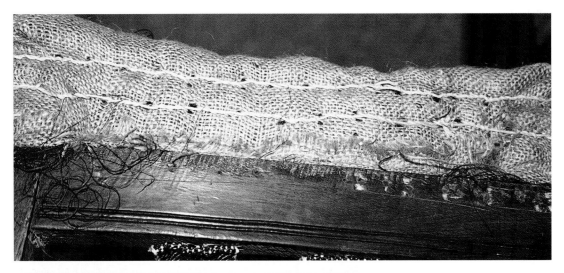

(Above) *The side view shows that hair is trapped under the hessian and might show through.*

Infilling the hollow behind the edge roll using scraps of cotton wadding.

(Below) *Filling in a deep well in shaped pad top.*

second layer of stuffing loops and
hair inside well of stitched pad

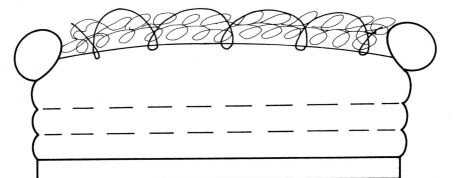

top hair not normally hessian covered

With the single or double layer of hair finished the next stage is to apply a layer of cotton felt. This normally comes in two grades. On very large pieces of furniture the heavier 4oz grade may be used, but for most chairs the 2½oz is all that is needed.

The felt should be cut to the size of the top platform. The edges of the felt therefore correspond with the outer edge of the top of the seat pad. The felt is then placed on the seat and working from the underside of the edge of the cotton it is feathered down to blend in with the top of the wall.

Now is the time to make a final assessment. You will normally have done enough to get the shape and smoothness right so that you can move straight onto the calico layer. You can also rely on the thin layer of skin wadding on top of the calico to iron out the last tiny imperfections. However, you may also decide to also cut and fit a layer of heavier grade skin wadding to go on top of the cotton felt before the calico. This is not normal practice, but it does offer one advantage. The skin wadding can be taken over the top and down the side walls to provide a very smooth platform for the calico.

The edges of the layer of cotton felt are feathered to give a smooth taper.

FIXING THE CALICO LAYER

In the chapter on drop-in pads we spent some time covering the fixing of the calico layer. It was cut to shape and lightly tacked in place and was then articulated with the heel of the hand and retacked one, two or three times until it was tight and perfectly smooth.

The same procedure is used when fixing calico over deep stuffing. There are, however, some added complications.

First, let's reconsider the two forms of covering where the materials are fixed directly to the chair's frame rather that onto a drop-in pad. In one, as detailed earlier in the chapter, the finishing fabric wraps under the frame and is fixed to the underside. On the other, the fabric comes down to a line on the face of the frame, and is fixed there. That line may be an arbitrary one at some point down the frame or across the face of a leg; occasionally it may correspond with the bottom edge of the frame, but quite often it is the top of a step or beading on the frame's face.

Obviously the easiest of these is fixing under the frame. Both the calico and the finishing fabric (and possibly the skrim) are wrapped under and are then simply tacked down with a row of close-spaced fine tacks – No. 10 ordinary tacks are adequate. No folded edge is made with the material – by allowing a sufficient margin, and recognizing that the tension is not too great, a safe fix can be achieved without a fold in all cloths except the hessian.

With the face fixing the task is not quite so easy. First, we wish to avoid any thick edges that will look ugly so we do not use folded seams. Second, we do not want any of the white of the calico peeping out below the finishing fabric. For this reason it is quite normal to tack the calico ¼in (6mm) above the line of the finishing fabric. For fitting the calico a good working edge is provided as this

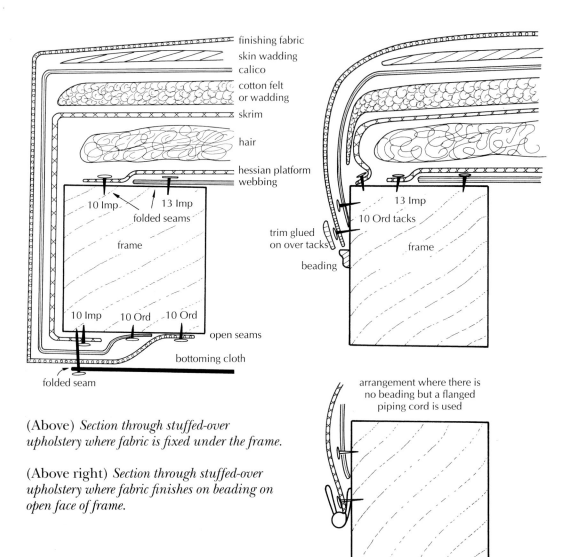

finishing fabric
skin wadding
calico
cotton felt
or wadding
skrim
hair
hessian platform
webbing
10 Imp
13 Imp
folded seams
frame
10 Imp   10 Ord   10 Ord
open seams
bottoming cloth
folded seam

13 Imp
10 Ord tacks
trim glued
on over tacks
frame
beading

arrangement where there is
no beading but a flanged
piping cord is used

(Above) *Section through stuffed-over upholstery where fabric is fixed under the frame.*

(Above right) *Section through stuffed-over upholstery where fabric finishes on beading on open face of frame.*

allows the pulling and articulating that is required. However, once this has been completed a close-spaced row of tacks needs to be driven in and the spare material cut away to about ¼in (6mm) below the tacks. The finishing fabric will be fitted in the same way but this time the spare is finally cut to the step or required finishing line.

The other problem with the calico and the finishing fabric is that the material has to be properly fitted around the legs and the back verticals. The techniques that you use may be the same as those that you employed on the hessian layers. Obviously they are executed with much more care, but in fact calico is much easier than hessian to deal with. We will consider the details of the various methods of making corners in Chapter 11, which deals with finishing fabrics.

In the next chapter we will examine the techniques of building up a spring subframe upholstery.

9

A Young Man's Fancy
Springing

When we were talking about stripping down an old chair for reupholstery, a number of points were made. First, it was stated that we did not reuse old materials (with the exception of washed animal hair). We also said that you make notes of the sequence in which the layers were fixed and of the points to which each was attached. You were also advised to put one of each size of the old springs to one side to assist in reordering. It is now time to look at the springs.

Certainly old seat springs are not reused. Some will have been more heavily loaded than others and will have lost some of their resilience. You can rarely get old springs to tie in evenly and although they may look right they will probably give differential support. New springs should cost you less than £1 each, so a new set will not break the bank.

CHOOSING YOUR SPRINGS

The springs used in traditional upholstery are double coil. They were first patented in the UK in 1828 and now come in various 'lengths' and are coiled from different thicknesses or 'wire gauge' of spring steel. The name 'double coil' stems from the fact that the spring is coiled narrowly at the centre and is of much wider diameter at each end. They are, therefore, often also called 'hour-glass springs'. There is no simple formula to determine which springs to use, but you will eventually develop a feel for the number, weight and length of spring for a particular piece. For the time being, however, it is best to keep back an old spring so that you can replace it with one of similar size, gauge and number.

The table on page 116 will provide a guide only and you will find individual pieces of furniture that differ widely from the recommendations shown.

Springs are not always easy to obtain. There are only a few suppliers who stock them and often the local shops that sell hair and fabric do not carry springs. They may or may not be prepared to get them for you – as they may have to buy in minimum lots of fifty, they can be reluctant. Some local upholsterers may be prepared to sell you a set. If you do have a source, take in an old spring and ask for similar. Otherwise, and most often the case, it is a mail-order job. This means that you have to determine the 'wire gauge' of your spring – this in turn will mean accurately measuring the diameter of the wire and translating that into 'WG' from the table overleaf. The length is determined by taking a spring that is obviously not squashed and standing it beside a ruler and reading the average height of the top of the coil (not necessarily the highest tip).

As you will see from the table, the thicker the wire the lower the wire gauge number. A 9 WG spring can be compressed under the hand to about half to two-thirds of its full height. A thinner 12 WG spring will compress to a quarter of its full height.

Springs Table
Double Coil Upholstery Springs (showing sizes normally available at suppliers)

Wire Gauge	Diameter		Lengths available		Typical uses
	in	mm	in	mm	
8½	0.152	3.9	6	152	Heaviest grade for seating
			9	229	
			10	254	
			12	305	
9	0.144	3.7	4	102	General seating
			5	127	
			6	152	
			7	178	
			8	203	
			9	229	
			10	254	
9½	0.136	3.5	8	203	Softer seating
10	0.128	3.3	4	102	Soft seating and chair backs
			5	127	
			6	152	
			7	178	
			8	203	
			9	229	
12	0.104	2.6	4	102	Lightest for soft backs and arms
			5	127	
			6	150	

Do not skimp on the springs. Never put in less than there were, and you may often feel that a better support pattern can be achieved by using one more rather than one less spring. A sprung dining chair will rarely have less than five, an armchair may have nine on the seat and six on the back, but that can quickly become twelve and nine. A chaise often requires twenty-four and a sprung-back Chesterfield may well have three dozen in total across the seat, arms and back. These bigger pieces and some old armchairs use the very largest 8½ WG by 12in.

You may, of course, be unfortunate enough to be starting with a carcass that has already been stripped down. You know it was sprung because the tack marks for the original webbing are on the underside of the frame. Now you really do have to look and think. The first clue is the arrangement of the webbing. You will see a little cluster of slightly larger holes at regular intervals under each of the frame members. This is where the webbing was anchored. Work out how many runs of webbing there were. At each point where a front to back length crossed a side to side piece, there was probably a spring. Springs are most frequently fixed where webbing runs cross. However, be a little cautious. Although the norm is for a spring to sit on a crossing, on

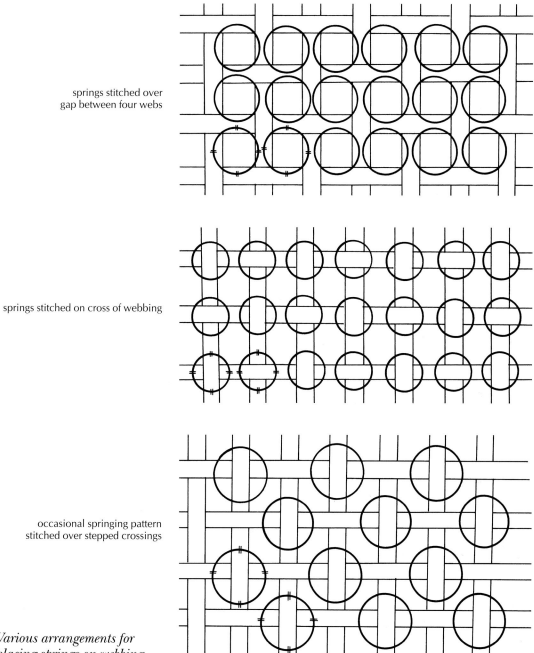

springs stitched over
gap between four webs

springs stitched on cross of webbing

occasional springing pattern
stitched over stepped crossings

*Various arrangements for
placing springs on webbing.*

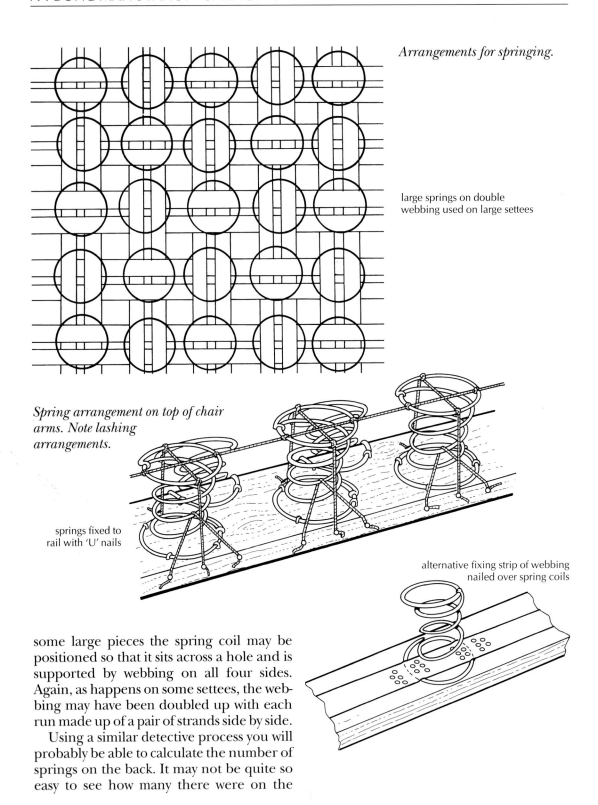

Arrangements for springing.

large springs on double
webbing used on large settees

*Spring arrangement on top of chair
arms. Note lashing
arrangements.*

springs fixed to
rail with 'U' nails

alternative fixing strip of webbing
nailed over spring coils

some large pieces the spring coil may be
positioned so that it sits across a hole and is
supported by webbing on all four sides.
Again, as happens on some settees, the webbing may have been doubled up with each
run made up of a pair of strands side by side.

Using a similar detective process you will
probably be able to calculate the number of
springs on the back. It may not be quite so
easy to see how many there were on the

arms, but by allowing a spacing of about 6in (15cm) it will usually come down to three along the top and perhaps four on the inside face (where there were any at all). Some roll arm tops may have three pairs of springs set in V-shapes, but as these are often fixed with a couple of U nails direct to the wood you will not see the telltale cluster of nails marking a webbing fixing point.

So, for various reasons it may be difficult to determine precisely where the earlier webbing was fixed or what the springing pattern was. Your best guide now is to measure the diameter of the wide end of a suitable spring, allow up to about 3in (7.6cm) between the outer rim of one spring, and that of the next, and then work out a suitable webbing arrangement and the number of springs required to fill the void with the calculated spacing. But again, be cautious. Sitting in my workshop at the moment is a pair of old square armchairs with small wings – each has nine 8½ by 12s and the tops of the coils are only 1¼in (3.2cm) apart.

In most chairs the outer springs are between 2–3in (5–7.6cm) in from the frame, and on settees this can increase to 3–6in (7.6–15cm). There is an exception.

On some armchairs and settees you will find that the upper rail on the front of the frame is a few inches lower than the rest of the frame around the seat area. On these,

(Above) *Springing on the arm of a settee.*

A very light springing on the settee backrest. When reupholstered, another row of light gauge springs was added.

The spring arrangement on a deep armchair. In fact, the springs were of settee gauge – 12in (30cm) by 8½WG.

(Below) *Another form of springing on a modern wing chair.*

there is a row of short springs along the front and these are fixed directly onto the top of the front rail. As these form the front edge of the seat they are usually lashed to a cane to give a firm edge.

Sometimes you will find that chair seats can have slightly stronger (lower WG) springs than some settees. The weight on a chair is more concentrated and usually comes on the same area every time. The grade of springs used in the back is always much lighter than that used on the seat, and where the arms are also sprung this will use either the same weight as the back or even lighter.

As a starting point you will usually find that the length of spring used (uncompressed) is twice the depth of the frame in which it sits. Hence a chair seat with a frame that is made of 3in (7.6cm) deep timbers will use springs of 5–6in (12.7–15cm) long. A 5in deep chaise frame will use 10in (25.4cm) long springs.

When considering frame depth we have to recognize that not all frames are of solid timber – often they are constructed of two or three parallel members. Hence we are

concerned with the depth from the underside of the lowest frame member (onto which the webbing is attached) to the upper side of the highest member where the hessian and hair will be fixed. An Inferior chaise may have a frame of two lengths of 2×2in (5×5cm) timber with a space of 2in between them – a total frame depth of 6in (15cm). A typical springing arrangement might involve twenty-six springs (three rows of eight to ten) of 10–12in

(25.4–30cm) long by 8½ WG, (plus two or three in the bow end) and there would then of course be a generous hair stuffing on the top of that.

FIXING THE WEBBING

While the springs on the seat and back are always supported on webbing tacked under (or on the back) of the frame, the springs on the arms, particularly on the top of the arms, are fixed directly onto the timber. These may be fixed directly onto the wood of the arm top, but sometimes there is a piece of webbing or a fold of hessian under the springs. Often there is also a fold of hessian pushed into the lowest coil of the row of springs. This is to dampen out any twanging sound if the springs are over-compressed (for instance if someone sits on the arm top). Arms are not designed to be sat on, hence the springs are of a lighter gauge and much shorter.

Standard webbing is used to support the main springs, and it pays to use the best quality black and white jute for this task. It is stretched and tacked to the frame in the normal way (a folded end and five 13 Imp tacks.) As was mentioned above, on some large pieces of furniture – big wing chairs and settees – a double webbing pattern is used. If the children use the furniture as a bouncy castle, then double webbing is a must!

STITCHING IN THE SPRINGS

With the webbing lattice established and tacked down you can start to place the springs. It is a good idea to position all the springs and check that the arrangement looks sound, and that each spring sits squarely on a webbing cross.

The springs are sewn onto the webbing – there are four knotted loops to each spring. The student has done a very neat job in routing the stitches.

Each spring is now sewn in place onto the webbing. This usually means working with the piece on its side so that you have access to both sides of the web. A strong spring needle and Barbour 6 twine is used. The ideal needle is a curved, bayonet point (very sharp), 5in (12.7cm) long and 8 wire gauge.

The first stitch starts under the webbing, passes through, over a coil of the spring and back down through the webbing. The free end is then knotted off as a slip knot and is pulled tight. From here, the four quadrants of the coil are sewn to the webbing with a double half hitch under each of the second and third loops; last loop is again knotted off. From there, the twine runs to the next spring along the line and again four stitches (two of which are knotted) are made. It is a matter of pride amongst upholsterers that the spring sewing is done in a continuous run of Zs without ever recrossing the line and with the twine only ever lying under webbing – that is it never crosses a gap in the lattice.

LACING THE SPRINGS

The real fun in springing is when we come to the next stage. Here, the tops of all the springs are tied or laced together. This serves two functions. The first is to lock the springs so that they cannot move sideways when the seat is sat upon. The other is to pull the springs down to an even level of tension.

The tensioning and locking are both very important. If the springs are able to move significantly – under whatever compression load they are subject to – then the whole stuffing would move and quickly become misshapen. It would also be possible for the springs to become intertwined and be unable to return to their normal position. At best, the fabric cover would wrinkle permanently; at worst, there would be a hollow in the seat.

Of course, by lacing the springs so that they are always evenly spaced you also prevent them twanging together when someone sits down – or perhaps musical chairs would be fun!

There are few tasks in upholstery as important as that of properly sewing the springs to the webbing, and then fully lashing them into a tensioned, rigid form. In many saggy sofas it is not that the springs have lost their tension, but rather that they have broken loose. Occasionally they will have come adrift from the webbing, and sometimes the lacing will have pulled out an anchoring tack. The most frequent problem is that they were originally badly lashed. On one recent piece I worked on one-third of the 12in (30cm) long springs had just keeled over, having been only partially lashed at half height, and this with sewing twine. They had then been 'fixed' by merely sewing the top coils to the covering hessian. Hessian ages and denatures and with the load of the springs it had just torn apart. Of course, if springs do come loose the only way to fix them is to strip the seat completely and reupholster it.

There is always a lashing pattern interlinking the tops of each spring, and this is done with the strong, heavy duty, waxed jute, known as lacing or lashing cord. Even a single row of springs as on an arm top are laced together and the tops fixed in position by cords down to the frame.

So runs of lashing cord are tacked onto one side of the frame and then tied along the rows of springs before again being fixed down to the opposite side of the frame. Cords run front to back, side to side, and sometimes diagonally corner to corner as when there are five springs. On springs of up to about 9in (23cm) long the lacing is usually confined to the top of the springs only. On longer springs there is often a secondary lacing at about mid-height.

To get compression into the springs the cords need to be anchored firmly, pulled very tight and knotted onto each spring; at the same time, the springs should be pushed down underneath the heel of the free hand. Obviously the cord needs to be strong; ordinary Barbour 6 is not adequate.

To get a good anchor we need to use large tacks, normally 16 Imp, which are driven in on a slant to provide maximum leverage against the slope of the lacing cord. To start with, the tacks are not driven right home so that the cord can be wrapped round and knotted. The lacing should be completed before you drive home any tacks, which will allow you to undo and re-tension any line of cord. Only when the lacing pattern is complete should you finally drive in the tacks. Sometimes you will not have clear hammer swinging access to a springing tack and the use of a nail punch is required.

Each line of cord should be continuous, and in order to allow for the knots on each spring and the tying back of the cord tails this means cutting lengths of cord which are about twice the length of the span being covered (the rail to rail distance). There is no special starting point – some

Note: all cords are tied to both sides of each spring; cords
crossing in centres of springs may also be tied for extra rigidity.

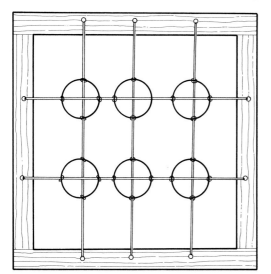 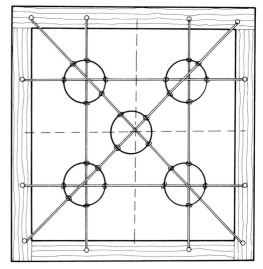

six (and even number) arrangement runs
straight across and up and down

five-spring pattern picks up centre spring with two
diagonals or uses extra crosslines as shown dotted

Lacing arrangements in five and six spring seats.

Driving a tack in with a nail punch. Often there is not room to swing a hammer in tight corners.

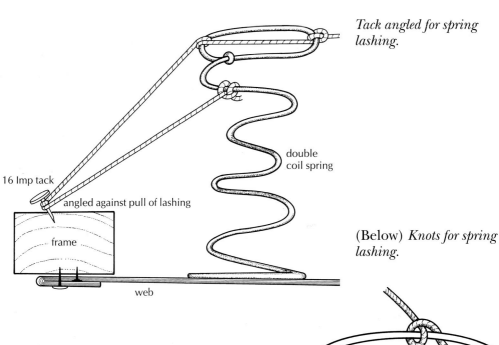

Tack angled for spring lashing.

16 lmp tack

angled against pull of lashing

frame

web

double
coil spring

(Below) *Knots for spring lashing.*

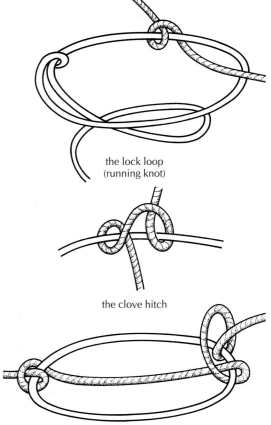

the lock loop
(running knot)

the clove hitch

one side of spring has a lock loop for
adjustment then a clove hitch to fix the position

upholsterers prefer a corner start, while others start with the middle row, and a good argument can be made for either. My preference is for middle row first. However, complete all rows in one direction before going to the cross lacing. The diagonal lines are fixed last.

Start by tying the cord using two half hitches or a slip knot to the spring one coil from the top (*see* Chapter 14 for details of knots). Take the cord to the starting tack and wrap round twice. Now loop the cord round the top coil with a spring locking or running knot. As you tighten the cord press the spring down. Once you have a satisfactory level of compression put the index finger of the pressing hand on the cord as it crosses the top coil and pinch hold the cord to the spring coil so that the locking knot will not slip. Now, holding it tight, tie the cord off to the far side of the spring coil using a clove hitch. As you release the compression the spring will rise slightly and will tilt out towards the frame against the pull of the cord; this is what it should do.

Now take the cord to the next spring in the line, loop it round the top coil and pull it tight as you compress the spring down to the same height as the first spring. Tie down this side with the running knot. While retaining the compression on the spring take the cord to the other side of the coil and tie it off with a clove hitch. The tensioning of this second spring will have pulled on the first spring and will have reduced the slant.

Move on to the next spring in line; compress it and tie off with a running knot. Let's now assume that this is the last spring in the line (on small and medium-sized chairs this will be the case). Tie the cord to the top coil close to the frame, using the clove hitch. Carry the cord on and take two wraps round the finishing tack. Now compress the spring to the height of the other two. As you now pull the cord tight watch the movement of the springs that you have tied together. The centre spring(s) should be upright and evenly compressed. The two outer springs should both lean out at a slight angle towards the nearest frame member. The side of their coils adjacent to the centre springs should be at almost the same height as the centre spring(s) – the outer side of the coils will, however, be dipping towards the frame.

If the spring lie is not satisfactory go back down the line, slackening off as many knots as necessary, and retension and retie. Once you are satisfied with the lie, tie the tail of the lacing cord to the second coil down of the outer spring; again use two half hitches. Trim away any excess cord.

Complete tying all the rows of springs in the same way. If you started with the side to side runs, now do the front to back lines. This time, the end springs in each of the outer rows will be pulled to slope outwards towards the corners. Finally, if there is an odd number of springs (five) there will be one spring in the centre and this does not lie on a front to back or side to side run. It is therefore laced to the corners of the frame and the corner springs using two diagonal cords. These rows are tied in in exactly the same way as the others.

At this stage, you should not really be able to hand compress the springs any further, and it is time to drive the 16 Imp tacks right home. This will pinch and lock in place the wrapped-around cord. You will probably also have learnt a lesson – it is much easier to tie off the lacing cords to a clear arc of the top coil. This means placing the springs so that you are always tying the knots on a clear length of spring wire.

The process of springing the back rests of chairs is basically the same. The springs will, however, be lighter and they will be compressed less. They may also be lashed with a slightly lighter weight of cord.

8½ WG springs will be compressed by at least a third of height, 12 WG springs by half

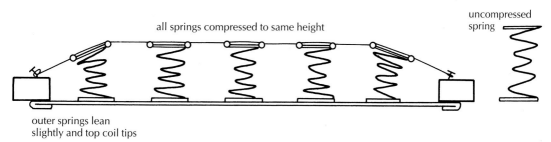

all springs compressed to same height

uncompressed spring

outer springs lean
slightly and top coil tips

Compression of springs.

The springs along the front rail are lashed independently of the main springs. A cane is whipped to the front to provide a firm edge.

(Below) *Sets of five springs may have additional diagonal lacing.*

Even a single row of springs on an arm top have to be lashed along the line. They are also fixed down to the frame with a loop of cord from the frame, up over the top, and back down to the frame again. Here you often need to think about the lashing arrangement. You need always to

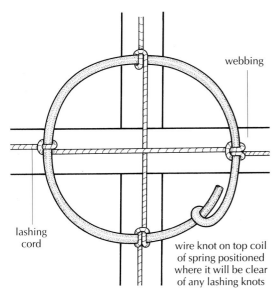

webbing

lashing cord

wire knot on top coil of spring positioned where it will be clear of any lashing knots

Orientation of springs to clear lashing knots.

bear in mind that the function of lashing is to ensure that under compression the springs, collectively and individually, can only move up and down in a limited vertical plane and certainly cannot lean over or bow sideways such that they might touch or trap an adjacent spring. This will indicate where the fixing point for the lashing cords should be placed.

Working with these principles in mind you should always be able to calculate the best springing and lacing pattern for any piece of furniture.

CANE EDGING

Mention has already been made of the fact that the front rail on some carcasses is lower than the rails around the side and along the back. This allows a row of smaller, but still full gauge, springs to give a soft front edge. Here, the top outer rim of the coils of the row of springs is lashed to a length of rattan cane. This arrangement gives a soft leading edge to the seat, but the cane ensures that when sat upon the edge compresses evenly.

This problem is, however, sometimes dealt with in a different manner. Here, the front row of main springs is positioned close behind the front rail of the main frame and is lashed so that they lean out forward a little. A length of cane may or may not be used. You do need to watch that the lashing ensures that when these springs are fully compressed none of their coils actually touches the frame. Often with this arrangement a dug roll is built in during the hair laying stage.

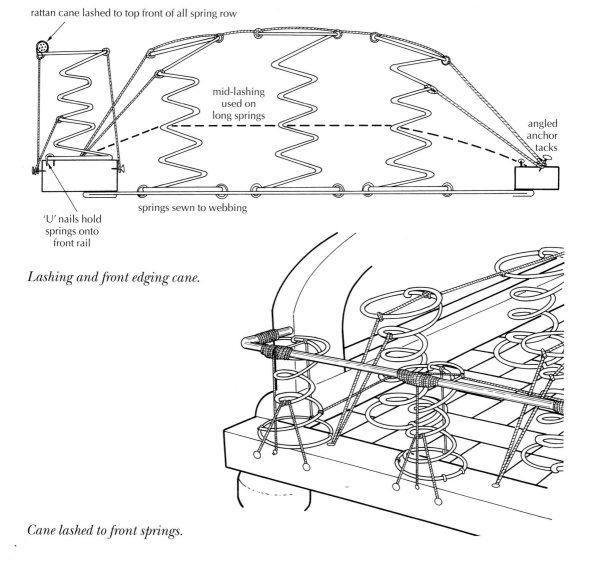

Lashing and front edging cane.

Cane lashed to front springs.

Stuffing seat with sprung front rail.

through roll stitch

3 blind rows

platform hessian

hair filling in stuffing ties

cane laced down to front rail to form valley which allows independent movement of front edge

FINAL STEPS

So the springs are in place, and the next steps are to fix the platform hessian and to do the top stuffing. The process is basically the same as for stuffed-over seating, although there is one point of minor difference.

The tensioning and lacing of the springs will have left you with a structure where the centre is significantly higher than the outer edges. The difference in height must be at least reduced if not eliminated during the stuffing stage; there will therefore be much more stuffing around the perimeter than at the centre. This must not, however, be achieved by making the centre stuffing thinner as this would allow the springs to be felt through the cover.

It is possible to achieve a flat top with a sufficient depth in the centre using a single layer of hair (allow generous stuffing loops). Alternatively, you may consider building up the outer edges with a dug roll, or even fixing two layers of hessian and hair. All methods are satisfactory, but it is sometimes a little more difficult articulating and through stitching a nice vertical side wall using either the double layer or the dug roll approach.

Probably the most frequently encountered compromise is the one detailed in the chapter on stuffed-over seating. To recap: in this, you fixed the platform hessian and built up with a substantial depth of hair around the edges. This was then covered with lightly tensioned skrim. The required shape was developed using two or three rows of blind stitches. At this stage, a smaller dug roll can be built up and this is tack-stitched in place to give a nice sharp corner to the edge.

The one thing that the doming effect of springs and the deeper stuffing involved does require is the use of through stitching from the top to the underside, and that the twine used must be strong enough to withstand the tensioning forces.

It is up to you whether you wish to create an absolutely flat seat top, or to have a very slight doming. With drop-in pads, and even with stuffed-over chairs, a dome is not desirable, whereas the use of long springs – even the strongest 8½ gauge – does add a considerable give, so that a dome on a settee will deform under load.

10

They Are Not All Alike
Frame Variations

So, traditional upholstery is the process of building resilient pads onto wooden seating frames. This is done using webbing, possibly some springs, hessian, hair, and cotton felt. The whole is then covered with calico and finally an upholstery fabric. There may, however, be some difficulties in this apparently simple task, and these concern the precise sequence in which the various parts of a chair are covered.

If there is just one padded area there is unlikely to be any problem; even two pads, seat and back, may not present any trouble. Three may still be easy, although they can sometimes be most awkward. It all depends upon the design and construction of the frame.

There are some immediate issues to consider. Without frame complications, you have a free choice. You could decide to complete each area separately, working right through from webbing to finishing fabric and completing each area before you move on to the next. This is quite logical, but a better case can be made for doing all of one process – say, fixing the webbing – to all the parts of the chair before moving on to the next task of tacking on the platform hessian. This way, you have fewer tools or types of material around you at any one moment.

You will, of course, not wish to put on the finishing fabric until the last minute because it might get soiled while you are doing cruder, earlier stage work on another part of the carcass. Unfortunately, this is not always possible.

In fact, there is not a standard approach. Some pieces will need to have some parts completely finished before you even start on other areas. Many modern high-backed chairs have to have the seat completely covered before the back is started, the reason being that the material (webbing through to fabric) for the back is anchored over the top of the finishing fabric at the back of the seat platform.

It is these sequence inconsistencies that make it so important, during your early days of upholstery, that you identify and note down the order of layer build-up while the piece is being stripped. Later, with a fuller understanding of the principles, you can quickly work out the sequence for yourself.

Equally, when you start to re-cover, you soon learn to look not only at the immediate area you are working on, but also at all adjacent panels. You work out how those panels will be covered and what interaction they are likely to have with the part that you are currently working on.

Let's now work through some of the more common problems and variations.

COMMON PROBLEMS AND VARIATIONS

One of the first problems that you may encounter are chairs with a hollow between the two uprights. In other words, the back rest is concave. Obviously, if you fully tensioned the webbing in both planes

When webbing a concave back, the verticals are fixed first and are fully tensioned. The laterals are then mounted behind these and are only lightly stretched.

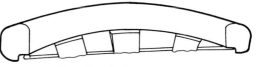

effect of tensioning cross webs

vertical webs on curved backs
fitted first and tensioned

horizontal webs then fitted behind
and drawn firm but not stretched

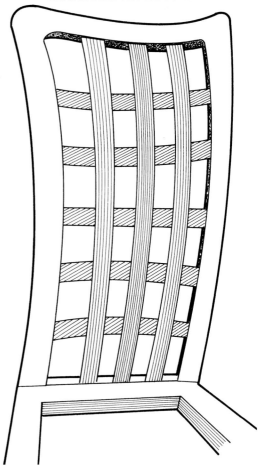

Webbing a curved back rest.

you would flatten out this hollow. To do this, the straight vertical webs are fixed first and these are tensioned as normal. When the lateral webs are run they are threaded such that the centre of each web is behind the centre vertical – thus they adopt the concave. They are then drawn to only the minimum of tensions so that they do not exert any pull on the verticals.

Some dining chairs have padded back panels. On some of these, the fabric on the panel in the front wraps over the top of the frame and spans across the back of the back rest, thus hiding all the inner workings. No problem!

The backrests on some chairs do not wrap right round the chair back.

(Below) *The stuffing of the window starts by laying a piece of finishing fabric facing to the rear.*

On others, the panel is covered on the front face only. Looking through a wooden frame from the back of the chair (as you might when approaching the back of a chair pushed in under a table) you would therefore be looking at the 'underside' of the webbing and hessian. You need to introduce a cover. On some chairs a backing panel is applied on the back of the frame, but on some it is not, The back masking panel is, in fact, applied directly as a backing within the back pad.

Normally this is done using the same material with which you will cover the face. Hence the first layer to apply on the face is a piece of finishing fabric with the pattern turned to face out to the back. With this in place you then proceed to cover the back of it with web, hessian, hair, and so on.

The carcasses of some modern wing armchairs present an interesting challenge. The wings themselves are made of solid board. Some of these can be a nightmare, while others are a 'doddle'. The easiest to deal with are the quality chairs.

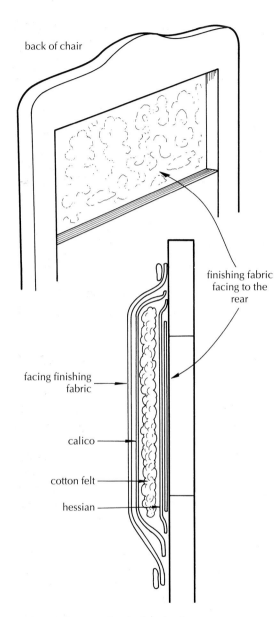

Back of chair with window back.

RE-COVERING A PARKER KNOLL CHAIR

One student recently bought a Parker Knoll carcass that I had picked up at an auction. This was the best-made piece of furniture that we had ever seen. All the frame members were of quality timber and all were shaped, sanded smooth and satin varnished. The joints were well engineered and sound; and the whole design neat. Above all, it had been made with the probability of reupholstering in mind.

The wings were of solid board, but then they sat on two large diameter dowels on the arm tops, and were fixed to the sides of the back frame with three massive screws. Once the outer cover of the wing had been removed, the screw heads were revealed. Undo these and the wing comes right away.

The seat, inner back and arms can be completely covered with the wings off. The inside of the wings can be easily reupholstered with the boards on the workroom table. The wings can then be repositioned, screwed home and finally the fabric back panel can be sewn on.

RE-COVERING 'SHORT-LIFE' CHAIRS

Against this, the same student had earlier brought in a wing chair which was extremely poorly made. The frame was of rough sawn wood – it could even have been rough poplar (often used for matchsticks). The wings were cut from chipboard and were glued and stapled to the back frame. There was a top and two bottom rails across the back – there should have been four as both bottom rails were part of the seat frame.

Personally, I would not have wasted time on it. It had been made for its original one-off covering in a factory environment and probably had been 'designed' to last about three years. We discussed how to progress on a cost/benefits basis. She wanted it as a bedroom chair that would get little wear, but above all thought that re-covering it, with all its problems, would be a good

Stripping a well-made Parker Knoll wing chair. The springs used here are coiled tension springs.

(Below) *The wing is a detachable board. It is held on two dowels and by three long wood screws. It can be removed and separately upholstered.*

learning experience. She was right! We both learnt from it.

Her solution to covering the back and the inner face of the wings was first to cover the seat right through including the covering fabric. She replaced the tension springs with a lattice of double-coil cone springing ('for practice!'). The back was then cone-sprung and covered. At all stages the lower end of the material panels that would eventually be tacked over the back of the seating material were left free so that subsequent layers could be pulled through. Once the finishing fabric was in place on the seat, the loose edges on the lower back were pulled tight and tacked down.

She tacked the sides of the backing layers onto the front face of the back frame tight into the corner between the back and wings. The inner wings were then covered, tacking down onto the edge of the backing material. Finally, a braid was fixed over the tack heads. The braid, being deep in the recess, did not look too unusual.

In the end the finished piece looked acceptable despite the unconventional

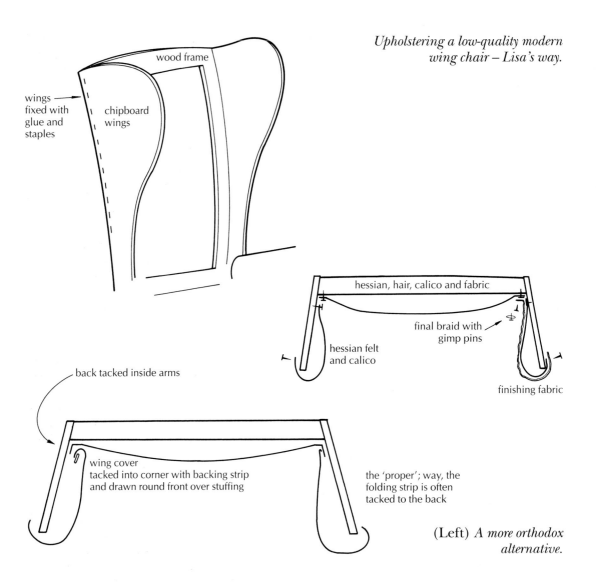

Upholstering a low-quality modern wing chair – Lisa's way.

wood frame

wings fixed with glue and staples

chipboard wings

hessian, hair, calico and fabric

hessian felt and calico

final braid with gimp pins

finishing fabric

back tacked inside arms

wing cover tacked into corner with backing strip and drawn round front over stuffing

the 'proper'; way, the folding strip is often tacked to the back

(Left) A more orthodox alternative.

methods. The student agreed, however, that she would not do it again!

It was interesting when the Parker Knoll chair was stripped down to discover how many hand-sewn seams there were on the piece. Much of the rear back panel and the outer facing panels on the wings and arms had sewn seams. In fact, in terms of the finishing fabric there were far more sewn-in than tacked-on panels.

The problem with the cheap chair was that with only the three rails across the back (and in the positions that they were), the seat and back face both had to be anchored to the same piece of timber. While this is passable from a construction point of view it does not always give the best shape, particularly at the lower part of a back pad. There are times when you use an artificial rail – a run of webbing is fixed so that the materials can bend over it and are loosely supported.

Many students bring along nursing chairs. Often these are relatively modern, but because of the associations that they have, they are much cherished. However, for exactly the same reasons they are now well worn! When they are stripped, often modern factory-style upholstery is revealed – cheap springing and a lot of foam. The reaction of most upholsterers would be either to scrap the chair, or just to bung on a new bit of foam and re-cover. To the owners, however, this is totally inappropriate. Again, because of the associations, the chair has to be given the best possible treatment – coil springs, hair stuffing and all. To make the piece suitable for a first-time student, it is not unusual to have to insert at least one additional timber – a stile or stuffing bar for the bottom of the backrest, so as to provide an anchor for the webbing.

THREE METHODS OF DEALING WITH A CHAIR WITHOUT A STUFFING RAIL

Let's consider how we might approach a chair that has no rail across the base of the backrest. As indicated a moment ago, this can mean leaving layers hanging or inserting an extra rail or seeking other alternatives. There are a number of these, and different upholsterers adopt different methods. There are three alternatives that are worth considering – each with their own advantages and disadvantages.

METHOD ONE

The first is to cut and fit a stuffing rail. This is my preference whenever possible. It usually means using a piece of beech of about 2in × 1½in (5 × 3.8cm) thick (or lighter for a nursing chair). This is cut to an exact size to fit snugly between the two upright side frame members. It is pushed into position

2–4in (5–10cm) above the back top rail of the seat platform. The size of this gap is varied according to the proposed thickness of the seat pad. It is towards the 2in for simple stuffed-over pads, and towards 4in for deep-stuffed sprung seats.

With the rail in the right position, two 10mm diameter holes are drilled through each side frame member and into the end of the new stuffing rail. The rail is removed, the ends glued and the rail replaced, making sure that the dowel holes line up. Glue is now squirted into the dowel holes and 10mm dowels are driven right home. An extra dowel is added if necessary so that you finish up with ends of the dowelling sticking out beyond the sides of the frame members. When the glue has set these ends are cut away and sanded flush and smooth.

The advantages are clear. Upholstery can now be built up easily and in the normal sequence. The back is independent of the seat and can be worked separately, although you end up with the fabric of the seat in contact with the bottom edge of the fabric of the back. The disadvantage is that in drilling through the frame members you introduce a possible weakness. This could be a danger if the main frame is insubstantial. However, the use of glued-in, tight-fitting, through dowels minimizes the weakness and does actually make a considerably stronger job than simply driving screws through the frame and into the rail ends. One of the greatest advantages of this method is that it is equally suitable for stuffed-over and sprung seating.

METHOD TWO

The second option for a simple stuffed-over pad is one that is widely used, but personally I do not recommend it. Here the seat area is completed including the fixing of the finishing fabric. The webbing of the back is now fixed with the cross webs fitted first. These are tacked and tensioned on the front face of the frame in the normal way with an extra strengthening run where you might expect to find a stuffing rail.

The vertical runs are placed next. These are fixed at the head of the back only woven into the cross runs and cut so that there is a tail at least 9in (23cm) longer than the length to the nailing point. This will allow the later use of a webbing stretcher.

The platform hessian is tacked on along the top and down both sides, with the bottom edge being left free. It is tensioned as far as possible. Stuffing loops are sewn, the stuffing completed, and skrim, wadding and calico fitted.

Once the finishing fabric has been fitted along the top and down the sides, it is pulled tight from the bottom and tacked over the seating fabric into the top rear rail

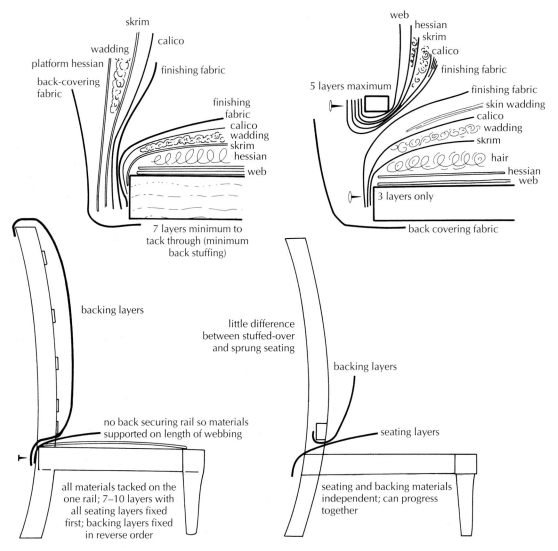

The back fixing problem: stuffed-over chair with no lower rail.

The back fixing problem with extra support rail.

of the seat platform. You will certainly require 13mm tacks to penetrate the layers already fixed to the rail. The calico is then pulled down and tacked off.

At this stage, it is fingers crossed time! You hope that the hair and wadding layer has a good even finish because once it is tensioned you have no means of smoothing out any lumps. Pull it tight and tack off.

The bottom ends of the webbing are fixed last. You left tails on each piece so that they may be tensioned before being nailed home.

The only advantage of this approach is that it is generally slightly easier to do than the third option. It is not, however, so effective. Obviously its particular disadvantage is that it is difficult to ensure a smooth finish; this is almost impossible to achieve if you are using springs. It is also particularly bad when you have a concave back, as you cannot tension the lateral webs so it is now almost impossible to build up an even hair layer.

METHOD THREE

The third alternative is really a reverse of the second, and although a little tricky can give good finished results. You work back from the finishing fabric, but this time it is fitted and tacked home along the bottom only. It is then folded to sit on top of the seat. The subsequent material layers of calico, skrim and platform hessian are each generously cut, and are also tacked along the bottom only.

You now start by placing the vertical webs, fixing them along the bottom, and tensioning each from the top. The side webs are then woven in, tensioned and tacked home.

From this point on, you build the layers as you would on an open frame, the only difference being that you start with each layer of material fully fixed along its bottom edge. Obviously you articulate and tension in three planes only – side to side and upwards.

There are minor disadvantages. First, you have to be sure that the bottom of the materials is firmly fixed and is laterally taut and wrinkle-free. You cannot later sort out any defects. Second, you have to allow a safety margin in the cutting of fabric, calico and skrim – you do not have the facility of a finished stuffed layer to measure from.

The advantages, however, are many. First, it is an ideal method if you are springing the back – the only caution is that it is safer to use 16 Imp tacks for the lower fixing of the vertical webs as you will be nailing through four layers of material. There is now no difficulty with curved backs – each layer can be fixed, shaped and articulated in a normal manner. Achieving nice edges – stitch-shaped if required – is easy; and the whole process is much more controllable.

There is another springing alternative that is sometimes practical. Here, the vertical webs are fixed first, but the lower ends are drawn right down to the lower rail of the seat platform and are fixed either to the rear face or even wrapped round and fixed under. The tops are also fixed and tensioned. The laterals are fixed in the normal way and the springs are then sewn in.

The materials are, however, fixed as in option three. That is, they are tacked to the back of the upper seat rail over the top of the seating fabric. This does mean that access to the tacking area has to be between the runs of fixed webbing, and a nail punch may be required.

A MIXED APPROACH

A typical example of a piece that required the use of some of these techniques arrived in the workshop some time ago.

It was a (very) Inferior Victorian chaise. The seat frame was a simple box rectangle of 3 × 2in (7.6 × 5cm) timbers. There were long straight front and back members and a short straight piece at the head end. At the tail was a similar short rail, but a carved, rounded end had been fitted outboard of this. All the timbers were sound, although overall they did look flimsier than I would have liked. The joints were dowelled and glued. Stuck onto the side rail at the open end of the seat were two profile cut timbers to round off the end.

The back of the seat had a single rail 'back rest' and this was supported on a row of small turned spindles, two of which were missing. The end support of the rail had broken away from the frame. Some heavy gentleman had obviously tried to use the rail as a backrest to lean against expansively!

The real problem was the 'arm' – this would of course be the backrest when you were lounging languorously or were stretched out with an attack of the vapours!

At the two ends of the arm (the front and back) were two profile-sawn boards, and 3in (7.6cm) below the top of the curve of these arm pieces was a 4in (10cm) wide sawn board cross member set as a platform for a vertical row of small springs. At about mid-height down the outboard face of the arm was a second cross member, the main function of which was to provide strength. At about seat height on the front of the arm rest was a lateral run of webbing. The finishing fabric and some other layers were fixed on top the underside of the outer facing edge of the spring platform. It then wrapped over the top (being pulled in to form a roll) and came down the face, bent round the web and was finally anchored onto the seat frame. This meant that the seat had to be completed before the arm could be covered. The whole arm structure looked flimsy, and in fact the front joint to the frame (dowelled) had broken loose.

It was a simple job to replace the web with a timber cross member. This was positioned about 3in (7.6cm) above the frame of the seat. Fixed here, it meant that the seat stuffing and covers would come up to the bottom of the timber, while still allow-

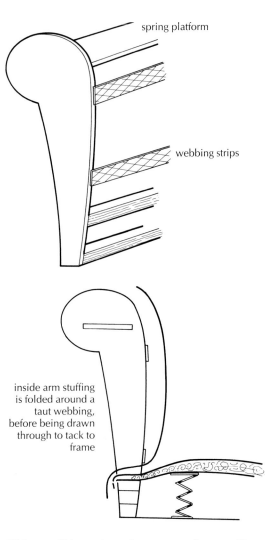

Using webbing where there are no frame rails.

ing the arm covering and seating fabric to be drawn through. The arrangement gave a much firmer support to the arm stuffing, but it also meant that all intermediate layers could be tacked around the back of it. It was now possible to build up the seat platform to the calico level and at the same time build up the stuffing on the arm face. The roll top of the arm could also be brought to the calico stage. A strip of hessian was tacked to the top of the back rail

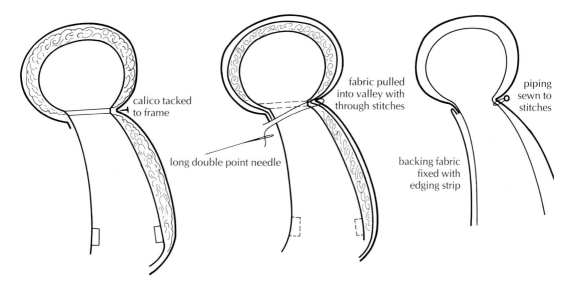

Labels within figure:
calico tacked to frame
long double point needle
fabric pulled into valley with through stitches
backing fabric fixed with edging strip
piping sewn to stitches

Pulling in the valley under the head roll.

and this was loop stuffed. Only when all had been covered in calico was the velvet finishing fabric brought out of its protective bag.

This all had a wonderful later spin-off, after a flying spark had burnt a hole in the centre of the seat. Replacing the whole panel now meant only the removal of the bottoming cloth, one row of tacks on the bottom of the outer arm material, and the tacks on the seat panel itself. Without the wooden rail it would have been necessary to dismantle a considerable part of the arm covering.

While we are studying this chaise let's look at some of the other problems it presented as they are elements that occur on many armchairs and settees. Some, as this one, have a roll on the top of the arm rest. This means that the fabric between the roll and the facing of the back has to be pulled in, requiring the stuffing to be held apart sufficiently to allow you to manoeuvre in a fold of the material and a length of edging strip.

An alternative is to stitch right through with a long needle and twine. If there is any danger of the twine being seen, then it can

be coloured to match the finishing fabric. Permanent colour marker pens can be used. However, a third solution was the one to be adopted. A piping cord with a reduced flange was made of the finishing fabric. The shape of the valley was achieved by through stitching with No. 6 twine. The piping cord was then pushed in progressively and was stitched onto the twine with a curved mattress needle and matching thread.

OTHER SEQUENCING PROBLEMS

Another problem that you meet on some modern and several earlier styles of settee and chair is that the stuffing on the top and inside face of the arm is brought round to the front where a roll is formed. Normally it is covered with the skrim of the arm, but sometimes the roll is made by building around a semicircular dug roll. Both the calico and the covering fabric have to be fitted over this roll and need to be multipleated or ruched.

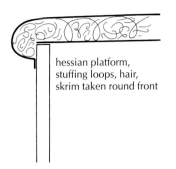

hessian platform,
stuffing loops, hair,
skrim taken round front

dug roll on front,
platform hessian on arm,
stuffing loops, hair,
skrim over front and roll

dug roll on top front,
platform hessian,
stuffing loops, hair,
skrim on top of roll
(roll may be tacked
onto arm top)

Roll around fronts on arms.

This has now left you with another problem. Inside the roll and down the front of the arm is an area that now needs covering. There are a number of ways of doing this.

On many Inferior chaises the 'upholsterer' may have chosen an easy option and fitted a wooden profiled panel infill with crude detailing carved onto it. You can understand why this was done when you remember that the piece was probably made by a local carpenter. It would have been much easier to carve a simple panel than to finish this front inset in upholstery fabric!

A second method developed at that time is to cut a thin wooden profiled infill panel and to drill this with three pairs of holes: top, middle and bottom. A cord or leather thong is threaded through each pair of holes. The front of the panel can now be separately upholstered. Next, the front of the carcass arm is drilled and the cords pulled through and tied to hold the finished panel in place. Although this idea works, the panels can sometimes become somewhat loose, and you may have to remove an outside cover to get at the cords to tighten them.

The third idea is a development of the second. Again, a separate infill panel is cut and this faced with a thin stuffing and finishing fabric. The whole is tacked in place using long, fine tacks. Finally, a length of braiding is fixed around the edge of the profile to cover the heads of the tacks.

The fully upholstered solution certainly looks the best. First, the roll and side panels are covered and the fabric tacked to the front face of the arm. A piping cord is made or a length of flanged cord is fitted and this is tacked in place inside the roll and out to the edges of the front panel. Finally, a piece of fabric is slip-stitch sewn inside the piping.

Let's return, however, to the webbing/extra fitted timber issue. There are several occasions when you do not need the extra

ply infill panel covered with wrap-round fabric before being tied on; suitable for chaise armchair or settee arms

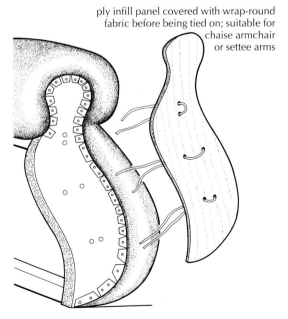

Tied on infill panels.

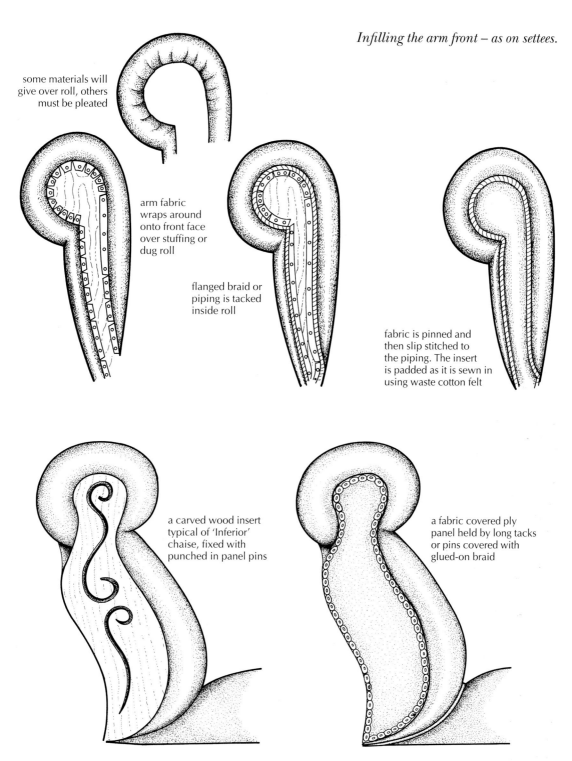

Infilling the arm front – as on settees.

some materials will give over roll, others must be pleated

arm fabric wraps around onto front face over stuffing or dug roll

flanged braid or piping is tacked inside roll

fabric is pinned and then slip stitched to the piping. The insert is padded as it is sewn in using waste cotton felt

a carved wood insert typical of 'Inferior' chaise, fixed with punched in panel pins

a fabric covered ply panel held by long tacks or pins covered with glued-on braid

Infill panels – typically on chaise.

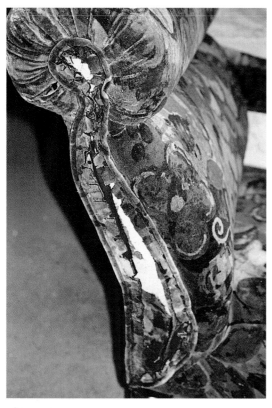

Infilling the front fascia on a chaise. A similar process is used on many settee and deep armchair arms.

(1) The arm facing and backing materials are wrapped round the front and the edge is tacked down using a flanged piping cord (left).

(2) The hollow inside the piping is filled with wadding and here a piece of covering fabric has been pinned in place (above).

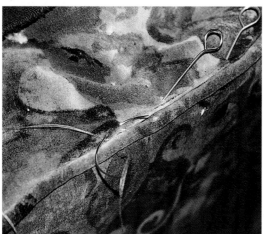

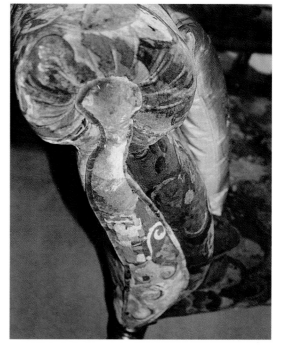

(3) The folded-under edges of the panel are blind slip-stitched through to the flange of the cord (above).

(4) A few tack stitches will finish shaping and fixing the fascia panel (right).

timber, and both support and shaping can be achieved by using a run of webbing.

Very often, the outside face of the arms on an armchair or settee are covered with a piece of lightly tensioned finishing fabric. The back of the backrest is treated in a similar manner. There is nothing under this, but there are times when you think a little support might make the fabric less vulnerable to tearing. You certainly do not need a lattice of webbing, but two or three lengths could be useful.

However, the inside face of the arms do need some support, and three vertical runs of webbing are often used. They are then probably skrim-covered and fitted with a layer of cotton felt. It is unusual to cover these with hair. There will, of course, be a layer of calico under the finishing fabric.

Frequently you will encounter the situation where one tensioned run of webbing is essential. This you will see on the arms of several designs of chairs and in the wings of early wing chairs. The purpose of the web is to provide a support for the fabric before it bends in to fix to the frame.

Another sequencing problem occurs in that there are times when the skrim (and all subsequent layers) cannot be merely laid on the top and then wrapped round the sides with or without pleats. This particularly occurs where the back and the seat form part of a continuous curve. The two sides have to be cut and fixed in as separate panels. With the skrim, the side pieces will be stitched to the edges of the top panel using twine and a curved spring needle. On this style of chair there is usually extensive shaping stitching (blind and through). With the calico the three panels should be cut, pinned together in position on the chair, then removed and machine-sewn. Similarly with the finishing fabric cut the three pieces – top cover and the two side panels – place them on the calico and pin them together with skewers. You may wish to introduce a piping along each seam. Make sure in pin-

ning that when the two side panels are tensioned, the seams will lie precisely along the apex of the corner. Take the pinned fabric of the chair and machine sew all seams.

Now in fitting the sewn-up cover, start in the centre of the curve between seat and back. Pull the fabric down until the seam is in the right place on one side at the centre of the curve and immediately go to the other side, again pulling the material down here until the seam is correctly positioned. Work out in both directions from the centre, developing each side of the chair as you go.

Another covering problem is that there are a number of places where the top fabric cannot be tacked on without the tack heads showing unless you are prepared to have runs of braiding around every edge. This would both look strange and could add considerably to the cost. To avoid this, many panels are hand-sewn – either joining the two panels corner to corner, or, as with the inset panels referred to a moment ago, a run of piping is tacked on and the finishing panel is then sewn into the piping.

Finally, we must re-emphasize a point made much earlier. There are few standard sequences, and nor is there a text book covering all of the eventualities that you are likely to encounter. For many pieces of furniture you will have to rely on applying the sorts of ideas that we have been discussing here, while modifying the techniques to suit each particular piece of furniture. Because you may be working on, say, a sofa, don't think you need necessarily to seek information on sofas. You may look at 200 different sofas before you find one even vaguely similar to yours. Look at basic methods and work out how they can be applied or modified. Look at what other people are doing on other pieces of furniture – see how they have dealt with the problem of, for instance, no anchor points for the back fabric, and then apply the idea to your piece. It is the variety of problems that makes upholstery so fascinating, and so frustrating!

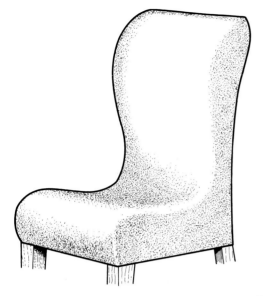

section across the seat
(and back)

the nursing chair, originally moulded foam pad,
upholstered had slightly rounded 'square' corners;
it was now to be stuffed-over; the top fabric
would not wrap down the side without excessive
relieving cuts and darts

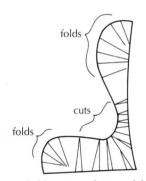

folds

cuts

folds

probable pattern of cuts and darts;
this would require several backing gussets
and would be impossible in open weaves
such as hessian and skrim

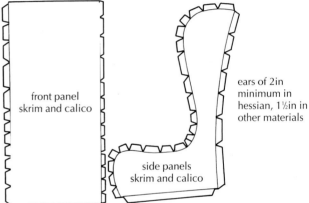

front panel
skrim and calico

side panels
skrim and calico

ears of 2in
minimum in
hessian, 1½in in
other materials

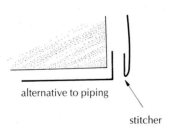

alternative to piping

stitcher

edge flanges turned and folded
over/under; stitched through to
form right angle seams then blind
and through stitched to give
squared corners and vertical side
walls

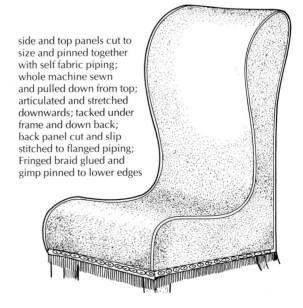

side and top panels cut to
size and pinned together
with self fabric piping;
whole machine sewn
and pulled down from top;
articulated and stretched
downwards; tacked under
frame and down back;
back panel cut and slip
stitched to flanged piping;
Fringed braid glued and
gimp pinned to lower edges

11

A Cover Story
The Finishing Fabric

You may be congratulating yourself upon how reasonable (cost wise) it has been to re-cover the chair yourself – so far! Now comes the 'Ouch!' factor. It scarcely matters how good or poor your work has been to this point, as the whole process can be made or (broken) by the fabric that you put on as a final cover. Of course, much of it is a matter of taste, but pocket does come into it. For a single small dining or bedroom chair where you may only need a half metre square, the remnants bin can often yield what you want for 50p. A six-metre length for a wing arm-chair, however, will cost. You are very un-likely to find even a roll end of suitable upholstery material at less than £10 a metre and £15–£20 is more likely to be the norm. And from here the sky is the limit. Some fine upholstery materials such as Liberty cloths are in the £50 per metre bracket and it is not difficult to double or quadruple that. There are several in the swatch books that we have in the workshop in the £30–£40 per metre bracket (others are only £8).

CHOOSING THE RIGHT FINISHING FABRIC

I quite enjoy abstract art and am therefore not averse to bright, contrasting, geometric patterns, although not, at present, for my own upholstery. As I now live in a black and white cottage my judgment has been condi-tioned and I tend strongly towards tapestries – often with a floral or medieval motif. Cer-tainly I rarely use a simple, single colour fab-ric. Many of my students live on farms, while others live in modern houses in the local towns, some of their choices of material are superb. Some, however, are not! Some stu-dents choose totally inappropriate materials – not only for the piece they are working on, but for any piece of upholstered furniture.

Let's start with a few basic principles – some you would have thought obvious, but you quickly learn this is not always the case when you see some beginner's mistakes. Upholstered furniture gets sat upon – many times. It takes bodies of various weights. Some sit relatively still, while oth-ers wriggle and squirm frequently. Some people position over a chair, hover, and then, bending their knees, they sit straight down. They may get up in the same way – a clear straight-up rise off the seat. Others, however, find the edge of the chair with the back of the calf and then slide on; they may even slide forward to get off. The differ-ence in wear can be considerable.

In some houses and particularly in some rooms people sit on chairs while wearing their work clothes – maybe not oily overalls, but often the suits they have worn to com-mute on dirty trains, or the clothes they put on for an hour's tidying up in the garden.

It is important, therefore, that you recog-nize where the chair will be placed and what its purpose will be. The materials chosen must suit the style of the chair; the decor within which it will be placed; and, above all, the pattern of use. Oh! and don't forget the cats – very few fabrics are cat-proof!

First, you do need to choose upholstery fabric. Essentially, curtain material will not do. The cloth you need will be of heavier weight with any patterning woven in. Many printed fabrics do not wear well. But let's qualify these last two statements: some boudoir chairs are subject to virtually no wear, and on these you can get away with lighter weight, purely decorative fabrics. Here, printed chintzes and cottons can be quite satisfactory and some better quality curtaining may well now be adequate. However, most of the chairs that you will wish to cover will be subject to daily usage.

Lighter colours are very nice, but unless you reserve the lounge for high days and holidays only they are not very practical. Only rarely do I recommend single colour plain fabrics. Patterns are much better for hiding the occasional mark, and they do not shine as badly on much rubbed or worn areas. On the other hand, a heavy pattern can be distorted out of all recognition if the piece is then buttoned. Some large motif patterns can also look distinctly odd on smaller chairs.

Lightweight cloths may pull away from the tacks if heavy bodies slide on and off them. Good fabric shops will be able to tell you what the wear factor is for given materials. They are classified by the number of 'rubs' they will withstand before wearing through. Clearly for a heavily utilized piece you need to look for between 10,000 and 30,000 rubs. Several fabric manufacturers now classify their materials by 'wear codes' – pay particular attention to these.

PILE AND GRAIN

Most materials have a 'grain' – this is particularly evident on velvets. If you rub your hand across the width of a piece of velvet it probably feels the same in both directions. Equally the pile will look the same both ways. Now stroke the velvet along the length. In one direction the hand slides easily and the stroked area takes on a sheen as it reflects the light, but when stroked in the other direction you can feel that you are going against the grain; the pile rises, the sheen vanishes and the colour apparently deepens. Almost all materials have some grain, and in most cases you do need to take account of this as it affects pattern, lay and strength.

All fabrics are woven in long lengths (on to rolls). The threads that run down the length are the 'warp' threads and these are usually of a stronger yarn than the cross or 'weft' threads. The 'grain' lies along the warp and often has a directional element – one way you run with the grain, and the opposite is 'against' it.

In fact, in cutting and laying the fabric it is the grain that will guide you – it will also help you to orientate the pattern. Basically, you should always have the grain running from front to back on the seating area and then straight up and down on the backrest. Ideally, too, the pile should lie down when stroked (with the grain) from the front to the back of the seat and rise when stroked forwards. In appearance, a chair looks odd where the panels have differently orientated grain. Clearly in a set of matching chairs it is important that the grain and pile run in the same direction on each seat.

If you get the grain always in the same orientation, then you will obviously also have the pattern the right way round. There will, however, be times when you are not quite sure which side of the material is the 'top'. On a few occasions it may not matter, but usually it does. Where there is a woven pattern it is often the case that the stitches on one side of the weave are all short – this is usually the top. On the other side, there may be long stitches or loops – this is normally the underside. If the long stitches side is used as the top, the threads can catch and be pulled out, leading to a rapid deterioration in the material's appearance.

Working to grain orientation means that any materials with a continuous stripe pattern will always have the stripes running front to back. Note, however, that some modern hand loom weaves do have weft stripes, but these are usually irregular in size and colour distribution.

MATCHING THE PATTERN

The pattern of the material can cause some difficulties, and a lot of waste in the cutting. Many materials have an across-the-width pattern. This means that the motif – whatever it is – will repeat at regular intervals down the length of the cloth.

Ideally, you should position the main motif, or a distinctive element of the pattern, so that it sits on the centre of the seat. The same arrangement of a centrally placed motif should then be used on the back of the chair. You may even extend the centralized motif idea to the outside faces of fabric-covered arm pieces (*see* picture on page 24).

Most designs, however, do not have a single central motif but a pattern which repeats (often with an offset) either side of the centre. You can often be lucky with 54in (137cm) wide materials in that a half width will cover the seat and another half width the backrest. Even with an offset in the drop of the pattern cutting can be quite economical.

Obviously you will try to place the seat and back panels so that the pattern flows continuously from one plane into the other. A flower on, say, the bottom left corner of the back may disappear into the valley where it abuts the seat, but you should cut the material so that the missing part of the flower reappears in the top left corner of the seat. Lines, straight or curved, on one panel should continue across the divide onto the next panel.

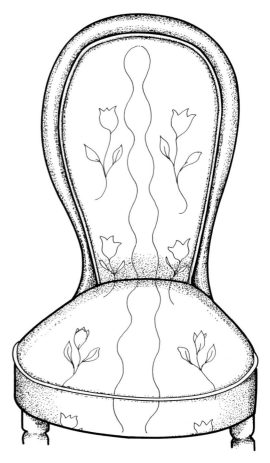

the material panels are cut so that when fitted the same pattern appears to run across from back to seat, and on to front panel

Continuous pattern elements.

On some patterned materials the motif on one side of the centre of the weft is repeated on the other side of the centre, but as it crosses the centre it is not an exact repeat but a mirror image (reverse) of the other side. This means that you cannot place two halves of a width one above the other. (A manufacturer's ploy to make us buy twice the length?)

Today it is extremely difficult to get material wider than 54in (1.37m). With some designs of settee – particularly three-seaters – this can be a problem, as you may need widths of 60in plus (152cm plus). Ideally, you do not want a seam down the centre of the back (and the problem is usually the back), so to avoid this you need to make up panels. Often a separate centre panel is the answer, but three seam-joined panels can cause you all sorts of problems with some patterns. This is why so many larger settees use materials with a more diffuse pattern, and are often single coloured.

Estimating material requirements is not difficult where there is no pattern to confuse the issue. When we talked about stripping down you were advised to retain the old top fabric, and the pieces will certainly now help.

Do not try to estimate requirements from a bare carcass; if you do not have the old fabric pieces wait until you have finished fitting the calico layer before taking any measurements.

FITTING THE FINISHED FABRIC

In earlier chapters, particularly the one on drop-in pads. some comments were made about fitting the calico layer, with particular emphasis on tacking off the corners before cutting to make the folds. We are not now going to detail separately the process for cutting and fixing calico as the methods used are exactly the same as those which we are now going to cover regarding fixing finishing fabrics.

THE CALICO LAYER

However, when working at the calico stage there are three general factors to be taken into account. Fundamentally, the calico is the platform on which the finishing fabric sits. Whatever the calico-covered seat is, so will be the finished chair. If it is soft and lumpy, then the chair will be soft and lumpy. Second, any imperfections in fitting the calico itself will show through the top cover. For instance, if the tacks on the tensioned calico are too well spaced little wave bulges will appear between each, which will certainly show through the finishing fabric. Hence the close tacking of calico and finishing fabric.

So the work done in fitting the calico needs to be carried out carefully and well. But, on the other hand, it does not need to be perfect – a slight misalignment in a row of tacks does not matter, as this will certainly be hidden by the final layer of skin wadding under the finishing fabric.

The third factor is that we should regard the fitting of the calico as our dress rehearsal. You can work out how to get the corners right before you have to risk the expensive final finishing cloth. Do the corners exactly as you would the top fabric. Cut the calico generously to give yourself plenty to work with. Partially tack it in place, articulate it, tension it and retack it. *Then* make up the corners. We will be going through these steps in a moment.

THE SKIN WADDING LAYER

Once you are satisfied with the calico, fit a thin covering layer of skin wadding. This will hide any tiny imperfections and cover the heads of tacks. To hold the wadding in place, give the top of the calico a couple of quick blasts of spray adhesive. Cut the wadding so that a neat glued butt joint is made at the corners. Actually, although we should not be saying this, you can compensate for slightly bigger earlier mistakes (such as a wavy top edge) by sticking on multiple layers of skin wadding over offending areas. Cut the lower edge of the wadding so that it stops just on the heads of the calico tacks and then tear the edge of the wadding to feather it out.

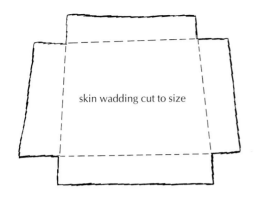

skin wadding cut to size

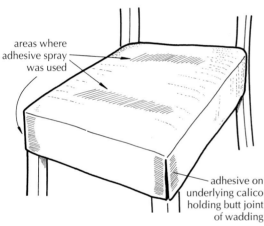

areas where
adhesive spray
was used

adhesive on
underlying calico
holding butt joint
of wadding

Fitting skin wadding.

ESTIMATING FINISHING CLOTH REQUIREMENTS

There are various approaches to estimating finishing cloth requirements. One way is that you now have the calico shape to give you exact measurements. Another way is to trace out on the floor the width of the material that you intend to choose. Two long wooden boards can be used to mark the edges of the imaginary material. Set these boards to the known width of the cloth you intend to purchase. If it has not yet been chosen set the boards to 54in

(137cm), and hope that you do not have to recalculate!

Now if you retained the pieces of the original cover, first place these on the chair over the calico and check to see that you have not dramatically altered the dimensions. If they are still all right, place the pieces of old top cover between the boards. Move them around until your 'jigsaw' gives the best fit, noting the grain orientation so that all pieces are laid in the right direction. Where your trial fit on the chair showed a deviation, allow a margin around the old pieces to accommodate this.

If you did not have the original fabric on the carcass then you have two alternatives. One is to get a large piece of squared paper, draw on it the width of the chosen material, measure the elements of the chair and draw these to scale on the paper. The second method is to make brown paper patterns, tracing them off the carcass once you have reached the calico stage. These paper patterns can then be placed between the two boards set to the material width.

When you have traced it all out and got an idea of the total length, add half a metre for safety!

Many texts on fabric estimating show a neat rectangle with all the panels placed on it. Each panel neatly abuts the next and there is not a scrap of waste. In your dreams! This takes absolutely no account of pattern.

With a strongly patterned fabric, it is best to use the squared paper approach. Find the 'drop' (the distance between pattern repeats) in the material that you are planning to use and mark on your graph paper the positions of a regularly occurring feature motif. Now as you place the elements of the cover, you can match these to the position of the motif. It is time-consuming but it does help to avoid expensive mistakes – particularly if you are buying an unrepeatable end of roll. Even with very careful measuring and drawing, a spare metre is a better safety margin with a long drop pattern.

Having a paper pattern or an old piece of fabric is obviously a great help to the beginner, and students are often advised to cut a pattern. Later, as you gain skill in measuring and laying off the process becomes less frightening.

You may gather from these notes that although in life I am generally a risk-taker by nature, I always play safe and overestimate on finishing fabrics. That is why I have a useful sideline in patchwork quilts!

CUTTING AND PINNING THE CLOTH

So now you have the cloth. Lay the fabric on the floor or a cutting table, smooth it out, lay on the pattern and mark the cutting line with tailor's chalk, allowing what working folds or margins are required (even now a handling and trimming margin is added round an old panel pattern). Normally 1in (2.5cm) is allowed for a simple folded-over edge, and 2in (5cm) for edges that are going to have to be pulled and tensioned. On the other hand, allowing too much is not only wasteful but it makes it very awkward to work, particularly around corners and folds.

Usually, given the measuring, preparation and cutting that you have already done, you may now proceed to fix the panels one after the other. There may be occasions, however, when you are still not quite sure of pattern match so as a final check, position the cut panels on the carcass and pin them together with upholstery skewers. Certainly when fitting panels for hand sewing, these should always be pinned fully in place before stitching begins.

With the panel placed on and positioned for design orientation, tack down all the edges, leaving a couple of inches clear either side of each corner. Moderate tension is applied and 10 ordinary tacks are used at about 2in (5cm) spacing. The tacks are, however, only driven halfway in.

ARTICULATING THE CLOTH

The top surface of the material is now articulated – stroked with the heel of the hand to push out any wrinkles. Work the whole

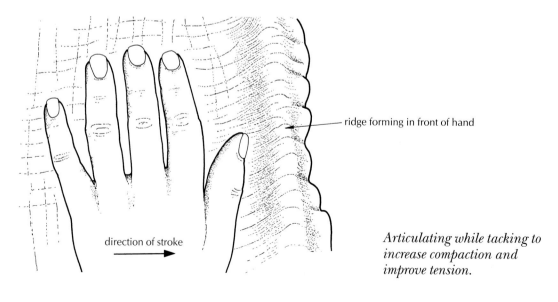

ridge forming in front of hand

direction of stroke

Articulating while tacking to increase compaction and improve tension.

surface in one direction – from back towards the front. As you approach the front edge there will probably be a small wave of loose material in front of the hand. Draw out the tacks in front of the wave, pull the cloth down and retack. Now stroke the top in the opposite direction, again retensioning and tacking. Next work side to side – one direction, retack; then the other direction and so on.

Test now to see if further articulation creates any waves of loose material. If it does, draw out the tacks, pull out the wave and retack. If not, then all the tacks can be driven right home.

MAKING CORNERS

It is now time to make the corners. We looked at some of the basic cornering techniques when discussing the calico layer, but let's now look at all aspects of making corners in more detail.

There are basically three types of situation to consider when dealing with front corners. First is where the corner is a vertical right angle, or nearly so. The second is where the corner is rounded but the radius is fairly sharp. There is probably both a vertical and lateral rounding to the corner – it is rounded from one side to the other; then rounded from the flat seat top over the edge and down to the vertical facing of the corner itself. The third type is where the wall either side and the face of the corner is vertical but the corner is formed by a long radius curve. This type of arrangement often appears on the open end of a chaise.

Basically, with a square corner we aim to create a single seam in the finishing fabric running vertically at the apex of the corner. On short radius corners it is also sometimes possible do draw the sides together in a single, central, vertical seam. As the radius reduces it is more likely you will have two seams. These will meet at the bottom of the corner but will slope to diverge as you move upwards. With long radius curves you may have two, three or four vertical seams or pleats, evenly spaced around the radius.

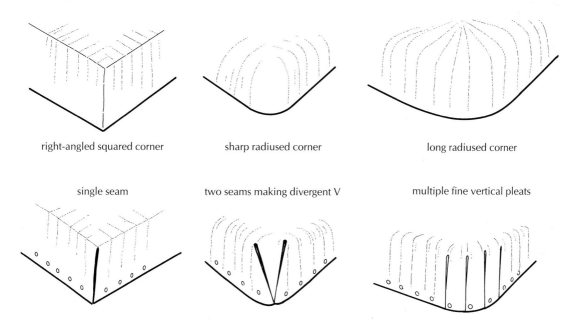

right-angled squared corner   sharp radiused corner   long radiused corner

single seam   two seams making divergent V   multiple fine vertical pleats

Three main front corner arrangements.

The single seam has two variants – the single or the double fold.

With the single fold the material from the vertical face on one side of the corner (say the left side) is drawn tight around the corner and to the vertical face to the other (the right) side of the corner is tacked down. The tack is set back ½in (15mm) or so from the corner. A V-shaped notch is then cut from the material to the right of the tack – the apex of the V angles towards the top of the corner. The material to the right of the cut is then folded under (and poked in with a regulator if necessary) until the fold lies vertically down the apex of the corner. A tack is now placed on or under the corner to hold the fold in place.

If this single seam corner is on a shallow drop-in pad it may now be left as it is. If it is on a deeper pad such as a stuffed-over seat the fold may be sewn down to the under layer with a run of simple slip stitches.

On short radius vertical-faced corners a similar approach with a single fold and seam may be possible.

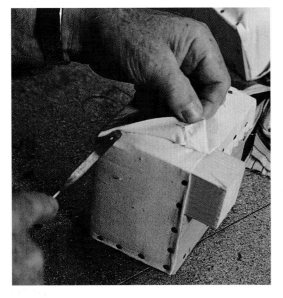

A single-fold front corner. The seam may be left open or may be slip-stitched down.

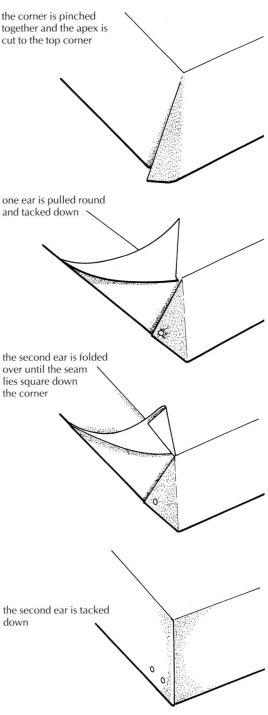

the corner is pinched together and the apex is cut to the top corner

one ear is pulled round and tacked down

the second ear is folded over until the seam lies square down the corner

the second ear is tacked down

A single pleat pinched corner.

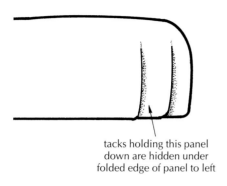

tacks holding this panel
down are hidden under
folded edge of panel to left

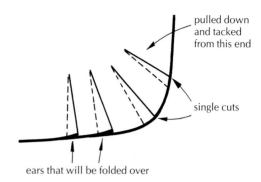

pulled down
and tacked
from this end

single cuts

ears that will be folded over

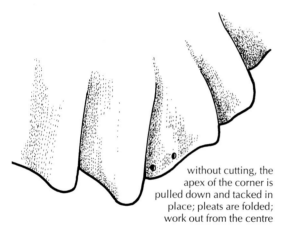

without cutting, the
apex of the corner is
pulled down and tacked in
place; pleats are folded;
work out from the centre

Cut or fold methods of making multi-pleat corners.

More frequently, even with a single seam, a twofold approach is used. Here, the corner of the material is pulled straight outwards from the apex of the corner on a line diagonal to the seat pad. It is then pulled downwards over the corner and tacked down a few millimetres either side of the apex.

This time, two V-shaped notches are cut, one to the left of the left tack and one to the right of the right tack. The material outside the notches is then folded back on itself and is moved until the best lie is achieved. The lie may be where the two folds meet in a vertical seam down the apex of the corner – and this will always be the aim on a squared corner – or the folds meet at the bottom and then slope upwards as a divergent pair of folds. They are manipulated until the angles of slope mirror each other

and the folds lie equidistant from the apex of the corner. This is the pattern usually found on a double rounded corner.

On long radius corners the approach is really a multiple of the single fold. The corner is started from the centre, pulling the material out diagonally and then downwards. It is tacked to the frame. The material either side is then multiple V-notched and a series of single folds are made.

Back corners are far more simple, and broadly speaking there is only one satisfactory method.

With the front corners made, turn to the first of the rear corners. Here, in most cases, the calico and then the fabric have to fit around the side members of the back rest. The process is simplified if the point of the corner of the material is trimmed away.

The material is first cut diagonally from the centre of the corner of the material back to where it meets the inside corner of the frame. The two wings either side of this diagonal cut are then trimmed back with a cut at a right angle to the material edge but leaving a folding margin. This is then folded under and pulled down to tack off.

Making a double-seamed corner on a rounded frame.

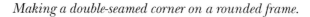

(1) *The point of the corner of the material is pulled down vertically at the apex of the corner.*

(2) *Two loose wings are formed* (above right).

(3) *The wings are drawn into pleats. Here they form two parallel vertical seams.*

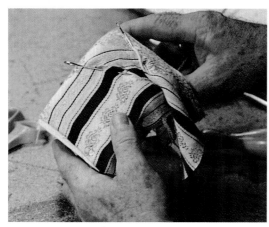

(4) *An alternative is to arrange the folds to form a V which meets at the bottom.*

(5) *To help form a tight V, two regulators are used.*

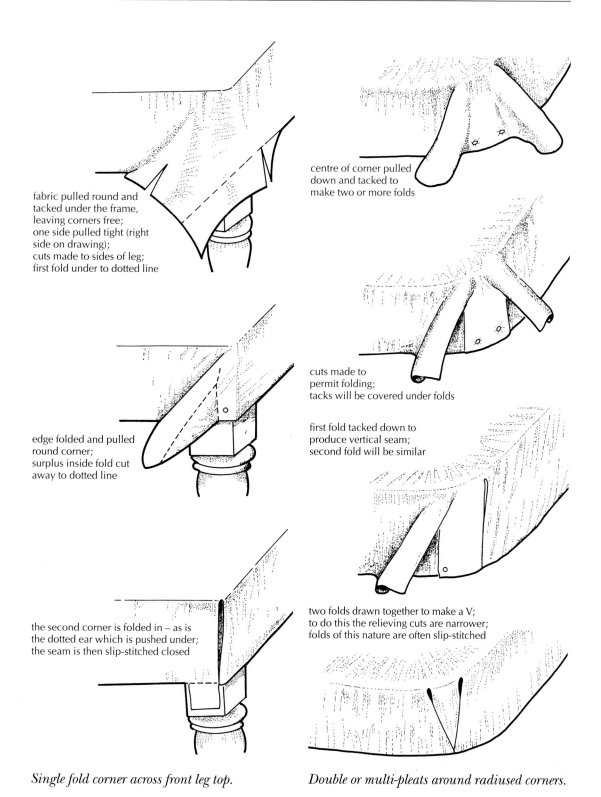

centre of corner pulled
down and tacked to
make two or more folds

fabric pulled round and
tacked under the frame,
leaving corners free;
one side pulled tight (right
side on drawing);
cuts made to sides of leg;
first fold under to dotted line

cuts made to
permit folding;
tacks will be covered under folds

edge folded and pulled
round corner;
surplus inside fold cut
away to dotted line

first fold tacked down to
produce vertical seam;
second fold will be similar

the second corner is folded in – as is
the dotted ear which is pushed under;
the seam is then slip-stitched closed

two folds drawn together to make a V;
to do this the relieving cuts are narrower;
folds of this nature are often slip-stitched

Single fold corner across front leg top.

Double or multi-pleats around radiused corners.

155

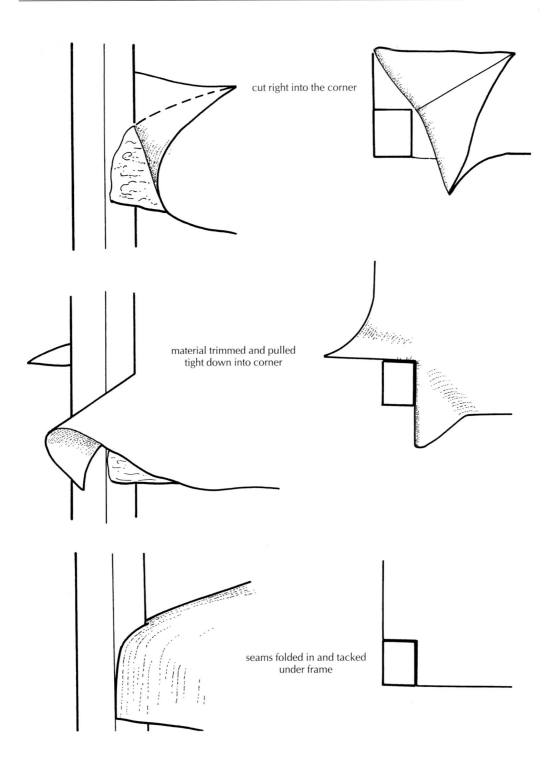

cut right into the corner

material trimmed and pulled
tight down into corner

seams folded in and tacked
under frame

A corner around a rear leg.

The folds of the wings are now aligned down the side of the frame.

OTHER ASPECTS OF THE FINAL FITTING

So far, we have been talking about the basic techniques of selecting, cutting and fitting the finishing fabric; but, of course, there is a lot more to finishing off a chair than that.

First, let's go back over some of the points touched on in earlier chapters. These concern the fixing points and the problems of working around legs and backs.

We have identified that there are fundamentally two forms of fixing. In one, the material is drawn down the side of the seat (or back) and then on to the underside (or round the back). It is finally tacked down to the underside of the frame. In the other form the material finishes in a line, usually on top of a bead which runs right round the face somewhere down the front cross member and the side rails.

Let's now explore each of these and their implications a little further.

Where the material is taken and fixed under the frame we noted that with the calico layer we allowed about a 1in (2.5cm) margin beyond the row of 10 ordinary tacks. This margin was not folded as the inch allows sufficient fabric to give an adequate grip on the tacks. The finishing fabric is fixed in the same way. Again 10 ordinary tacks are used with about 1in spacing between each. The fabric edge is not folded, so about a 1–1½in (2.5–3.8cm) margin is allowed. Usually, the fabric is taken just to overlap the edge of the calico.

A piece of bottoming cloth is now fixed over the base. This is cut so that the edges can be folded under to form a seam about a ¼in (6mm) in from the edge. As it is tacked down it is lightly stretched. Where it fixes around a leg a diagonal cut is made and the two ears are folded under and tacked down. The tacks used to hold it in place do, of course, provide an additional fixing for the calico and the finishing fabric as they pass through both.

Many backrests have to be dealt with in a similar way. The facing fabric passes round the two uprights and also over the top, and is tacked down to the back of the back frame. The difference is that here the back is then covered with another piece of finishing fabric. With the exception of the top and occasionally the bottom edge of this backing piece, the side seams have to be folded in and hand stitched in place. In fact, on some wing chairs there is almost as much stitched edge as there is tacked. We will come to the details of fixing backs in a moment.

Whether the fabric was under the frame fixed or open faced (beaded edge) fixed you have two problems to deal with on the seats. You will have had to make a corner around the front corners of the seats, and had to work the material around the inside of the two uprights that frame the backrest.

The work is finished off by covering the bottom. Here a thin stretch nylon has been used, and although recommended for this job, the stretchiness makes it difficult to tension. It is obviously thin, as the photo flash has penetrated it and the webbing can be seen through.

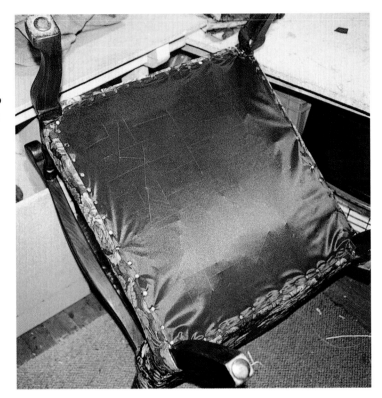

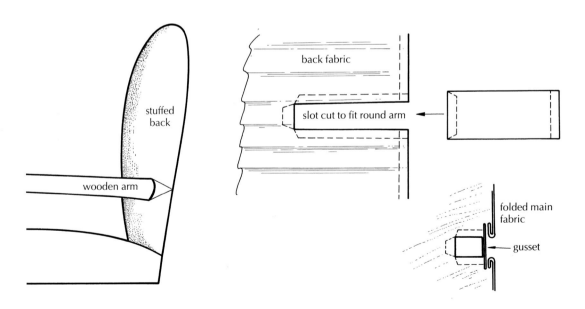

Fitting back fabric around wooden arms.

Many chairs have wooden armrests and padded backs. Here a gusset has to be used where the finishing fabric is cut to go round the arm.

A little earlier we talked about the basic methods of folding corners, including drawing the material under and tacking it off. This is fine where the legs are set some distance back from the corner itself – as on the front legs on settees and chaise. On stuffed-over chairs, however, the leg will be an extension of the seat frame corner. Even where the fabric is drawn under for most of its length it will have to finish in a neat folded edge on the open face of the front legs. Hence as the folds of the corner are drawn together the bottom edge of the fabric has to be folded under for fixing on the open face. Obviously you will not want the heads of the tacks showing. To avoid this, the folds are pinned together and the seam is sewn with a slip-stitch. The whole is held in place by the tacks used to hold the first pulled-down piece. The slip-stitching may also pick up on this material.

There is not the same problem with the back supports, as there is usually no fixing of material across the face of a frame member.

An open V-front rounded corner in a printed Dralon velvet. The seams could be made tighter by slip-stitching.

The rear leg corner on the same chair.

alternative arrangement
of seat/back interface

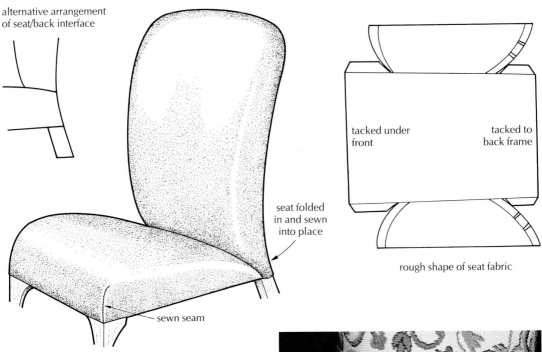

seat folded
in and sewn
into place

sewn seam

tacked under
front

tacked to
back frame

rough shape of seat fabric

Joining seat fabric to side of back rest panels.

However, on some chairs – again such as those with wooden arms – the back panel wraps around the side and is fixed to the back of the chair. It also runs down to meet the side of the seat panel which also wraps around the back. There now has to be a join between the two side panels. This can take several forms. Sometimes it will run straight across from front to back. At other times it may follow a curved line which is a continuation of the sweep of the backrest. At times, the join may be defined by using a piping, but often it is a simple fold-over join which is then slip-stitched to lie flat.

Now let's consider the other form of fixing where the edges of the whole length of the seating fabric terminate on the open face of the seat frame. Here, obviously, the

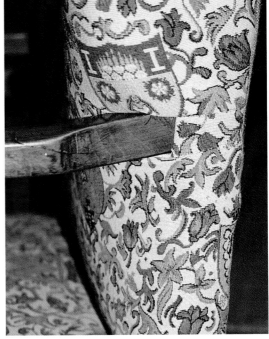

The finishing fabric on a fully covered chair back has to be fitted around the wooden arms. It is cut and folded as fitting round a back rest corner (see page 158).

A beautifully finished chair from Michael, a first-time student. The gusset behind the arm, and the junction between back and seat are all perfectly aligned.

tacks can be seen. You have two alternatives – one is to make a feature of the tacks and the other is to cover and hide them.

In order to be able to tension the material a working edge is left and this is then trimmed to the final line once it has been tacked in place. Because there is not too much loading, and because the holding tacks will be fairly closely spaced, the edge of the fabric is not folded under.

If the tacks are to be featured we use dome-headed upholstery nails. These are available in a huge variety of finishes. Some are also embossed and patterned. For antique furniture it is normal to use one of the metal finishes – often an antique bronze. On modern furniture painted, brightly coloured tacks can be used. Normally these

are placed so that each touches the next and you get a continuous row right around the seat.

Actually fixing the tacks is simplified if you first tack the cover in place with a few well-positioned small standard tacks (10 ordinary). You then make yourself a little tack holder to hold the dome heads while you hammer them home. You should also cover the head with a piece of cloth or supple leather so that the hammer does not damage the top of the dome.

Much more frequently, however, you will fix the top fabric with standard upholstery tacks and then hide the row of tacks with a braid or fringe.

In this case, the fabric is fixed, corners and all, using 10 ordinary tacks at 1in

(2.5cm) spacing. Particular care needs to be taken to place the tacks in a straight line ¼in (6mm) in from the final edge. When all the tacks have been driven home, the edge is carefully trimmed to its finished line using fine, sharp scissors or a new-bladed Stanley knife. A braid is chosen to match or contrast the finishing fabric. On some chairs you may prefer a trimming which incorporates a fringe and/or tassels. The braid is held on by Copydex glue and gimp pins (Copydex is by far the best adhesive for this task). The gimp pins can again be obtained in a range of colours and although you part the top of the braid to hide the head of the pins, a matching colour does make them even more invisible!

A fireside stool being releathered. The leather is tacked at the back of the frame rails.

Decorative dome-head nails give a good finish. These are knocked home with a plastic hammer to avoid damaging the bronzing.

162

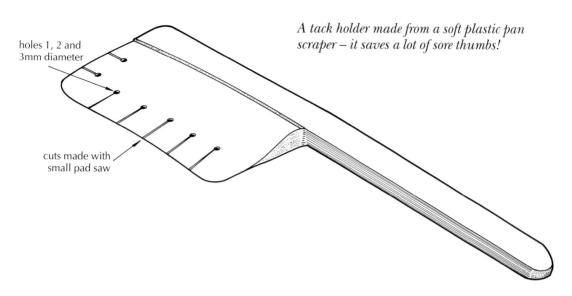

holes 1, 2 and
3mm diameter

cuts made with
small pad saw

*A tack holder made from a soft plastic pan
scraper – it saves a lot of sore thumbs!*

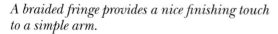

*A braided fringe provides a nice finishing touch
to a simple arm.*

(**Right**) *Not so good! The infill panel is merely
a piece of finishing fabric wrapped around
hardboard. The holding down tacks are hidden
under the glued-on scalloped braiding. The
ruching of the head leaves a lot to be desired.*

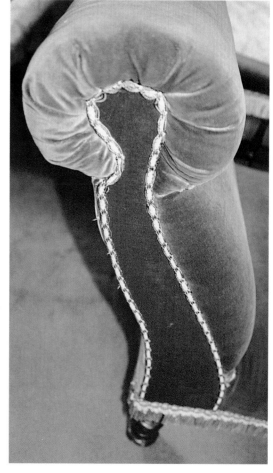

There is a third alternative which is really a mix of the previous two. Here you make an edging strip and then fix this with spaced dome-head nails. The back tacking strip that we will be considering in a moment is ideal. This is ½in (1.3cm) wide and a narrow strip of your finishing fabric can be glued around it. The strip is then glued and nailed along the edge of the fabric, covering the ordinary upholstery nails. Dome heads spaced at about 2in (5cm) intervals will suffice.

As was mentioned a little earlier there are a number of panels which may be partially sewn in. These frequently include all or some of the seams of the back panel; the outer facing of the wings of wing chairs; the outside facings of the arms; and decorative inserts on the front of arms.

It is sometimes possible to fix one edge with a neat fold using back tacking strip. This is a vulcanized, cardboard-like strip. It is placed on the back of the fabric near to the edge and is then tacked through to the frame (13 or even 16 Imp tacks will be needed). It may be positioned along the top of the back, or in the seam on the underside of the arm roll. The fabric is then turned over the strip,

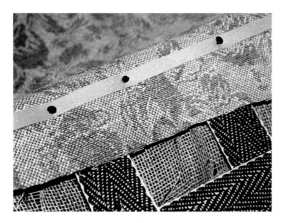

Some panels can be given a neat folded edge using edging strip – here along the head of the back fabric. The fabric folds over, hiding the tack heads within the fold.

thus hiding it. Obviously it now gives a clean, straight, tack-free edge to the panel. The other edge of the panel is taken under the frame and loosely tacked in position.

The side seams now have to be folded in and through stitched (slip-stitches) to the edge of the adjoining panel. Often the stitched seam also incorporates a decorative piping.

PIPING

Piping can be bought to match most braids and fringes; alternatively you can make your own, often from the same fabric as used for the chair cover. Strips of fabric to make piping are traditionally cut on the bias of the material, but with many fabrics this is not absolutely essential. The strips are then folded round a length of piping cord and are stitched in using a sewing machine with a one-sided piping foot (*see* chapter 14).

There are two methods of fixing piping. One is a bit fiddly, involving pinning the strip and fabric in place and then stitching right through to the material of the adjacent panel. The second is to nail the piping to the previous material and pin the folded edge of the panel to it, and stitch through.

An edge finishing arrangement which can sometimes be useful incorporates a double piping. Here a piping is made with two lines of piping cord, the space between them being just sufficient to accommodate a width of braid. The piping is first tacked in place over the material edge and the braid is fitted last, again using Copydex and gimp pins. On an Ottoman chest, one student made a double-piped piece incorporating within it a length of edging strip. The whole was then fixed with matching exposed dome-head nails. This strip went right round the outer face just under the lid and hid all the tacks that were holding the covering fabric in place.

And that will be all that you require for 90 per cent of the chairs you ever wish to

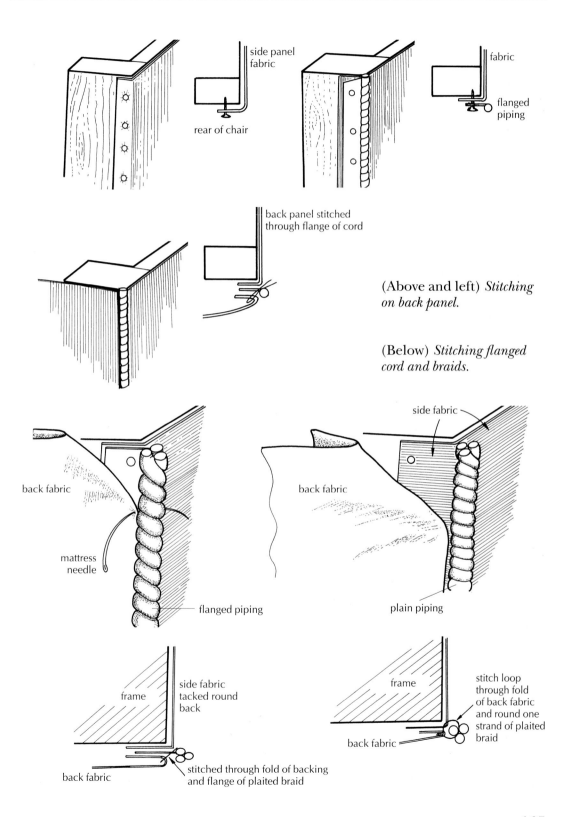

side panel fabric

rear of chair

fabric

flanged piping

back panel stitched through flange of cord

(Above and left) *Stitching on back panel.*

(Below) *Stitching flanged cord and braids.*

side fabric

back fabric

mattress needle

flanged piping

back fabric

plain piping

frame

side fabric tacked round back

back fabric

stitched through fold of backing and flange of plaited braid

frame

stitch loop through fold of back fabric and round one strand of plaited braid

back fabric

upholster. You will meet some difficult problems, but practically all can be solved by using a variety of the basic methods that we have been discussing. In front of me at this very moment is a wing chair that I know will be difficult. It has upholstered scroll arms with compound curves on the edges. There will be a lot of fitting, hand working and sewing – but it was done at least once in a previous life, so it can be done again!

A double-flanged piping has been made from the finishing fabric. This is tacked in place and the braid is then slip-stitched over the tack heads.

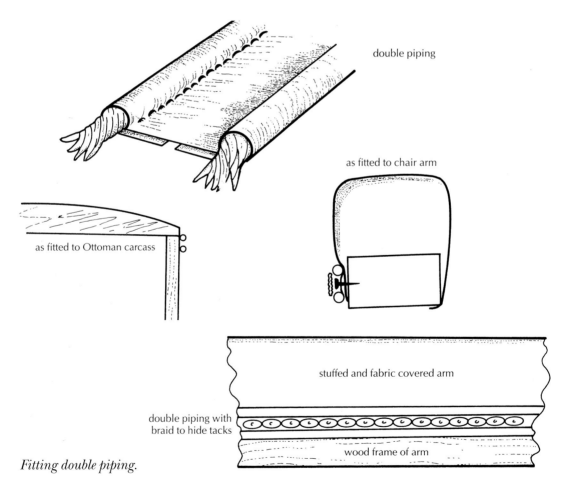

double piping

as fitted to chair arm

as fitted to Ottoman carcass

stuffed and fabric covered arm

double piping with braid to hide tacks

wood frame of arm

Fitting double piping.

12

Added Comfort
Cushions and Pads

Cushions and removable pads play a big rôle in upholstery. They take a number of forms – let's start with the most common.

Many armchairs, particularly several of the designs of wing armchair, and almost all settees, have a separate pad or squab to provide the seat. Sometimes these are simple rectangular shapes, but on many wing chairs and the outside pair of a set of three on sofas, they are often rectangles with one or two small ears sticking out at the front of the sides. These ears fit on the platform where it sticks out beyond the arms. Usually the slabs are box-shaped in that they are 4in (10cm) or so deep and have crisp square sides. Occasionally the pads are softer and a little thinner, and also have ill-defined side walls.

The seat squab of this chair is formed by fitting a pre-sewn cover over a block of fire-retardant foam cut to shape. Most suppliers will cut foam to your template.

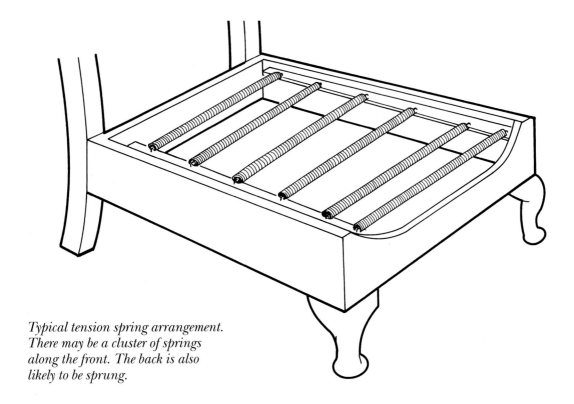

Typical tension spring arrangement. There may be a cluster of springs along the front. The back is also likely to be sprung.

Many settees have two or more removable squabs to form the seat and usually the number of pads equates to the stated seating capacity of the unit. Hence a three-seater has three pads.

A second form of cushion or pad is the removable back. Again, this is found mainly on high back armchairs and sofas, and it is most usual on chairs with exposed wooden frames. Back squab cushions are usually softer and more yielding than seating pads and are less clearly box-edged.

After these forms of cushion that are an integral part of the whole seat, we have also to recognize loose lumbar rolls and even scatter cushions, both of which are an intrinsic part of the design of some pieces.

As upholsterers we are concerned with providing, replacing or simply re-covering the pads or cushions that are already there; general cushion-making is not usually part of our bailiwick. As you look at the cushions and pads that we are concerned with you will find that various forms of construction have been used and we need to be able to replicate these if we are to do authentic restorations.

But let's for a moment take a step back and consider the platform on which the pad sits. With some modern furniture, and particularly those pieces with exposed wooden frames, we often find that the platform is simply a piece of strong material tacked across a number of close coil tension springs. These are clipped into metal brackets at either side of the frame. Sometimes the springs are individually covered with material and there is not a platform cloth. There are also chairs where instead of coil springs the suspension is made up of lines of a form of rubberized webbing. *Always* start by replacing these springs or webs as they are very easy to stress and they can stretch differently.

There are also times with some modern pieces where you find a spring unit which is made up of a number of light springs lashed together into a wire mesh cage. These are sometimes reusable, but if there is any doubt, replace them. Blocks can be made up to your own specification by most of the better upholstery materials suppliers (*see* picture on page 16).

There is one other issue that we need to touch upon before we look at the making of cushions. This again concerns the seat platform. If you lift the cushions on many chairs you will find that the finishing fabric which is clearly visible at the front of the seat soon gives way to a plain, coarser cloth. The reason is twofold. First, if the cloth under the seat squab is never seen, why use expensive finishing fabric? The second is that the platform cloth can be chosen not only for its cheapness but also because you can use much coarser but strong cloth to provide a longer lasting sub-base.

If you do adopt this route, the seating cloth is machine-stitched to the front finishing cloth and the whole is then stretched and tacked into place as one. The material used is known as platform lining and one of the best choices is a fire-resistant Bolton twill.

Some of the squabs themselves are also constructed using preformed spring units. Others have foam cut to the required size and shape. On older furniture we may find squabs that are entirely stuffed. Although we occasionally meet animal hair stuffing, the more common is down and feather. On the some modern pieces, fully stuffed cushions may incorporate kapok or one of the microfibre synthetic fillings. Whatever the original form of stuffing it can still be replaced with like materials. Some are, however, more difficult to obtain and are certainly much more expensive than others.

In the worst-case scenario we may have two tasks. The first is to recreate the basic squab, and the second is to then produce a cover for this. Almost always the stuffing of a hair or feather-filled cushion or squab is self-contained in a material case which is separate from the cover of finishing fabric. Often the outer covers are zippered so that they can be removed and cleaned. It is also easier to fit a machine-sewn zippered cover than it is to hand sew a cover over a made-up cushion or squab.

The pre-built spring cages appear a little more frequently in factory built chairs made up until about 25 years ago. In addition to the core of small springs the wire cage often has a top and bottom facing of a woven wire mesh. Obviously you would not wish to put a finishing fabric straight onto the top of this mesh so the cages are usually encased in hessian, may even be given an overall stuffing of hair, and certainly have a layer of felt wadding. They are then covered in calico. The finishing fabric is made up into a zippered envelope to slip over the whole pad.

Although these made-up spring frames are themselves relatively modern, they have now been almost entirely replaced by preshaped blocks of a foam compound. It is here that there has recently been so much trouble. Amongst the first foams to be widely used was a rubber-based product which once ignited and burnt fiercely, giving off masses of clinging black smoke. Later, urethane-based foams took over, but many of these again proved to be a fire hazard, producing very toxic fumes. Stringent regulations now govern the type of foams to be used in furniture and the compounds involved have to be to a Fire Resistant (FR) specification. You may, of course, use anything you like provided you do not wish to sell the piece on, but it is a wise precaution to insist on fire-resistant materials for any upholstery that you undertake.

There is another point to bear in mind. Much of the cheap plastic foams sold from stalls in the local market soon degrade and will break up inside the case. In no time at all you are remaking the squab.

Feather-filled squabs, and microfibre-stuffed loose lumbar rolls completed this Knowle settee.

On the other hand, the beauty of foam is that it can be cut to a well-defined shape, retains that shape when sat upon, and does not require any intermediate covering layers. The finishing fabric envelope can be pulled straight over it.

On older pieces, and therefore more frequently used in traditional reupholstery, the squabs are made of fabric and are filled with a loose stuffing. The best is a down and feather mix. This provides a very comfortable, 'squashy' seat cushion. The downside is that it has to be knocked back into shape and squared off after it has been sat upon.

Almost as difficult to handle are some of the modern and microspun fillings. They have an advantage over feather in that there is a greater resilience and they hold their shape better. But the Hobson's choice is yours – would you rather fill the air in the workshop with down or microfibres?

So, although they are beautiful in their accommodation to the human frame, feather and fibre-filled squabs are not the easiest to make. For the faint-hearted, deliverance is at hand. Many upholstery suppliers and some of the better stores will make up squabs and cushions to your measurements and will fill them with almost any conventional material that you require. Here mention has to be made of John Lewis in Oxford Street who never even blink when you ask for quite extreme feather-filled one-offs!

MAKING CUSHIONS AND SQUABS

However, many of us wish to do it ourselves.

Stuffed squabs are made using a compartmented box. The material for such boxes does need to be feather-proof and therefore a waxed cambric or feather-proof ticking is normally used. First, a strong box form is sewn to the overall dimensions of the squab required. The base and all four sides are sewn together on a machine, but the lid is sewn in down one end only. The box is then turned inside out to put the seams inside. Compartment dividers are now fitted and these are sewn in along their bases and up the side walls. A single-seater squab would probably have three dividers.

The back compartment is filled first. The edges of the top of the section are then turned in and through stitched to close them. Similarly, the top of the first divider is sewn to the lid.

The middle compartment is stuffed next and again the lid and seams are sewn down. Finally, the third compartment is filled and the seams sewn together. A typical seat pad may use 3–3½lb (1.4–1.6kg) of feather mixture at a current price of about £5 per pound, dependent upon supplier.

Roll and tube cushions feature on some old furniture. They are particularly important on those pieces where the design does not really offer a good lumbar support. You will have to decide whether to use the same fabric as the body or to go for a contrast. Roll cushions are not usually compartmented, but again it is normal first to make up a capped stuffed tube and then to have a separate covering envelope of finishing fabric.

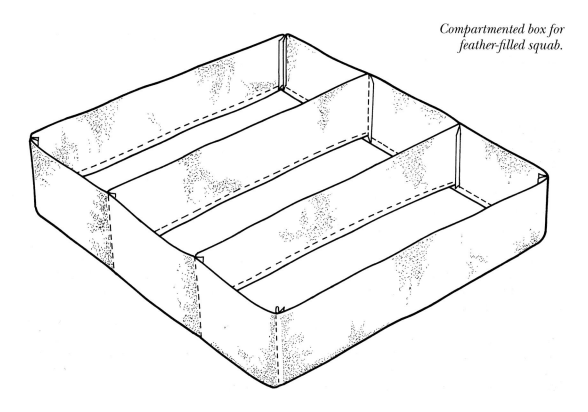

Compartmented box for feather-filled squab.

PIPING

Very often, some or all of the seams of squabs and cushion pads are finished off using a piping or flanged cord. The cord will usually be chosen to match the braid or cord used in the covering of the main frame of the piece. In making the envelope or finished cover, the first task is to acquire or make up the flanged cord or piping that you require. The second task is to check and adjust your sewing machine. I cannot envisage making up the final covers without a sewing machine, and the machine and needle have to be capable of stitching through at least four layers of finishing fabric, and possibly even a length of piping cord.

MAKING THE COVER BOX

The actual cover box for a squab is made up inside out. It consists basically of five pieces. There are the two main top and bottom rectangles that are pattern matched and cut to a good inch (2.5cm) wider (on all sides) than the required finished size. This is a generous sewing margin so as to allow tolerance in assembly.

The third piece is a long strip which will do the front and the two side walls. It makes things easier if this can be cut from a single length. If it is to be a jointed length try to make the joins down the side wall. Obviously you do not want a join on the front face, and making the joins at the front corners only adds to the sewing difficulty. Again, allow a reasonable sewing margin (a good ½in (1.3cm)) all round plus an extra inch (2.5cm) at both ends.

The final two pieces are the two halves of the back which are joined by a full length zip. Sew up this piece complete with its zip before fitting to the box.

How confident are you in your measuring? If you have been careful, you may now make the front and side strip and the zippered back into a complete circle. The total length must be exactly that of the sum of all four sides of the finished seat. Don't forget that the box is still inside out and that the zip should therefore be facing in towards the centre of the box or circle.

Still working inside out and starting at the centre of the front and working out, pin the top and bottom fabrics to the side wall. Into each seam pin the flanged cord or piping as you go. Working inside out the piping will be inside, and the pinned sewing seam will be facing outwards. It is here that the 3 and 4in (7.6 and 10cm) long upholstery skewers really come into their own as you will be pinning through anything between four and eight layers of material.

As you work around the corners you will have to cut small relieving notches into the edge of the wall fabric and the flange of the piping cord. If all your dimensions were exact, you should find that the edges of the top and bottom fabric extend about ½in (1.3cm) from the edges of the wall materials and the flanged cord. A one-sided 'zipper foot' on the sewing machine will allow you to sew right up to the bulge created by the cord of the piping. Again, it gives you the facility to make adjustments if you stitch from the centre of the front outwards. With the seams completed all the way round unzip the zip and pull the envelope inside out. Hey presto! Doesn't it look wonderful?

If the cover that you have made is a nice tight fit, you will find it a little tricky to insert the pad. A spring frame will need compressing and a second pair of hands can be useful. Foam blocks are easier because they can be bent as well as compressed. Feather-stuffed pads are the easiest of all because they give in all directions. Of course, what we have been talking about here are flat top pads. On some pieces of furniture the pads are buttoned; so let's look at the process of buttoning next.

—13—

Button Up

It is some time since a chair or settee requiring buttoning came into the workshop. One student keeps threatening to bring in a Chesterfield, but so far her furniture-carrying capacity or her nerve have failed!

The process is not difficult, just a little fiddly. It does have to be said that the job is easier on foam pads than on hair stuffing, and even many traditionalists tend to put a foam layer on top of the hair to assist in the shaping and making the necessary buttonholes. Certainly the finishing fabric with all its pleats sits better on a thin foam layer.

PREPARATION

The process starts in the same way as for sprung or stuffed-over upholstery. The platforms are almost identical up to the skrim-covered stage. It is important, however, to ensure that the pad is well formed and that the hair layer is generous. For a deep-buttoned pad you need a stuffing layer of 2–3in (5–7.6cm) thickness as a minimum. To reach this stage use enough stuffing ties just to hold the hair within bounds but not to compress it down too much. In fact, the buttoning ties will lock the hair in place and provide sufficient compression once the seat is finished. You do not need any separate through-the-seat stitching if you are going on to button the pad.

You do, however, need to make a very good job of stitching shape into the pad if you are going for a square-walled platform. For a seat this deep, it is likely that you will need three blind rows and one through row. Nothing looks worse than a neatly buttoned seat, the sides of which are randomly rounded and lumpy!

Even with a rounded-edge seat you still need the overall depth and you might still consider a row or two of slightly less tensioned blind stitching to draw the hair against the wall.

It seems almost a contradiction to suggest that the stuffing ties should not be so tight and yet we are now recommending very firm stitched side walls. In fact, there is no problem. The outer rows of buttoned diamonds will just miss the area of hair that is drawn against the walls by the blind stitches, so the buttonholes will be in an area of looser hair that will mould to the desired shape.

Regulation, too, becomes very important. Work over the whole top to ensure that the platform is absolutely level and evenly stuffed.

BUTTON PATTERN AND POSITIONING

You need carefully to work out your buttoning pattern and the exact position of the buttons. The normal way is to set them in diagonal rows so that the pleated top covering forms a pattern of diamonds across the surface. The first decision is what will happen on the centre line. Will there be a diamond on the centre line on the outer rows or will the centres fall halfway between two diamonds? The size and spacing of the diamonds must fit within the frame and look balanced. Above all, you must be careful to ensure that the buttoning pattern on the chair back, the seat and the inside of the arms follows the same format and line ups and works together to form a whole.

When buttoning the back rest of a chair it is usual to position the two lower lateral rows of buttons so that the ridge between them falls in the right place to provide lumbar support.

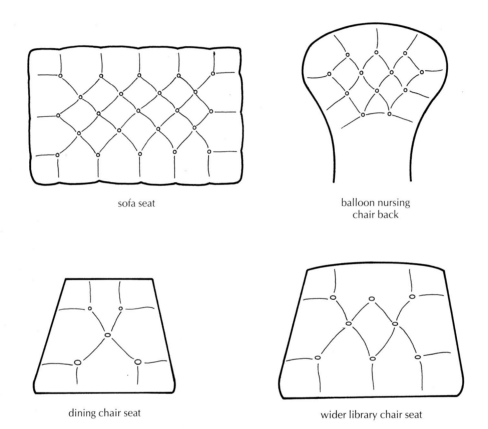

sofa seat

balloon nursing
chair back

dining chair seat

wider library chair seat

hooped back nursing chair

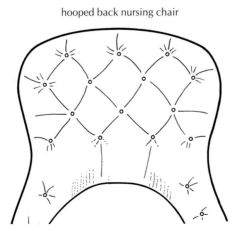

Buttoning patterns.

174

FIXING THE BUTTONS

Once you have worked out the pattern you require, measure carefully and using a straight edge mark off the position of each button with a marker pen. Cut small cross slits into the skrim at each button point.

If you are proposing to do a number of pieces of buttoning, and particularly if you are working on a set of chairs, it is a good idea to make one or more hardboard templates where the position of the buttons is marked and drilled out with a 10mm hole. These templates are positioned on top of the seat pad and are lined up on centre markings. The position of the buttons is then marked on the hessian with a marker pen pushed into the holes. The beauty of templates is that they can be used for each layer and make it much easier to place accurately the later holes when the first hessian holes have been covered with wadding and calico.

Making buttoning holes in the hessian.

Now to continue with the buttoning – with a pair of sharp pointed scissors work into these slits, cutting into the stuffing and then, poking in a finger, work the stuffing to either side until the tip of the finger reaches the underlying platform hessian.

The next layer is cotton wadding. On some chairs you will wish to take the wadding down over the side walls. If this is the case, put on one layer of 2½oz wadding which reaches right down the side. Then cut a second layer which comes out only as far as the edge of the top of the seat. If not taking the wadding down the side, then a single topping layer of 4oz wadding will suffice.

In both cases, you now need to pull wadding away over each of the holes cut into the skrim and stuffing. Mark the positions of the holes with the template. You will find that the best method of making these holes is to press down lightly on the seat with one hand so as to hold the wadding in place. Then, using the finger and thumb of the other hand, gently pull the wadding away in small pieces at each hole.

Finally, a piece of polyester wadding is cut to fit over the top and walls of the seat pad. This is positioned, marked off with the template, and small holes (1in (2.5cm) in diameter) are cut through it to correspond with each of the holes in the wadding and skrim. The pad is now covered with a generous piece of calico, but at this stage the calico is not tacked around the edges.

Start with the centre hole in the back row, and with your finger push the calico down into the hole. Take a long straight needle (it is less fraught to use a single point needle) and a short length of twine (about 15in (38cm) of Barbour 4 or 6). Working from the top of the pad push the needle into the centre of the hole and through to the underside. If the needle passes through part of the webbing then this is fine; if not, thread a small offcut of webbing onto the needle. Draw through about half the length of twine, take the needle off and rethread it onto the twine above the seat.

Now push the needle back down the hole to enter the material about ½in (6mm) to the side of the first entry. This makes a small stitch. Push the needle through until you can grip the new tail again, making sure that it passes through the scrap of web. Tie the second tail round the first in a slip knot. When you now draw up the slip knot the webbing will prevent the knot sinking into the platform hessian. In fact, I recommend both belt and braces. As you draw up the knot, put a small twist of material into the underside loop – this will also make it easier to undo in the unlikely but just possible event that you should wish to do so later. Pull the slip knot down tight; this will draw the calico deep into the hole, thus forming a deep button pocket.

Work out sideways from the starting hole until the row is completed. Move then to the next adjacent row and work this out from the centre. As you go, ensure that the calico is pulled outwards to keep it taut.

As each hole is sewn in, carefully fold the material to produce pleats along the line of the diamonds. Use the spade end of the regulator to shape the pleat. While you do not need to be exact because this stage will not show through, it does provide useful practice for the much more precisely worked final layer of finishing fabric.

With all holes made and sewn in, you now tack the calico round the edges. Here, too, while you are maintaining tension, you will have to make folds in the material. The folds from all central holes are angled towards the next hole producing diamonds, and they are thus diagonal to the edges of the seat frame. The fold out from the outer row to the edge, however, should produce a single small pleat which meets the seat side walls (and therefore the frame) at right angles. Tension off the whole seat, articulating outwards from the centre. Drive home the tacks and make off the corners. At this stage, slip-stitch the pleats going out to the sides – it helps to retain the required shape.

You will probably wish to have buttons that match your finishing fabric. Most upholstery suppliers have a button press and they will make up buttons for you of the size required, but using a little of your fabric. (Your own press will cost between £120 and £200.)

The dedicated traditionalist will now apply a layer or two of skin wadding. It is, however, much easier and controllable if you use a fire-resistant polyester wadding at this stage. This should be cut large enough to cover the top and side walls, plus of course enough to pull down into the holes. Again, mark off with the template and cut small holes at each of the button recesses. You can now cut and place over the upholstery fabric, checking for grain orientation or pile.

This time, the buttoning work is started at a central hole on the front row (I can't remember why, but that is what I was taught years ago!).

A new 15in (38cm) length of twine is now threaded onto the needle and again the entry is made from the top of the pad and the twine is drawn in for half of its length. A button is threaded onto the twine above the pad, the needle rethreaded to this end, and the second entry is made and the needle is pushed through. Once more, a slip knot is tied and the loop is drawn up tight. At this point, the knot is left and the next hole along is buttoned.

This time, of course, great care is taken in folding and pleating the fabric on the seat top. The pleats are made and pushed into shape and placed again using the spade end of the regulator needle. As you work, develop a pattern for the lie of the pleats – fold them all in the same direction, or all inwards for one row of diamonds, and so on.

With all the buttons in place and the fabric loose tacked to the frame, articulate it outwards until it is taught, tack it home and make the corners.

Diamond and straight out pleats.

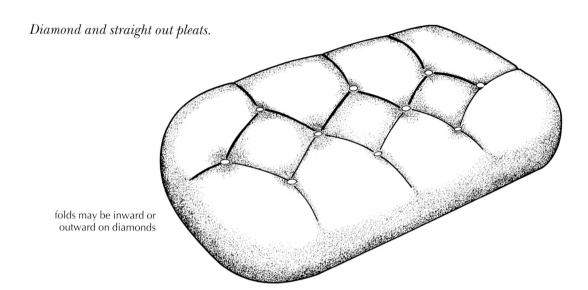

folds may be inward or
outward on diamonds

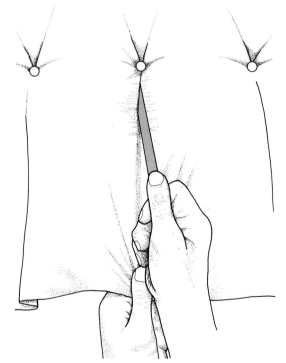

Using regulator to shape buttoning pleats.

A reasonable first attempt at buttoning. If perfect, there would only be the main diamond folds without all the short secondaries.

The final task is again to work from the underside. Give each of the button ties a final pull and lock off the slip knot. This can be done in one of two ways. Either working on the button tie alone, tie it off with a double knot; or pull the button and the earlier calico tie loop tight, and tie the two off together. Some upholsterers actually remove the calico tie at this stage, but I feel that it is this one that carries most of the tension and with the double ties there is much less likelihood of a button coming adrift at a later date. A frequent workshop or customer site visit task for an upholsterer is that of replacing a couple of buttons!

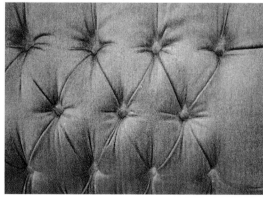

So the actual process of buttoning is not difficult. Beginners find that the making of neat diamond pleats gets very much easier with practice. Do not expect your first attempt to be perfect, so if you do have a treasured leather-covered Chesterfield to re-cover you should first get an over-stuffed chair and button that – even if it was not buttoned in a previous life.

BUTTONING ON LEATHER UPHOLSTERY

The mention of Chesterfields here does prompt another subject – leather upholstery. Fundamentally, leather is little more than a slightly thicker, and slightly less yielding, upholstery 'fabric'. It is therefore not quite as easy to get the diamond pleats to lie flat. The only significant difference is that leather is much more difficult to obtain (in the UK), is more expensive and can be very wasteful.

Unfortunately, cows do not produce their skins in 54in widths and long lengths on a roll. You have to buy leather in whole or part hides. Purely to get pieces of a suitable size for a settee you may need a hide for the front, another for the back and maybe even one for the two arms. As offcuts, you will have enough to keep a native village crafts shop in raw materials for soft handbags for months. (It does, however, make useful material for releathering old fire bellows!)

Leather-covered furniture can be treated in exactly the same way as a fabric-covered piece right up to and including the calico and skin wadding stage. The leather itself is initially fixed in much the same way, although folded corners and seams are fewer. Stitching is rare except on factory-made items. The small areas where the amateur reupholsterer may find it necessary to use a needle and thread can often be replaced with a few dabs of balsa cement

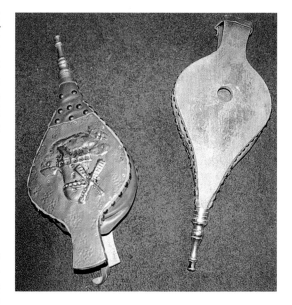

A use for offcuts. 'Reupholstered' bellows.

from the local model shop (try UHU). Stretching and articulation are very important, but gloves should be worn for handling and clean dusters for articulating – leather marks easily with the natural oils on the hands.

Where the leather finishes on an open face it is usual to hide the tacks with a leather strip held in place with decorative dome-head tacks. These come with plain round and embossed domes, are available in a range of sizes and are either bronzed, antiqued, coppered or coloured.

Some of the bigger upholstery suppliers (particularly two wholesalers) stock leather, or will certainly obtain it to order. They do not, however, sell direct, so you may have to go through a local supplier and lean on them to order for you. Do not take no for an answer; leather can still be obtained. Similarly with the dome tacks – several shops have said they are no longer available. Nonsense! They are, but you may have to search for a supplier who will take the trouble.

14

Getting Knotted and All Stitched Up

This chapter gathers together a number of threads. At various times we have said 'make a slip knot', or 'draw together with slip stitches', but not everyone will know what this means. As an ex-mountaineer and sailor I am often very surprised to find how many male (and female) students cannot tie simple knots, and how much difficulty some (of both sexes) experience when using a needle and thread.

As an upholsterer you undertake many tasks where thread or twine has to be tied – sometimes with commonplace knots, but sometimes with upholstery specials. As you then come to the final stages of each piece some seamstressing skills become highly desirable. If you are not sure of your ground in this area, practice sessions on scraps of material of the knots and stitches detailed in this chapter can be very beneficial.

We are going to run through a range of the most widely used knots and then look at stitching. This is for a number of reasons. First, to put an official 'upholstery' name on those knots you have been using all your life – this will serve as a reference aid when looking through upholstery books. If you like, it is a jargon-buster (or trainer)! The second reason is to show some alternatives to the most frequently used knots and to suggest reasons why some might be better than others. The third aim is to increase the range of your knotting ability, and fourth to help develop skills for those individuals who have never dabbled in these fields.

KNOTS

THE HALF HITCH

Many knots incorporate one or multiples of a half hitch. The basic half hitch itself we first encountered in rush seating where we used it to join in new rushes; we also met it when tying off the ends in seat cane. It has two forms and many uses and adaptations. The simplest form is where the tail end of a line is laid beside the main line, is then wrapped once around the main line and is tucked under itself. It therefore has little strength and is certainly not load-bearing; it is really used just to tidy up and fix an end in place neatly. It is used in rushing/caning where a load bearing lock-in is achieved by other means – pegging in caning and twisting in rushing.

The more regular form of the half hitch is more secure. Here the tail is wrapped round, tucked under and then pulled through the loop it has made. This secures the tail of a new line to the end of the main line but will not lock it in a fixed position. The half hitch can slide along the main line. If, however, the tail of the new line is half hitch knotted round the end of the original main line, and then the main line is half hitched round the tail of the new line, the two lines can be pulled away from each other and the two knots will bind up and prevent the ends from slipping apart. This is a very good knot for joining a new length onto the end of a line where you wish to tension or load the line. It is very

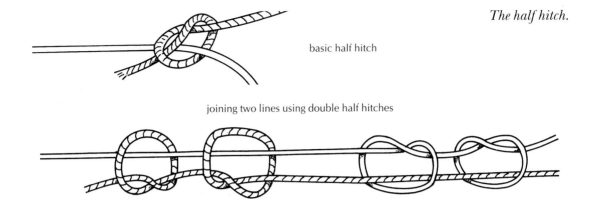

The half hitch.

basic half hitch

joining two lines using double half hitches

useful in adding lengths to the twine used in making stuffing loops.

With cord, including twine and sewing threads, the back-to-back, two half hitch knot is fine. If joining two nylon monofilaments (as in single strand transparent fishing lines) the half hitches can slip and undo themselves. (Such line is sometimes used by some upholsterers and furniture-makers because of its strength and cheapness.) Here a double half hitch in each end is the minimum required and you are better looking at the more complex knots such as a blood knot.

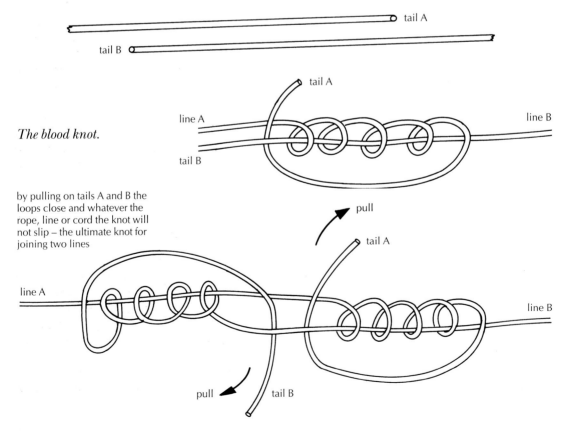

tail A

tail B

tail A

line A

line B

The blood knot.

tail B

by pulling on tails A and B the loops close and whatever the rope, line or cord the knot will not slip – the ultimate knot for joining two lines

pull

tail A

line A

line B

pull

tail B

THE REEF KNOT

Most people know of the reef knot, and this again is useful for tying two ends together. Here a loop is made in one end. The end of the other line is brought up through the inside of the loop, taken out to the side across the first leg of the loop, curled round underneath where it passes under both legs of the loop, is then brought up outside the second leg and is pushed back down through the middle of the loop. You now have two interlocking loops. By gripping in

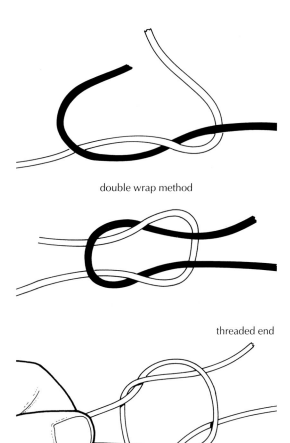

double wrap method

threaded end

pinched loop method

Reef knots.

one hand (pinched between finger and thumb) the line and tail of one loop, and in the other hand the other loop's tail and line, the two can be pulled outwards to tighten up on each other. In most cords, the reef will not slip, and yet it is relatively easy to undo.

Making a loop in one end greatly simplifies the tying of reef knots, although most people do not bother. They make a simple wrap over half hitch one way and then a second reversed. Sometimes they get all the right sequences of overs and unders, but often they do not, and so they end up with a granny knot which can slip apart.

The reef knot is again good for joining two similar lines of woven or spun materials. On monofilament it pulls straight apart. To reduce this problem, the tail of one loop can be half hitch-knotted around the line of that loop, with the other side being treated similarly.

To make absolutely sure there is no slip in monofilament, there is a better knot. Here you start by making a plain reef knot. You then bring the tail down along the line and loop it over. The tail is then wrapped around the line three or four times inside the loop and the tail is then drawn up tight. The same is done at the other end.

Making these multiple wraps inside the tail loops gives huge non-slipability. Pulling on the line may cause it to try to slip in the reef, but this now clamps the multi-loops even harder on themselves. We will see this principle again in a moment.

THE SHEET BEND

Where the two lines you need to join are of substantially different nature or size, we use a knot which appears to be an adapted reef knot – it is called a sheet bend.

Start with a pinched loop made in the thicker cord. The tail of the thinner cord then starts as in a reef knot. It comes up through the loop, bends out over the first leg of the loop, passes under both legs of

reef knot with two locking half hitches

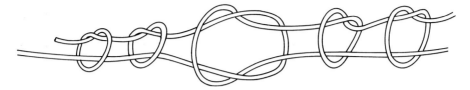

reef knot with internal wrap loops

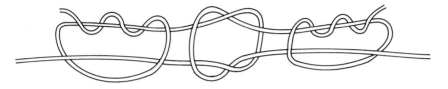

Secured reef knots.

Sheet bend.

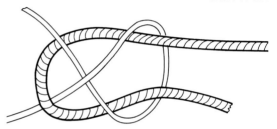

the loop, bends up outside the second leg (so far exactly as a reef knot), but now passes back under the loop of itself and out to the side over the top of the first leg of the heavier cord.

Again, if in doubt the two tails are taken in half hitches around their own lines.

joining together two lines of significantly different diameters

THE SLIP KNOT

One of the most frequently used knots (in cord, twine and thread) is the slip knot. This is used where the starting end of a line needs to be firmly anchored. It can also be made out in open space and then drawn up tight into difficult corners.

In fact, there are several approaches to this most basic of knots. The simplest method is to make the loop in the end of the line – probably by threading it through or round something, and then tying the tail around the line just behind the loop with two half hitches.

A better slip knot, widely used by fishermen and the one normally demonstrated in my studio, uses the internal wrap loop we saw a moment ago. The thread is drawn through the material, the tail is then

passed over and back under the line and is pinched to form a loop. The tail is now passed through the loop to form a couple of wraps. When the tail is drawn tight, this closes the loop down on the line, but the line can still be drawn through the loop. By pulling on the line the knot slips down and tightens onto the surface of the material.

There is then the official 'upholsterer's slip knot'. This is effective, but it is complicated. However, some students are perfectionists. The line is threaded through the material or passed around a coil of a spring. A tail of about 4in (10cm) long is left free. The line and tail are pinched together at an inch (2.5cm) or so from the material. The tail is now turned back and is passed over the pinched tail and line to form a loop. The tail now does two internal wraps

this end may be tied off with
a half hitch around the
main line

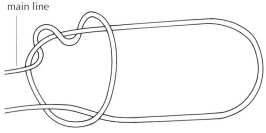

loop made by double internal wrap

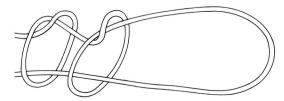

loop made as two half hitches around main line

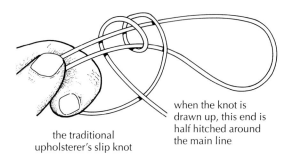

the traditional
upholsterer's slip knot

when the knot is
drawn up, this end is
half hitched around
the main line

Three patterns of slip knot.

around both lines inside the loop – it is
drawn tight to close down the loop. The
loop is drawn or pushed down to the surface of the material. Finally, the line is taken
round in another half hitch around the tail.

THE BOWLINE KNOT

The last of the general purpose basic knots
is one that is sometimes used, particularly
when you want to make an end loop with a

non-slipping, permanent position knot. It
is that old friend of mountaineers and
sailors, the bowline. It is the fact that it does
not slip or tighten up on itself that is important to them. In climbing, it is used to tie
the rope around the waist. If you fall and
are going to be held on the rope, you certainly do not want it to tighten up and saw
through your midriff! We use a little cou-
plet to guide us while we tie it. The line is
in a loop – around your waist, around a
spring coil, or through some material.

Make an underhand loop in the line –
this means that the main line emerging on
the far side of the loop iies under the line
from the climber's waist. Then – 'The rab-
bit (the tail) comes up out of its hole
(passes up through the loop), goes around
the tree (passes under the main line and
comes up above the loop), sees the fox and
bolts down its hole again (goes back down
through the loop)'. The tail is then drawn
tight and the knot forms exactly where the
loop was. Now whatever you pull, nothing
moves or slips. The greatest beauty of the
bowline is that despite any direction of tension you have subjected it to, by bending
back the main line and pushing up on the

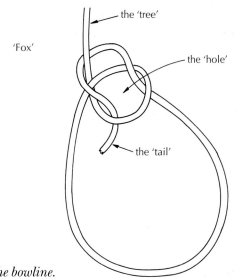

The bowline.

183

loop, the knot can be easily undone. A bow-line-tied loop makes a wonderful eye for a slip knot that stays tight while under tension, but which can be loosened and pushed apart with the greatest of ease.

Now we come to some knot applications that are exclusive to the upholsterer.

In the chapter on springing we detailed the procedure for tying in springs – starting on a second coil down, out to an angled 16 Imp tack, back to the top coil, and a running and a fixed knot on each spring. Let's now detail the two knots used.

Here comes the first problem! Across the upholstery literature you will find various names used for the spring lashing knots. Some authors even reverse the names used for the two primary knots. In general practice, the running knot is known as the lock loop; and the fixed knot is a common clove hitch. Some, however, call the lock knot the spring running knot and the clove hitch the spring fixed knot.

THE LOCK LOOP KNOT

The lock loop is so called because it is easily tied and it holds the spring in the required

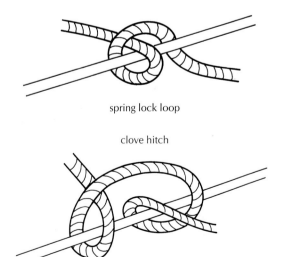

spring lock loop

clove hitch

Spring knots.

position while you make any adjustments. It can, however, be easily adjusted (hence my dislike of the name lock loop). The clove hitch is the one that finally ties the cord to the spring in a fixed position – and this knot is not so easily adjusted.

The lock loop is made by bringing the cord to the coil of the spring, passing it under the top coil, bending it back over the coil, looping it under the incoming main line, and then passing it back over the coil of the spring. By pulling the emerging line it 'locks' onto the top of the spring. However, by releasing the tension, the spring can be slid along the line to any desired position.

THE CLOVE HITCH KNOT

The clove hitch is made after the line has passed across the centre of the top coil of the spring. It passes over the outer coil, wraps around under the coil and is brought back up inside. It now wraps over its incoming line and is held in a pinched loop while the tail is again wrapped round the outside of the coil and is brought back up inside. The tail is now passed through the pinched loop and the tail is drawn tight. It will not slip, and has to be 'unpicked' to adjust the spring position.

KNOTS USED IN LASHING

Before moving on from springing, reference must again be made to chairs and settees where the front rail of the frame is lower than the rest of the seat frame. With some of these there is a row of short springs fixed to the top of the rail. With others there is a row of full length springs on a web just behind the front frame member. In both cases, a front edge to the seat platform is made by lashing a wire or a rattan cane to the front of the top coil of each spring.

The easiest way of lashing is first to tie a slip knot around the stiffener and the front edge of the top coil of the spring. This is

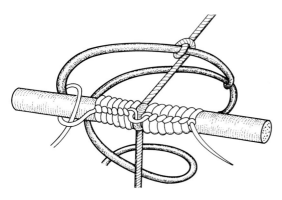

Cane front edge lashed to spring top.

drawn tight. The cord is then taken around the couple and is tied in a half hitch. A series of wraps and half hitches is made to give a lashing of a about ¾in (2cm) length. Some people tend to go over the top by doing a proper whipping with pulled-through internal loops and all. Don't bother, nobody will ever see how clever you are!

KNOTS USED IN BLIND AND THROUGH STITCHING

The second major area where upholsterers use a special set of knots is in the blind and through stitching used to shape the walls of stuffed over seats, so let's recap on the process.

The procedure is the same for both the blind and the through stitched rows. First, the long double-ended needle with the twine end (the short point) trailing is pushed into the pad on the stitching line on the wall. The needle's leading long point emerges on the top of the pad on the aiming mark line. The needle is then carefully pulled until the twine end has disappeared into the pad and is somewhere about halfway into the stuffing. The leading long point is pushed sideways so that the trailing short point is now aiming at the stitching line but about an inch (2.5cm) to the side of the entry point. The needle is

now pushed back down until the trailing point re-emerges on the stitching line. The needle is then drawn right out. The end of the twine is tied to the running line across the face of the stitching line. It is tied off with a slip knot which is tightened up by pulling on the running line.

The needle leading point is next pushed back into the pad at a point about an inch (2.5cm) further along the stitching line. Again, the twine is taken halfway in, the needle angled and the trailing point pushed back out again.

This time, as the point emerges the running line is wound twice or even three times around the needle trailing point. The needle is then pulled right out. As the running line is pulled through, the two twists made round the needle now tighten up into a knot. By pulling this knot down, the hessian of the wall is pulled back against the hair (and the hair inside the pad is pulled towards the wall). The line is pulled until the face of the wall is vertical to the side of the seat frame.

The through stitches are made in a very similar manner. The difference here is that the whole needle is taken right through

Blind stitch knotting.

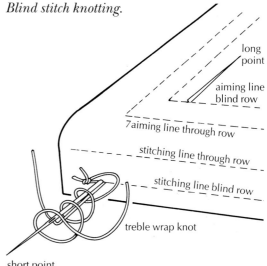

the pad from the stitching line to the aiming line and the needle is drawn clear of the top of the pad. The trailing end of the needle re-enters the aiming line about an inch (2.5cm) to the side of the point of emergence, pointing towards the stitching line to reappear about an inch along from the initial entry point. Again, it is tied off with a slip knot and is drawn tight.

Now there is a slight variation. The next entry is an inch along the stitching line and the leading point exits an inch along the aiming line from where the last re-entry was made. The needle is drawn right through and is moved back along the aiming line to be reinserted at the previous re-entry point; that is, it makes a back stitch which is locked by the double wrap. (*See* pages 104–6 for pictures and drawings.)

STITCHES

When we move on to the calico and finishing fabric stage we need to call on needle and thread, and develop more commonplace sewing skills. Very, very occasionally we may find use for conventional straight shank sewing or darning needles, but most of our seamstress work is done with curved mattress needles.

The actual hand needlework we do is all based around three forms of stitching – blind, slip or ladder, and lock – but we also need to be able to control a sewing machine. Most people can use a machine, but many fewer can actually control them! Before you get too far into upholstery a lesson or two in how to set up a machine, load bobbins, adjust tensions (absolutely vital), and changing stitch size are strongly recommended.

HAND SEWING

Let's deal first with hand sewing. Almost all our work revolves around mattress needles. These are 2 or 3in (5–7.6cm) long needles

of ordinary sewing needle diameters, but they are curved into near semi-circles. They enable you to work from the surface, penetrate the material, and then re-emerge from the surface. You can make a small stitch into, say, a piece of braiding, enter the main material (even when it is backed by a frame member), make a long tack and then re-emerge to make another small tack in the braiding. The small surface tacks are almost invisible but the braid is held firmly in place.

There are two hand sewing jobs that we have to undertake regularly. The first is the tacking or sewing in of pleats or folds on the front corners of seats. Sewing is not always necessary, but it does add permanence and 'finish'.

The second is the very tedious but unavoidable task of the sewing on of back and underarm panels on most armchairs and settees. The two side seams are always sewn, and occasionally the top seam.

There are then many odd jobs – facings and inserts into arm fronts; joining on a platform cloth on an underseat; fixing a particular piece of braid or cord; joining a folded edge. In almost all of these cases we use a blind slip or ladder stitch. This really is a simple process, but there are a few points to note.

Ladder Stitching
A length of ladder stitching starts with a small tack under a fold of the material. This tack is locked in, fixing the tail, with a slip knot around the running line. The needle then enters into the fold of one material, travels along inside the fold for a distance of ¼in (6mm) and then emerges out through the surface. From here, it is taken straight across into the fold of the second material, again travels ¼in (6mm) and re-emerges before re-entering the first material. The line continues. When the thread is pulled up the two folds are drawn together. Obviously by adjusting the entry points on

The many stitched seams on a typical chair.

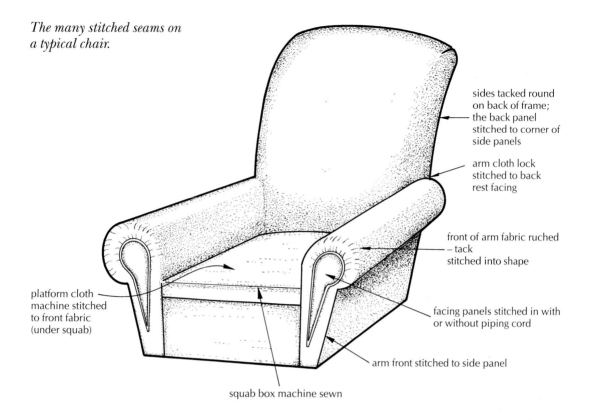

sides tacked round on back of frame; the back panel stitched to corner of side panels

arm cloth lock stitched to back rest facing

front of arm fabric ruched – tack stitched into shape

platform cloth machine stitched to front fabric (under squab)

facing panels stitched in with or without piping cord

arm front stitched to side panel

squab box machine sewn

the folds of the materials the amount of drawing together can be controlled. Also the tightness of the seam can be adjusted by angling the thread across the gap between the two folds. Instead of going straight across, the second stitch can be started slightly back from the emergence on the first fold. On very coarse weave materials the length of stitches can be increased, and up to ⅜in (1cm) is acceptable.

In dressmaking, pieces of material are often pinned together before being sewn (by either machine or hand methods). Tacking pins can also be used in upholstery. Our tacking pins, known as skewers, are large – 3 or 4in (7.6–10cm) in length and have an easy grip eye at the end. However, they are not always helpful; they are so big that they may limit the amount of tensioning 'adjustment' that you can make when drawing two folds together.

The Lock Stitch

There are times when you join two edges that could later be subject to some loading. A typical situation is the butting between the covering on the top of the arm of a chair and the cover of the seat back or wing. Here you could still use a slip stitch, but what happens if the thread later breaks at some point down its length? The whole seam could become loose. The answer here is a lock stitch where each tack is ended with a half hitch. Obviously the stitch is made as deep as possible in the fold or seam so that it does not show.

A sophistication of the lock stitch is used where the whole row of stitching is later to be covered. In many applications you could use a row of upholstery tacks, but these may not be as effective in trying to deal with curves and folds. Upholstery tacks are also not very good in gripping open-weave hessians. The device now used is a locking back

Upholsterer's stitches.

a locking back stitch uses a double wrap similar to that used in blind stitching

a French knot – a secure lock to end a row of stitches

simple slip stitch pulling two seams together with semi-circular mattress needle

lock stitch – the loop of the knot passes through the edges of both pieces of fabric; the knot is a simple half hitch

stitch. In fact, this is built up in a manner that is very similar to that used in blind stitching the side walls. Using a mattress needle, each stitch is a back stitch and the running line is double wrapped around the needle (as in the twine around the long needle in blind stitching).

It is worth noting at this point that when fitting compound curved facing inserts onto the front of chair arms and similar, slip-stitch sewing in enables you to mould the fabric to almost any shape.

Stitching on Trims and Piping

As we saw in the chapter on fitting the finishing fabric, there are times when you wish to add various forms of trim. Some of these may be hand-sewn in place.

The first to be fitted will be piping or flanged cords. These may be incorporated to edge the top and side of the back panel. They may be used on the front edge of the wing of wing chairs, and they are frequently found edging inset panels on the front of stuffed arms.

Flanged cord or piping can be fitted in a number of ways. The first, and probably the most simple, is to tack the cord onto an edge – say where the side panel wraps around the back of the frame – with 10 ordinary tacks and then to sew the folded-over edges of the back panel onto the flange of the cord. The second method is to pin the cord in place and then sew the back through the cord to the tacked down, wrapped round edge of the side panel.

The third method is the one fancied by more experienced upholsterers who can cut and make up to exact measurements. Here, the back panel and the side pieces are cut to size, and are pinned up with the flanged cord pinned into the seams. The cord is also taken across and pinned to the material at the head of the back. The pinned seams are now sewn on a machine, leaving a tacking margin all around the piece. The back is now positioned starting with the head of the back which is tacked in place through the flange of the top cord onto the top of the frame. The side panels are then drawn round and tacked to the front of the arms, making sure that the

cord down the side of the back panel sits neatly on the apex of the corners of the frame. Finally, the bottom of the back and side panels is wrapped under the frame and tacked down.

This sequence will be modified according to the format of the chair that you are working on, and will be particularly dependent upon the style of the top of the arms and the fitting of the side panels.

There will be times when you cannot obtain a flanged cord that precisely matches your colour requirements, but you may find an unflanged cord – this will have to be sewn on. It is advisable first to fit all panels and sew all necessary seams. The cord is now fixed by parting the strands slightly and sewing the under cord of the plaited braid through to the materials using a lock stitch.

The braids and tasselled fringes used to finish edges and to hide rows of nails are usually held on with adhesives (Copydex) and gimp pins (*see* Chapter 11). To improve the fixing, some upholsterers tack stitch their braids on. This is done by taking tiny stitches around loops of the braid with a long slip-stitch inside the underlying material.

MACHINE SEWING

We have already seen how more experienced upholsterers may use machines to speed up considerably the re-covering process. There are, however, at least two stages where we all need them, and these were noted in earlier chapters. Let's just remind ourselves of these and recap on a few points.

First, where the seat of a chair has a squab cushion, the fabric actually covering the platform of the main seat is not seen. Both to avoid wasting expensive upholstery fabrics and to provide extra strength, this area is often covered with a coarse platform cloth. The usual arrangement is for the fabric which faces the front of the seat frame to wrap over the top and to meet the platform

Various trims and pipings: home made flanged pipings on Dralon and tapestry; gold commercial flanged rope plait piping; various grades of rope plait piping; two coils of braids, one scalloped; fringed braid.

cloth some 6in (15cm) in under the seat squab. This hides the joint, yet allows the cloth to move and adjust to loading. Obviously the seam between fabric and platform is subject to considerable stresses; hence the seam needs to be particularly sound.

One good way of making this joint is to put the fabric and platform cloth end to end with the edges overlapping by about ¾in (2cm). A line of machine stitching is then taken through the overlap. A tuck is now taken in the joined piece so that the sewn join is folded in. A line of stitching is taken about ⅛in (3mm) in from the edge of the fold. The material is then turned over and again a line of stitching is applied just in from the exposed fold. An alternative is to place the materials on top of each other. Sew a seam and then double fold the seam in and again sew through the whole.

Woven braids and cords add finish to a piece of furniture. On the other hand, they can make some items look too ornate, yet a plain sewn edge would not be good enough. An ideal way of overcoming this problem is to make up a piping of the same fabric as used to cover the chair. There is also the option of a piping made in some suitable contrasting material.

The text books tell us that the material used to make piping should always be cut on the bias – that is, with the threads diagonal

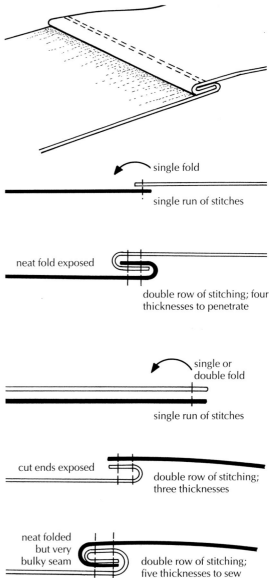

(Above) *Joining platform cambric to finishing fabric.*

A piece of strong buckram forms an ideal seat squab platform. This also saves some more expensive tapestry finishing fabric.

to the length of the strip of material. There are some fabrics where this does make a better job with less distortion or wrinkles, and it does give a stronger sewing edge to the flange. However, many upholstery fabrics will make very good piping when cut along the warp or weft, and often this is much more economical.

Strips of the material 2in (5cm) wide are cut and the ends of several pieces may then be sewn together to provide a continuous length. The strip is then folded around a length of piping cord and the flange is pinned together. A single-sided foot is fitted onto the sewing machine so that the row of stitches can be made tight against the side of the piping cord. It really is very simple.

A great deal of the machine work done in conjunction with upholstery is facilitated by using the single-sided zipper foot. Many of the machine-sewn seams are made against flanged cord or home-made piping.

The Sewing Machine Itself

If you intend to do a lot of upholstery I would strongly recommend keeping an eye on local auctions. Old Singer industrial machines often go for about £15, they are almost indestructible, and however old they are, parts can still be obtained from any Singer shop. You will be able to acquire readily any of the variety of feet that you require and these and a few spare shuttle bobbins will only cost you one or two pounds. Make sure that you also get a supply of heavy duty upholstery needles.

Only very rarely do these old machines go wrong, and if they do the shop will advise on how to contact a service agent. You can do most of the adjustments you ever have to yourself.

The first essential is to keep the shuttle mechanism clean and a little air puffer brush for camera lenses is very useful. Secondly, keep the moving parts oiled – there are usually holes with signs printed on the machine which tell you to 'Oil'.

Beyond this, it is all a matter of adjustment. You can tell when the adjustment is wrong by the look of the stitches. They should be evenly tensioned on both sides of the fabric and the loop 'knotting' the top and bottom threads together should be buried in the middle of the fabric. On most machines there are just two adjustments for achieving the correct tension, and in fact you very rarely have to touch one of these.

On the side of some shuttles (the part under the hatch below the needle) which holds the cotton bobbin there is a tiny screw. This controls the tension on the cotton coming from the bobbin. This one is normally left alone.

The main adjustment is on the pillar above the needle. This is the set of spring-loaded plates through which the cotton passes. There is a knurled knob on the front of this and by turning the knob you can adjust the tension on the cotton going to the needle.

Put in a piece of heavy calico, for example, and make a row of stitches. If, when you look at the run of stitches, the two sides are not even, then the tension on the cotton is not right. If there is a festoon of hanging loops on the underside then the tension on the cotton from the top was far too slack. Turn the knurled knob clockwise two or three turns. If on the underside there are no hanging loops but the thread is straight and taut, then the top cotton is only slightly under-tensioned. Try a half-turn clockwise on the knurled knob.

Take another run on the calico. If the underside is alright but the top thread is taut, then there is a little too much tension on the top cotton. Slacken the knurled knob with a turn anti-clockwise. Take a run on the calico once more.

On the initial setting up you may have to make several runs and adjustments before you get it right. Once it is alright on the calico, try it through a couple of layers of thick upholstery fabric.

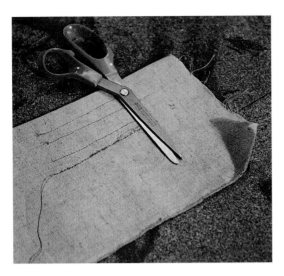

Machine stitching showing the underside of the fabric. The top row shows the machine tension just too tight. The next row is just about right with equal loops on both faces. The third row has the machine tension a little too loose, whilst the lower row has very little tension on the machine and results in festoons of loops.

However badly the machine ran when you first tried it, it usually comes down to tension adjustment. Only rarely is there a mechanical defect. If it did not run at all,

suspect the wiring; there is probably a loose connection – a burnt-out motor is also virtually unknown.

Lest you do not know, there is another adjustment on all machines. On the drive-end pedestal will be a lever against a scale. This varies the length of stitch, but otherwise has no effect upon the running adjustment. Incorporated into this, or as a separate lever there is usually a means of making the machine sew forwards or backwards. However, not all the older industrial machines have a reversing facility.

If you do try to find an old industrial machine at auction, do not bother with one on a nice cast-iron table – you will probably be bidding against someone who wants the table for the garden and who will be prepared to pay fancy money! (Of course, they might give you the mechanical parts for spares!)

I have my own old clunker of an industrial machine; it cost me £18 and I cherish it dearly. It does not blink at several thicknesses of upholstery fabric and even a zip fastener to sew through. I bought it because my wife would not allow me anywhere near her all-dancing, singing, lights flashing electronic wizard – which would probably have let me down anyway!

An old industrial Singer. They go on forever and spares are readily available. This was bought on its table for £18 at a local auction. It will sew through ten or so layers of upholstery fabric.

15

The Bare Essentials
Tools And Materials

Setting up an upholstery studio is not an expensive operation. There are no heavy machines required, and although a few power tools and maybe a small lathe will be of use in carcass restoration, most of your equipment will consist of simple hand tools.

Neither do you need great stocks of materials. Few of us carry much finishing fabric; it is usually bought a few metres at a time as required. Of course, there will always be that odd length that you just couldn't resist at a sale that now awaits the right frame, but the only quantities that you may have about will be webbing, hair, hessian and calico. It certainly pays to buy webbing by the roll and hair in as large a bag as you can get (usually 28lbs).

TOOLS

In this chapter, we will review the basic tools and look at a recommended starting kit. We will also recap on the various materials that we have been using so as to provide a reference summary.

Most of the tools that you need can be bought at the local ironmongers. In each case in the following tool lists, the optimum price/quality option is noted. Your kit will fit into a mechanic's toolbox, and this will be our starting point.

You need a box that is about 18in long by 10in wide by 10in deep (46 × 25 × 25cm). A suitable one will be found in most big DIY stores. The strong hard plastic boxes are more use-friendly than the metal ones. A box with fold-out trays will enable you to keep different types of tool separate. One particularly important thing is the hinges of the lid – simple plastic hinges soon give way, so look for those with a metal pin through the centre. The other element is the catch. This does need to be sound and to stay shut until you open it – in fact, one which can be padlocked is useful.

Into the box will go the following basic tools:

Tool	*Best Source for the Quality Needed*
Rubber or plastic head mallet	Market stall
Ripping chisel (*see* notes)	Upholstery supplier
Tack or nail claw	DIY store
Carpenter's pincers	Tool store
Hammer with claw	Market stall
Webbing stretcher	Upholstery store
Tack Hammer, magnetic (*see* notes)	Tool store
Nail punches $\frac{1}{16}$, $\frac{1}{8}$ and $\frac{1}{4}$in	Market stall
'Stanley' knife and blades	Market stall
Scissors, strong and sharp	Drapers

Measuring tapes (steel and cloth)	Market stall
Felt tip markers	Stationers
Emergency Superglue	Good model shop
An old magnet for picking up dropped tacks	from a broken loudspeaker

You will then add the following upholstery items:

Item	Best source
Tailor's chalk	Drapers
Various darning needles	Drapers
Tufting needle (buttoning)	Drapers (some)
Copydex	Ironmongers
Spray adhesive	Ironmongers (some)
Long bayonet upholstery needles 10 and 12in doublepoint	Upholstery store

Mattress needles 3 to 6in	Upholstery store Some drapers
Spring needles 5 and 6in	Upholstery store
Skewers (upholstery pins)	Upholstery store
Regulator needle 12in	Upholstery store
Upholstery sewing machine needles	Singer shop
Needle threader?	Drapers
A couple of stout thimbles	Drapers
Length of felt as needle/skewer roll	Drapers

For modern upholstery you may care to add a heavy duty staple gun – this needs to come from a tool store as it is a model beyond the range of the DIY stores.

Market stalls provide good value on average quality tools. For upholstery you do not need the best quality long-life items. The prices in big DIY stores can be beaten if you shop around but they do offer value and

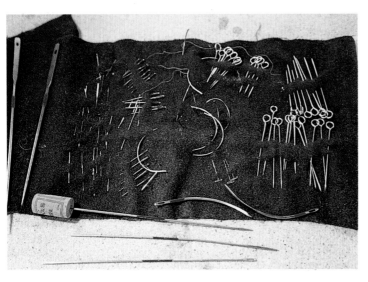

Needle roll with regulators, long upholstery needles, curved spring needles, semi-circular mattress needles, various large and small-eyed sewing/ darning needles, and various lengths of skewers for temporary tacking.

convenience. Unfortunately, some of the specific upholstery items have to be bought at specialist outlets – some of these are very reasonably priced, but some are extortionate (one marks up by well over 100 per cent).

Magnetic tack hammers can cost £12 to £25 from such outlets, yet some ironmongers and tool stores do a perfectly serviceable Draper brand tack hammer (with a nice hickory wood handle) for under a tenner. Webbing stretchers too have to be bought from specialists – or made for yourself. The same item can be variously priced from £4.50 to £14.

Ripping chisels have a chisel edge and a cranked blade; these are only available from upholstery suppliers. However, my tool box also contains three sizes of homemade 'ripping chisel' which were produced by sharpening up the tips of old screwdrivers on a grinding wheel.

There are several particular points worth noting regarding tools. Nothing appears to blunt scissors faster than upholstery! Get two or three pairs, and assign each to specific uses. The modern, domestic stainless steel scissors are a waste of time. I am afraid that you will have to spend a lot more money, and £10 to £15 each should be your minimum budget. If it is any consolation, one of my students is a hairdresser and she has to pay £160 a pair for her scissors! Get one particularly robust pair for webbing, piping and multi-layers of tapestry; and keep another pair of tailor's scissors sharp for finishing fabric. A pair of small, sharp-pointed scissors is useful for unpicking seams.

Now a point of caution. The long double-ended upholstery and the curved spring needles can be obtained with plain round or bayonet points. The bayonets are much stronger and more effective, but they are very sharp – and lurk just waiting for you to rummage in your toolbox! To avoid accidental injury, keep the points of all needles pushed into wine bottle corks.

WORKING FURNITURE

A good strong workbench (or kitchen table) is useful. You need something solid to hammer on. A useful item is a pair of trestles. These can be made up from MDF, chipboard or scrap shuttering ply. They need a recess in the top into which you slot the legs of the piece of furniture that you want to work on.

My trestles are 36in (91cm) long, and with the recess give a working height of 28in (71cm). Obviously you need to make them of a height to suit yourself, and by making one 2 inches longer than the other they can be conveniently stacked.

In the chapter on rushing, and again referred to in caning, is a platform trolley.

A pair of home-made trestles are very useful as they can accommodate any piece of furniture (and be moved out into the garden on sunny days!).

Workshop trestle.

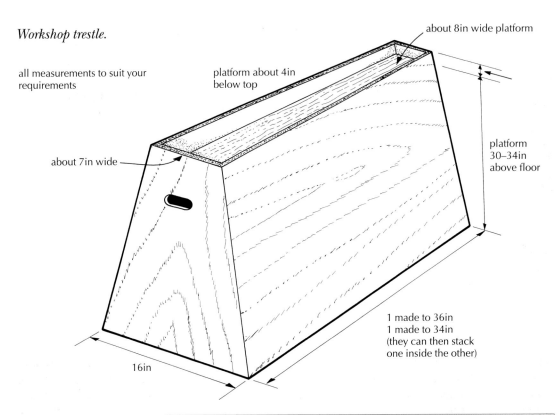

all measurements to suit your requirements

about 8in wide platform

platform about 4in below top

platform 30–34in above floor

about 7in wide

1 made to 36in
1 made to 34in
(they can then stack
one inside the other)

16in

Tacks				
Pin sizes mm	Grade	Kit items	Equivalent	Main uses
6	Fine		¼in Fine	Silks – finishing
10	Fine	*	⅜in Fine	Finishing fabrics
10	Improved	*	⅜in Imp	Calico
13	Ordinary		½in Fine	Calico
13	Improved	*	½in Imp	Hessian and webbing
16	Ordinary		⅝in Fine	Multiple layers
16	Improved	*	⅝in Imp	Spring anchoring
20	Fine		¾in	"
25	Fine		1in	"

Gimp pins
Gimp coloured in 10,* 13, 16mm braiding

*Upholstery twines.
Clockwise from lower left: soft
piping cord; spring lacing
cord; packets of grade 4 and 6
upholstery twine for all
stitching and shaping.*

This uses four big castor wheels (again bought in a box of junk at auction). This piece gets more use than almost everything else in the studio. Again make of all scrap materials, but set the height and platform size to suit yourself. Incidentally, the basic trolley is very useful for moving heavy pieces of furniture around – even pianos!

MATERIALS

Let's now look at the upholstery materials that we have been using throughout the chapters of this book.

TACKS

First the tacks. Almost exclusively we use blued-steel tacks and steel gimp pins as detailed in the table opposite.

The starred items are those normally carried in your kit.

Tacks can be bought in 250g packs at the local ironmongers, but you could need four packs for a big settee. Bulk quantities can be obtained at good woodworking and upholstery stores. Here they are available in ½, 2½, and 10kg packs and working with the 2½kg size offers huge savings over the small DIY packs.

CORDS AND TWINES

Next there are the twines and cords. Three cords are recommended.

First there is the general twine for stuffing loops, shaping stitching, sewing in springs, and so on. The most widely used trade name is Barbour twine. It is a waxed linen cord and comes either by the yard/metre or in balls of ¼kg (approximately ½lb) weight. Obviously whole balls are much, much cheaper than cut lengths. There are three grades readily available – buying by weight, you get much more of the lighter 3 cord than you do the medium-weight 4 cord or the thickest 6 cord. While a little of the 3 cord might be useful for sewing up hessians and so on, we now exclusively use the 6 cord. An alternative is a range of flax twines – these are about one third of the price of the linen Barbour, but are nowhere as nice to work with, and are certainly not as strong. A ball will do several average chairs.

The second cord is the much heavier spring lacing cord or laycord. This is again sold by the yard/metre or in 500g balls. Its sole use is in lashing the tops of springs so that they will not move in anything but a vertical plane. There are no worthwhile alternatives. One ball will deal with several chairs and settees. Note: working with this can be very hard on soft hands.

The last cord is used much less frequently – I think I am still only on my second ball. It is available in three thicknesses: 3, 4, and 5mm and is the cord used to form pipings. It is cheaper, softer and much more pliable that the other upholstery cords.

WEBBING AND TAPES

The basis of the platform which supports all traditional stuffed or sprung upholstery is a lattice of cotton or jute webbing. Modern chairs may use a polypropylene alternative or some elasticated material such as Pirelli rubber or elasticated polypropylene.

Early furniture used a plain brown, 100 per cent jute fibre webbing. This is still available in 2in and 2⅛in widths but although it is strong it does tend to stretch and lose shape. Today, most webbing lattices are built up of 'Old English Black & White' webbing which is made of a cotton/jute mix. Most is in rolls of 16m of 50mm width (nominally 2in), and although the quality is satisfactory you can occasionally find supplies of true 2in (often 30yd length) which is slightly heavier and is less likely to pull off the tacks if over-stretched.

Most retailers sell rolls or cut lengths. One roll equals several chairs, but may only do one settee.

The other 'tape' you will occasionally need is a vulcanized backtacking strip. It is obtained by the yard/metre or in 1.4kg coils of about 600ft (200m) length (a lifetime's supply!) and is ⅛in wide. It is used for fixing and holding folded-over edges in place. It will, for instance, permit a back panel to be fitted without having to sew the margin along the top edge.

On top of the webbing is a platform of hessian or a set of sewn-in springs. Let's take the springs first.

SPRINGS

Early chairs were not sprung. In the nineteenth century we saw the development of coil springs and their later sophistication to double-cone coil springs. Subsequently there have been pocketed spring units; mesh top spring units; transverse tension springs; Pirelli webbing; sinuous springs; and so on. With the exception of separate cone springs and Pirelli webbing and similar, most spring units have to be made up for you by a supplier.

In this book, we have focused upon the double-cone coil springs. They are coppered against rusting. These are readily available at most upholstery suppliers; and a table of sizes and typical uses is given in Chapter 9 (page 116). Bought wholesale, they come in bundles of fifty, but are usually retailed by the piece and are not expensive.

HESSIANS

Hessian of one grade or another is used at two or three stages of the upholstery process. Basically, it will be the heavy-duty platform under the hair and then there is a lighter but close-woven skrim grade capping the stuffing. Hence, as there is a layer of hair over any springs, the springs will always be capped with a hessian platform.

As with all fabrics, hessian (a 100 per cent jute material) is supplied in widths using Imperial measures. Hence there are four basic widths – 36, 40, 54 and 72in. There are then various weights – 5, 7½, 10 and 12oz. The heaviest grade of hessian is a 12oz close-woven cloth used for heavy-duty platforms on large settees. From wholesalers, it can be obtained in rolls of 50 or 100m (at prices of 30 to 60p per metre for all but the heaviest grades). From upholstery suppliers, many drapers and other sources it may be bought in any length. Skrim (or scrim) is a finer weave of pure jute hessian, normally 40 or 72in widths and in either 185 or 290g weights. It can be more than twice the price of other hessians.

The actual widths/grades used will depend upon the specific application and the preferences of the upholsterer. For platforms under the hair most upholsterers prefer the 10oz grade (12oz for settees). Usually there is a lot less overall waste in using the wider materials.

For capping the hair, the hessian needs to be pliable so that it can be pulled and stitched into shape: the 7½oz grade is preferred for this. However, it also has to withstand the ravages of the regulator. Skrim is better designed for such use. If you do buy any skrim as well as ordinary hessian, clearly mark which is which. It is easy to get them confused and you could end up using the more expensive material where ordinary hessian would have done.

STUFFINGS

When it comes to the stuffing, you really have four choices. You can buy old furniture and hair-filled mattresses, remove the hair and wash it. It is a dusty, dirty job that must be done outside. Put the old hair into old pillow slips, sew up the tops and drop them in the industrial washing machine at the launderette. Proper horse hair is a wonderful material, with a feel and resilience that is unequalled and it washes to an as-new quality. What you buy as new horse hair today is a mix of horse hair and hog and may even contain cow's tail hair. Any form of hair is hard to find and expensive

and other than for an authentic restoration, it is probably not worth the cost and difficulty.

Then there are two vegetable 'hairs'. One is an untreated brown coir (coconut fibre), and the other is a black coated coir. The black, though slightly more expensive, is much more resilient and springy. One of its trade names is Filair. Filair is fire-resistant and is less than half the price of mixed natural hair. It is available at most upholstery suppliers in bags of ½, 1, 5 and 13kg. You will use a kilo on an average stuffed-over dining chair and 10kg plus on a settee.

It is also possible to buy sheets of pre-formed rubberized hair in 1 and 2in thicknesses and two levels of density. The beauty of this material is the ease with which you can produce beautifully squared platforms; however, it is usually supplied only in whole 72in by 36in sheets and you have to cut it to shape. It is not for the traditionalist!

WADDING

Once the hair has been capped with hessian skrim, it is normal to put on a layer of cotton felt or wadding. In earlier times, this often took the form of a blue/grey mix of waste materials – in fact, engineers used to use it for cleaning up oil spills, and for many years I knew it as 'engineer's cotton-waste'. Today, most upholsterers use a processed cotton wadding that is something like unrefined cotton wool. It is produced in rolls and is backed by a crimped, absorbent paper. Cotton felt is available in rolls or cut lengths. It is 27in wide and comes in two grades – 2½oz and 4oz. The thinner grade is a nominal 1½in thick and the 4oz almost 3in. However, both compress, and so it is almost meaningless to talk about 'thickness'. You can still obtain black cotton mix, but as this is compact it is not as easy to work with as the cotton felt.

Cotton felt or wadding is normally cut to the size of the top of the seat platform, and is only occasionally taken down the side walls. It smoothes out the surface, and torn-off scraps of felt can be used to level out any hollows. The edges are ragged out to smooth the transition to the side walls. Cotton felt is an important element in ensuring that the hair does not work through the finishing fabric. Obviously a hairy seat can be irritating!

Just occasionally, a thin back pad on a dining chair may be 'stuffed' by simply laying cotton felt on a strong canvas platform.

CALICOES AND OTHER MATERIALS

On top of the felt goes the calico layer. Calico is a 100 per cent cotton material. It is this that provides the platform for the finishing fabric. It also locks in place the felt and all the under layers. A good taut calico layer is essential if a firm seat is to be built. It is not, however, suitable for the final covering, as due to the nature of the cloth, it soils very easily.

Few materials show so much variation in price, and it is worthwhile shopping around for your calico. Market stalls can be a good source. Be careful, however, in trying to do direct price comparisons. There are many grades and weights of calico, and until your 'feel' becomes highly skilled, the grades are not always easy to recognize.

The weights used by upholsterers are typically (dependent upon who your supplier is): 2¼, 2½, 3¾, 4¾ to 5, 5½ and 6oz. The widths are 37, 40, 48 and 54in. The heaviest grade is an odd 71in wide. For most dining chairs 2½ or 3¾oz are quite satisfactory. For armchairs 3¾ is my standard, but for settees the heavier grades are chosen. Of course, these are only guidelines and for particular reasons you might move some distance up or down the scale.

There are other materials that we sometimes call upon to finish off the seat, for example the 100 per cent jute fibre buckram used under separate squabs; 100 per cent glazed cotton cambric which is feather-proof; cotton or twill platform linings; and a range of bottoming cloths.

Finally, on top of the calico a skin wadding is often used. This comes in book-folded pieces of some 11m long by 18in wide. It can usually also be bought in cut lengths. It may be left loose or tacked to the top of the calico with a couple of blasts of spray adhesive. Its main purpose is in hiding any wrinkles, folds or seams in the calico and it is normally cut to cover completely the calico and particularly any tack heads around the edges. It is rather like multi-layered fibrous tissue paper and is easy to cut to make a box joint, or to feather out where two pieces overlap.

To obtain a perfectly shaped squab you may wish to use a cut-to-shape/size pad of foam. Again, most upholstery suppliers have this available and will cut it to your template/dimensions. Make sure that any foam you use is fire-resistant – seat pads are the most vulnerable to a dropped cigarette end or a fire spark. Be very careful about buying foam off market stalls unless they specialize in fire-resistant upholstery materials.

Traditional squabs are often feather-filled. Again, there are two grades of filling available. One is curled poultry feathers which do not hold shape particularly well; it is, however, three times cheaper than the better quality feather and down mix.

Scatter and lumbar roll cushions can be feather, kapok or microfibre-filled. Again, these are materials that can be found in any upholsterer and some large department stores such as John Lewis.

And finally, of course, comes the finishing fabric where the range and choice is almost boundless and there are suppliers on every high street. Here your tastes may require the support of a very deep pocket! However, by the time that you get to this stage of your reupholstery project you will probably be so delighted with what you have done that you will be quite happy paying for just the right fabric!

Appendix I
Step Sequences for Typical Pieces

REUPHOLSTERING A DROP-IN PAD

1. Strip all old materials and bin them.
2. Remove all tacks.
3. Repair frame as necessary.
4. Fix lattice of webbing.
5. Tack on platform hessian.
6. Sew in stuffing loops.
7. Stuff hair over top surface.
8. Fix hessian skrim.
9. Cover with layer of cotton felt wadding.
10. Cover with calico.
11. Place layer of skin wadding.
12. Cover with finishing fabric.
13. Fix bottoming cloth.

REUPHOLSTERING A STUFFED-OVER DINING CHAIR (also carvers and bedroom chairs)

1. Strip all old material and bin it.
2. Remove all tacks.
3. Repair frame as necessary.
4. Clean and repolish frame.
5. Fix lattice of webbing on top of frame.
6. Fix platform hessian.
7. Sew in stuffing loops.
8. Stuff hair all over top.
9. Cover with skrim.
10. Shape with regulator.
11. Sew in blind and through stitching to shape.
12. Regulate to smooth finish.
13. Cover with cotton felt.
14. Fix calico.
15. Articulate and tension.
16. Make back corners.
17. Make front corners.
18. Stick on layer of skin wadding.
19. Measure and cut finishing fabric.
20. Tack on fabric, leaving corners.
21. Articulate and tension and drive home tacks.
22. Make rear corners.
23. Make front corners.
24. Trim edges of fabric.
25. Apply braiding or fringe.
26. Fix bottoming cloth.

REUPHOLSTERING A SEAT WITH SPRINGS (sprung library or saloon chair)

1. Strip all old materials.
2. Retain top cover as pattern (do not reuse).
3. Retain sample of each spring.
4. Remove all old tacks and staples
5. Check all joints.
6. Repair frame as necessary.
7. Clean and repolish.
8. Fix webbing under frame.
9. Place new springs.
10. Stitch base of springs to webbing.
11. Drive in spring anchor tacks.
12. Lace in all springs.
13. Tack on platform hessian.
14. Sew in stuffing loops.
15. Liberally stuff with hair.
16. Fix hessian skrim.
17. Regulate.
18. Blind and through stitches to shape pad and walls.
19. Regulate.

20. Cover with cotton felt.
21. Tack on calico.
22. Articulate, tension and fix.
23. Make rear corners.
24. Make front corners.
25. Build up back pad (*see* below).
26. Measure and cut finishing fabric.
27. Tack on fabric.
28. Articulate, tension and fix.
29. Make rear corners.
30. Make front corners.
31. Trim edges of finishing fabric.
32. Apply braid of fringe if required.
33. Cover underside.

REUPHOLSTERING BACK PAD ON DINING/SALOON CHAIRS

1. Tack in backing material.
2. Fix webbing or platform cloth.
3. Fix hessian.

For deep pads	*Shallow pads*
4. Sew in stuffing loops.	4. Cut and fix cotton felt.

5. Stuff with hair.
6. Cover with skrim (or muslin).
7. Regulate.
8. Cover with cotton felt.
9. Fix calico.
10. Cut and fix front finishing fabric.
11. Braid all necessary edges.

REUPHOLSTERING A STUFFED-OVER CONCAVE SEATED STOOL

1. Strip away all materials and bin.
2. Remove all tacks.
3. Repair and repolish frame as necessary.
4. Fix (tensioning) four lengths of webbing front to back.
5. Weave in two cross webbings both going under the two centre front to back webs. Only hand tension these runs.
6. Fix platform hessian.
7. Sew in stuffing loops.

8. Stuff with hair.
9. Cover with fine skrim.
10. Regulate to required shape.
11. Cover with layer of cotton wadding.
12. Tack on calico cover.
13. Articulate, tension and fix.
14. Cut and fix top fabric.
15. Trim edges.
16. Braid all edges.

REUPHOLSTERING A NURSING, PRIE OR OTHER SPRUNG-SEATED CHAIR WITH SPRUNG BACK

1. Strip away all old materials.
2. Retain top cover as pattern.
3. Retain one seat and one back spring as pattern.
4. Remove all tacks.
5. Check joints and repair as necessary.
6. Web underside of seat frame.
7. Web the rear of the back.
8. Stitch springs to seat webbing.
9. Put in seat lacing tacks.
10. Lace in seat springs.
11. Drive home lacing tacks.
12. Put in back lacing tacks.
13. Lace in light gauge springs in seat back.
14. Knock home seat lacing tacks.
15. Cover seat with skrim.
16. Cover top face of back with skrim.
17. Sew in stuffing loops on seat.
18. Sew in stuffing loops on back.
19. Stuff seat, building up all edges.
20. Cover seat stuffing with 7½oz hessian.
21. Regulate seat.
22. Blind and through stitch seat to shape.
23. Stuff back, building up edges.
24. Cover stuffing with hessian.
25. Regulate.
26. Blind and through stitch back to shape.
27. Sew through seat and tension to level centre.
28. Sew through back.

29. Sew in second layer of stuffing loops if required to deepen seat.
30. Second stuff seat.
31. Fix second layer of stuffing on seat.
32. Cover seat with skrim.
33. Regulate.
34. Through stitch to required shape.
35. Cut and place cotton felt across the seat area.
36. Feather wadding over front and side edges.
37. Tack calico over seat.
38. Articulate and tension retacking as you go.
39. Make rear corners in calico and tack home.
40. Make front corners around legs and tack home.
41. Cut and place cotton felt across whole face of back.
42. Feather felt over side and top and bottom of the back.
43. Tack calico cover on back.
44. Articulate, tension and retack calico to back.
45. Cut shape, make corners in calico around head of chair.
46. Tack down back calico around back frame members at seat area.
47. Cut and glue in place (spray adhesive) skin wadding over top and sides of seat.
48. Test old seat fabric for fit and size.
49. If all right use old fabric as cutting pattern for new seat cloth.
50. Tack on seat fabric.
51. Articulate.
52. Tack down front edge and make front corners.
53. Articulate towards back.
54. Cut rear corners around back frame.
55. Tension and tack down rear of seat fabric.
56. Articulate and tack home sides.
57. Repeat steps 49 to 54 for fabric for facing of back.
58. Cut and tack home fabrics around head of back integrating piping or flanged cord where required.
59. Articulate downwards down face of back.
60. Tension and tack home bottom of panel.
61. Tension and tack home sides of back facing fabric.
62. Tack on piping or flanged cord all around sides and top edge of rear of back (if required).
63. Fix top of backing panel at head using edging strip.
64. Fold panel over and draw down and tack under the frame.
65. Fold in side seams of backing panel and pin in place.
66. Slip-stitch sew backing panel seams to flanged piping or direct to back corner of facing panel if cord is not being used.
67. Slip-stitch folded seams on front corners of seat.
68. Slip-stitch to finish any detail on head (Prie chairs).
69. Glue and tack with gimp pins any fringe or braiding around bottom edge of seat block.
70. Slip-stitch any cord being applied to any other seams.
71. Sit in chair and dream!

Obviously a similar sequence applies if the backrest is not sprung. Here the web would be applied to the face in step 7.

REUPHOLSTERING A CHAISE LONGUE, DAYBED AND SIMILAR

1. Strip all old material.
2. Retain seat and arm facing fabric as patterns.
3. Retain one seat and one arm spring as patterns.
4. Bin remainder of stripped materials.
5. Remove all old tacks.
6. Check joints and repair as necessary.

7. Add extra back timber if required.
8. Clean and polish frame.

Work on Seat Platform
9. Fix webbing under seat (probably double runs).
10. Place springs.
11. Sew in springs to webbing.
12. Fix spring lashing tacks.
13. Lash springs tight.
14. Cover springs with platform hessian.
15. Stitch in stuffing loops.
16. Stuff seat (possibly with dug roll round edge).
17. Cover with hessian or skrim.
18. Regulate.
19. Three blind and two through stitched rows to form outside walls.
20. Through stitch seat to flatten.
21. Second skrim layer if required (Repeat Steps 17–19).

Work on Back Rail
22. Tack hessian strip on back rail.
23. Stitch in stuffing loops.
24. Stuff rail generously with hair.
25. Cover with light hessian.
26. Through to back stitches to shape.
27. Regulate.

Work on Arm/Head Rest
28. Web the outside of the arm to form spring platform.
29. Tack strip of hessian on arm spring platform.
30. Place light gauge springs.
31. Fix arm top springs with U nails.
32. Sew in face springs.
33. Place lashing nails for all arm springs.
34. Lash springs and drive home lashing tacks.
35. Cover arm top and face with hessian (tacking into valley under head roll).
36. Sew in stuffing loops.
37. Stuff with hair bringing hair round front edge to form roll. Leave valley under head roll.

38. Cover with skrim forming front roll as you go and tacking back to frame under head roll.
39. Stitch roll into shape.
40. Through stitch through face to firm.
41. Regulate whole arm.
    Work on seat platform.
42. Cover whole seat with layer of heavy grade cotton felt.
43. Cut and tack on calico.
44. Articulate and tension calico.
45. Form corners and fit around legs and arm and rail supports.
46. Drive home all tacks on calico.

Work on Back Rail
47. Cover rail with wrap round of light cotton felt.
48. Cover with calico tensioning and fixing as you go.

Work on Arm/Head Rest
49. Cover top, face and roll front with medium cotton wadding.
50. Cut and tack on calico cover. Through stitch from back of rest to form head roll.
51. Articulate calico and tension, working out from valley.
52. Fit calico around rear rail abutment and rear of frame.
53. Finish front corners of calico fitting around side frame member maintaining roll round front edges.
54. Drive home all arm tacks.

Finishing
55. Cut and fix a layer of skin wadding over all calico areas. Tack wadding in place and make glued corner joints with spray adhesive.
56. Place on all retained panels of old fabric and check their suitability as cutting patterns now the piece is restuffed.
57. Measure and cut finishing fabric for all panels, carefully placing to ensure

pattern position, nap and working edges.

58. Place and tack finishing fabric to seat area. Leave all corners loose.
59. Articulate and tension.
60. Make the corners round the outboard end of seat platform.
61. Fold and fit to front legs.
62. Articulate and finally tension from front to back.
63. Make corners around back support and head frame members.
64. Drive home all seat tacks.
65. Tack fabric onto back rail using edging strip to form back edge (you may on occasions decide to form folded edge on front of rail).
66. Fold and make corner round outboard end of rail (some through stitching with matching cotton may be required).
67. Shape and fix fabric around rail abutment with arm rest.
68. Articulate and tension.
69. Drive home all rail tacks.
70. Determine whether you will use a tacking strip or through stitching in valley under head roll.
71. Tack fix fabric over head roll and down face of arm/headrest (possibly using tacking strip).
72. Sew through from back to pull down fabric into valley if adopting stitch through forming.
73. Articulate and tension up and down.
74. Fix under outside of head roll.
75. Cut fabric to fit around the two side members of the arm, draw bottom of fabric tight and fix to outside of lower member of seat frame.
76. Cut fabric to fit around back rail abutment and tack down to rear face of arm side member. Build up the

roll edge as you go. Cut darts to assist in rounding curves particularly on sides of head roll. Carefully make rouches or multi-radial folds as you round face of roll.

77. Repeat shaping and tacking down of step 76 on the front face of arm/headrest.
78. Cut, fold and fix fabric around front leg.
79. Cut panel of fabric for outside of arm/headrest.
80. Fix top edge of fabric under head roll using tacking strip.
81. Draw fabric under end of frame and tack down.
82. Draw side edges around frame members and tack down to face.
83. Decide what method of infilling you will use on arm faces – here we will follow the piping or flanged cord route.
84. Measure and make two pieces of piping of required length.
85. Tack piping inside hollow careful to get good round shape.
86. Cut to shape and infill centre of hollows with layers of skin wadding.
87. Make paper pattern of fabric required for infill.
88. Cut fabric to pattern allowing a folding/sewing margin; make relieving darts to assist folding.
89. Pin infill in place, folding under edges as you go.
90. Sew panels in using hidden slip stitches through base of piping and edge of fold.
91. Cut and fit braid along lower edge of back rail.
92. Cut and fit fringe (if required) around lower edge of seat platform.

Appendix II
Sources of Help and Materials

If you wish to extend your knowledge, start with your local library as they should have some books on upholstery. Look particularly for *Upholstery, A Complete Course* by David James. This work was designed as a text book for those interested in obtaining trader-based qualifications (City and Guilds etc.). A useful feature is the sectional drawings of most types of chair and settee; they are especially helpful if you wish to make your own carcasses.

David James has also produced two video cassettes, which give step-by-step instruction on simple stuffed upholstery. One looks at drop-in pads and the other at deeper stuffed over seats. The videos are very useful if you have difficulty in folding corners.

Should your chairs need major surgery, then there are a number of good books. A useful starting point is *Furniture Restoration – a Manual of Techniques* by Graham Usher, published by The Crowood Press. If you are faced with the need to turn new members there are two books: first *The Complete Spindle Turner* by Hugh O'Neill; and the other *Woodturning for Repair and Restoration* by Ian Wilkie. Both are published by The Crowood Press.

Today, many of the adhesives, stains and polishes are available in some larger DIY superstores. Not surprisingly High Wycombe, the home of English furniture making, is a good centre for anything to do with upholstery. For carcass repair tools and materials, Isaac Lord of Desborough Road is a good starting point, and just around the corner from them is T.R. Bush at 19 Desborough Avenue. Bush's supply webbing, hessians, hair, springs, etc. and do offer a mail order service. In the area, there are also some excellent fabric warehouses.

If you search Yellow Pages for your area you will usually find one or two local suppliers; but check out their prices! As mentioned on page 10, it pays to keep your eyes open as you drive around and also enquire from local antique furniture dealers.

Petco, with warehouses in Long Eaton, Brierley Hill, Bridgend, and St Austel are useful. They will do mail order on quantities of materials. They are good on foams and modern types of springing. They can also supply leather and ready-made carcasses, but, for reasons unknown, they do not do basic upholstery twines.

One of the best suppliers in the country is D.L. Forster of Great Dunmow. It supplies the full range of upholstery requirements, but it operates very strictly on trade, bulk orders, only.

Several of the better fabric shops can supply most of the cloths from hessian upwards; many also stock ranges of pipings and trimmings. If all else fails you cannot beat a trip to John Lewis in Oxford Street, London – if you cannot get it through them, then you cannot get it!

Cane and rush can be obtained from The Cane Warehouse in Westport, Somerset, but several of the larger craft warehouses also stock all standard items.

Do not accept it when a local trader says that something is no longer available. There is nothing that I have wanted that could not be found somewhere, but I had to do most of the searching myself.

Index

3 260